MANUFACTURING THE FUTURE

Manufacturing the Future is the first full-length history of the Western Electric Company, which was founded in 1869 and served for more than 100 years as the manufacturing and supply unit of the Bell System. Western Electric was a leading manufacturer in the communications revolutions of the nineteenth and twentieth centuries, making not just telegraphs, telephones, and switches, but radios, sound systems for motion pictures, and radar – even an early computing machine. As captive supplier for a regulated monopoly, Western Electric's situation was far from typical, but its story offers broader lessons – such as the difference between innovation and implementation. The aftermath of Western's 1882 acquisition by Bell Telephone, for instance, reveals vertical integration as a difficult process rather than as a single event. Western Electric's innovations in areas such as quality control and industrial psychology were adopted worldwide, yet the company was slow to implement these innovations itself. By contrast, in response to government initiatives Western Electric transformed itself in less than a decade from a laggard to a leader in equal opportunity. Western Electric disappeared as a separate entity with the 1984 breakup of the Bell System. Western's functions were dispersed throughout AT&T until they were spun off in 1996 as part of Lucent Technologies, a new company with a 127-year history.

Stephen B. Adams's first book, *Mr. Kaiser Goes to Washington: The Rise of a Government Entrepreneur* (1997), was based on his Johns Hopkins doctoral dissertation, which won the American Historical Association's W. Turrentine Jackson Award. Dr. Adams has an MBA in finance from the University of Michigan and is the Gordon Cain Fellow at the Chemical Heritage Foundation.

Orville R. Butler has a master's degree in the history and philosophy of science from the University of Notre Dame and a doctorate in the history of technology and science from Iowa State University. He is the historian for the Academy of Management's International Management Division and Visiting Assistant Professor of Management at Bond University.

MANUFACTURING THE

FUTURE

A HISTORY OF WESTERN ELECTRIC

STEPHEN B. ADAMS   ORVILLE R. BUTLER

CAMBRIDGE
UNIVERSITY PRESS

PUBLISHED BY THE PRESS SYNDICATE OF THE UNIVERSITY OF CAMBRIDGE
The Pitt Building, Trumpington Street, Cambridge CB2 1RP, United Kingdom

CAMBRIDGE UNIVERSITY PRESS
The Edinburgh Building, Cambridge CB2 2RU, UK
http://www.cup.cam.ac.uk
40 West 20th Street, New York, NY 10011-4211, USA
http://www.cup.org
10 Stamford Road, Oakleigh, Melbourne 3166, Australia

First published 1999

Printed in the United States of America

Typeset in Adobe Garamond 11/14 pt. and Gill Sans, in DeskTopPro$_{/UX}$®

*A catalog record for this book is available from
the British Library.*

Library of Congress Cataloging-in-Publication Data
Adams, Stephen B., 1955–
Manufacturing the future : a history of Western Electric / Stephen
B. Adams, Orville R. Butler.
p.   cm.
Includes bibliographical references and index.
ISBN 0-521-65118-2 (hardcover)
1. Western Electric Company – History.   2. Telephone supplies
industry – United States – History.   3. Electronic industries – United
States – History.   I. Butler, Orville R., 1952–   .   II. Title.
HD9697.T454W473   1999
338.7'6213'0973 – dc21   98-34294
CIP

ISBN 0 521 65118 2 hardback

CONTENTS

CONTENTS

PREFACE

On September 20, 1995, AT&T announced the spin-off of two companies. One was NCR, which it had acquired in 1991 as part of a strategy to bring together computers and communications. The other was Lucent Technologies, whose 1996 initial public offering would be America's largest to date. Lucent evolved out of the Western Electric Company, which acted as AT&T's captive manufacturer for more than a hundred years. This book is a history of a new company with a 127-year history.

There are, of course, major differences between Western Electric and Lucent. One difference involves Lucent's research arm, Bell Laboratories. Although it had its genesis in Western Electric's engineering department, Bell Labs was separate from Western Electric after 1925. Another difference involves the government. Western Electric was a captive supplier to a regulated monopoly. Therefore, although Western was not directly regulated, its behavior was shaped by AT&T's relations with the government. Lucent's biggest difference from Western is its independence. Its behavior is neither prescribed directly by a parent company nor indirectly by the government.

Western Electric was a manufacturing company, and this book emphasizes that aspect of the business. Although other dimensions, from distribution to installation to repair, were important to the success of the company, our focus is on what the company made, where, by whom, and how.

Manufacturing the Future could not have been written without the generous help of many individuals. Dan Stanzione, president and chief operating officer of Lucent and sponsor of the book, created ideal conditions for academic authors. He wanted a book that would convey the heritage of Western Electric both to retirees and to employees of the newly independent Lucent, one that would relate the human aspect of business enterprise. He also sought lessons from which both Lucent and the wider world could learn, and that meant presenting Western Electric's story warts and all. He provided the necessary resources to do the job and offered valuable advice along the way. He also demonstrated restraint, exercising no editorial control. Therefore, although Dan and the others who helped us made valuable contributions, the final product is ours and we take full responsibility for it.

Sheldon Hochheiser, the head of AT&T's archives and the company's historian, played a unique role in this project. Having written a corporate history himself, Sheldon knew how to realize Dan's vision. Trained as a historian of science and technology, Sheldon is a respected authority on the history of AT&T and telecommunications. He read the entire manuscript – some sections several times – and offered invaluable comments and suggestions.

Dan and Sheldon were both members of the project's advisory board, a panel of business people and academicians. Terry Seese, Lucent vice president and assistant to the president, excelled in the art of the possible. When the project encountered difficulties early on, he was a source of ideas and encouragement. Terry and his secretary, Sue Bacigalupo, helped by shielding us from administrative matters, allowing us to focus on the book. Don Procknow, Western Electric's last president, was exceedingly generous with his time and offered insightful comments and suggestions. Larry Seifert began his career at Western and is now a senior vice president at AT&T Wireless. Therefore, although his eye is on the future of communications, he offered excellent guidance on recent manufacturing developments. Ed McKeever, a vice president in Lucent's legal department, and Ed Eckert, Lucent's archivist, expressed keen interest in the project from the beginning.

We were blessed with a talented and enthusiastic academic advisory board that helped us frame the Western Electric story in a broader historical context. W. Bernard Carlson, who writes on the history of technology (including the invention of the telephone) and teaches writing, gave us detailed advice on both content and style. He was also a source of excellent practical advice, particularly on how to turn a manuscript into a published book. Naomi Lamoreaux read the entire manuscript, and offered helpful comments, during her transition from one university – and coast – to another. Ken Lipartito, who had written a book on the Bell System, joined our board on very short notice, but was able to point out quickly where the gaps were in the manuscript and what to do about them.

Our greatest disappointment with respect to this project is that advisory board member Roland Marchand never saw the finished product; he died in November 1997. Roland was a historian who effectively united cultural and business history and pushed us to explore the wider implications of Western Electric's story. His curiosity and enthusiasm were infectious, and his suggestions during the darkest days of the project were invaluable. Roland introduced Steve to business history at the University of California, Davis, in the mid-1970s, then helped steer him to graduate study in history in the late 1980s. Roland was a pleasure to work with, and it was an honor to have been his student and colleague.

Many people at the AT&T Archives contributed to this project: Joann Crawley, Dan Curtiss, Susan Eckert, Laura Graham, Ralph Hacker, Joan Jarrett, Roger Kief, Irene Lewicki, Leigh McClure, Norma McCormick, Virginia McLean, Christine Natale, Dana Neubauer, Joy Perillo, Judy Pollock, Sean Quilal-lan, Linda Straub, Barbara Sweeney, and Dave Wampler. At the Lucent Archives, Ed Eckert and Bunnie White led us to some great photos for the book. From Lucent's legal staff, Theodore Weitz provided us with material on divestiture, and Allison Schaefer and Kathy Olson helped us navigate copyright issues. Ghislaine Butrica of the Rutgers University Library found books we needed.

When Steve visited Chicago, Robert Jerich arranged two luncheons of Western Electric retirees, Harold Pedersen provided a tour of the area where the Hawthorne works used to be, Eugene Janicke hosted a dinner of the Hawthorne tradesmen, and Georgienne Becker guided a special tour of the Hawthorne museum. Howard Plunkett invited Steve to attend a luncheon of the Kearny chapter of the Telephone Pioneers of America, and Don Leonard, Bill Marx, and Don Procknow arranged for him to attend a luncheon of retired AT&T and Western Electric vice presidents. Liz Roach and Kim Meseck did an excellent job transcribing taped interviews.

We are grateful to those who were patient enough to consent to be interviewed for the book: Robert Allen, A. E. Anderson, Dr. Joseph Arnold, Guy Asnani, M. M. Ayoub, William O. Baker, George Bates, Charles Bergmann, Lee Bockelman, the late Floyd Boswell, Sherri Brunette, Don Chaffin, Frank Cihlar, Hiram Cody, William Cooper, Cuthbert Cuthbertson, Peggy Dellinger, Kathy Detrano, Irv Diamond, Carol Dill, Richard Dudeck, Eugene Eckel, Bob Ehinger, Joe Fullan, Charles Gayley, Helen Grefe, Ralph Hacker, Harrell Hill, Ann Hopkins, Ken Hopper, Sanford Jacoby, Elmer Janda, Eugene Janicke, Robert Jerich, Nancy Johnson, Val Jordan, Joseph Juran, George Koch, Chester Lasko, Margaret Lawson, Don Leonard, Robert Lewis, William Marx, John Mayo, Ed McKeever, Jack McManigal, George Merna, Art Miller, Lewis Moore, Jack Neustadt, Robert Newman, Jack O'Marra, John T. O'Neill, Harold Pedersen, Lee Perkins, Howard Plunkett, Robert Prescott, Don Procknow, Maybelle Rodgers-Smith, Mrs. Arthur Rogers, Charles Ruch, Mary Russ, Ray Russ, Larry Seifert, Alex Smith, Jerry Stocker, Morris Tanenbaum, Charles Taylor, Helen Tichauer, Mary Volango, Alvin von Auw, Wayne Weeks, Thomas Wharton, Jack Wier, the late Robert Yaverick, and Rachel Zampaglione.

Cambridge University Press worked wonders in both quality of product and in meeting a difficult deadline. Executive editor Frank Smith saw the potential in the project and was always there when we needed help the most. An anonymous outside reader gave us excellent suggestions that improved the book. Production editor Helen Wheeler and production controller Cathy Felgar transformed our difficult requests into possibilities. Manuscript editor Barbara Folsom and indexer Shirley Kessel both did excellent jobs under intense time pressure. Binghamton Valley Composition did an excellent job of typesetting.

All photographs in this book appear courtesy of the AT&T Archives.

Finally, our families deserve special mention. Madeleine Adams, Steve's wife, agreed to move to New Jersey so that he could undertake this project, and she offered excellent advice throughout. Xiaohua Yang, Orville's wife, endured a year and a half of a cross-country marriage. Hsieyun Butler-Yang, Orville's daughter, had to forgo opportunities to play while her father worked. They each have our deep gratitude.

INTRODUCTION

O N JANUARY 25, 1915, THIRTY-NINE YEARS after the first telephone conversation, the original participants reprised their roles: inventor Alexander Graham Bell, from New York, called his associate Thomas Watson, who sat in San Francisco. This time Bell and Watson were introducing transcontinental phone service, and their conversation marked the opening of the Panama Pacific Exposition. After some initial pleasantries, Bell said, "I have been asked to say to you the words you understood over the telephone and through the old instrument, 'Mr. Watson, come here, I want you.' " From across the continent, Watson reminded Bell, "It would take me a week to get there now!"[1]

The 1915 Bell–Watson conversation represented the fulfillment of a promise made by AT&T's chief engineer, John Carty. In a 1909 visit to the West Coast, Carty had pledged to introduce transcontinental telephone service in concert with the opening of the Panama Canal. Carty's promise was a continuance of the 1908 pledge made by AT&T's president, Theodore Vail, to continue "annihilating distance and bringing people closer to each other."[2] The result would be what Vail called "universal service." Transcontinental service, when fully implemented, would allow any of the more than five million telephone subscribers in the Bell System to speak to one another.[3] At about the same time, national advertising had first referred to the "Bell System," a network of local phone companies affiliated with or owned by AT&T, linked by AT&T's long-distance network and supported by the manufacturing capabilities of Western Electric.[4] The telephone

I

Figure 1. Opening of the first transcontinental telephone line on January 15, 1915. Alexander Graham Bell in middle; John J. Carty, chief engineer of AT&T on far left

was becoming America's communications device of choice; in 1909 the Bell System alone conveyed more than six billion conversations.[5] So, fifteen years after the historian Frederick Jackson Turner pronounced the American frontier closed, Theodore Vail's Bell System was promising to bring east and west together in a new way.

Linking Carty's promise with the Panama Pacific Exposition had tremendous symbolic value. The greatest public-works project of its day, the Panama Canal symbolized America's coming-of-age as a world power. In addition to offering increased naval mobility, the canal promised to enhance the country's economic expansion. Commercial ships sailing from the East Coast to the West would save 8,000 miles from a voyage that had previously included a trip around Cape Horn. This transportation revolution promised an economic bonanza. Many hoped it would allow America, with its agricultural resources, to play an intermediary role in European trade with China. Just as the Panama Canal promised to bring East and West together, so Vail was now promising a corresponding revolution in communications.

Observers could be forgiven, however, for interpreting the boast about transcontinental telephone service as a fait accompli. After all, they had seen the unmistakable combination of innate American self-promotion combined with can-do brute force before. Wasn't this the building of the transcontinental railroad all over again?

It was not. Carty's pledge required technology that had not yet been developed. Long-distance service had expanded with the development of balanced metallic circuits, mechanical repeaters, and most recently, loading coils. But the technological innovations existing in 1909 could not provide commercially feasible transcontinental communications. Voice distortion caused by each mechanical repeater limited the number that could be used in sending a signal from one point to another. Loading coils, the most recent breakthrough in long-distance telephony, would similarly find their limits in the New York-to-Denver line.[6]

It fell on the shoulders of the research staff at Western Electric to make transcontinental telephone service a reality. But, in 1909, the Bell licensees and Western Electric had barely been molded into the system that would coordinate telephone communications in subsequent decades. Western Electric's relationship with American Bell Telephone Company had its formal beginning in 1882, but through the remainder of the nineteenth century Western viewed itself and was viewed by Bell as a largely independent supplier bound by a contract but not vertically integrated into a system.

The process of integrating Western Electric into the Bell System was difficult. No clear models for integrating manufacturing into a service industry existed. The railroads, the earliest and most comparable big business, had neither relied upon a single manufacturer nor integrated manufacturing into their systems. As late as the 1890s, Western Electric was operationally viewed as an independent manufacturer with an exclusive contract to manufacture American Bell Telephone's telephonic equipment. Its role in the system evolved over time, until by 1914 Western would be described as the manufacturing department of the Bell system.

Even after the arduous process of vertical integration began, no structured research and development organization existed at Western Electric. Like most of American industry, the Bell System had depended primarily on outside inventors for innovation by purchasing their patents; research done inside the system resulted largely from individual rather than corporate initiative. The need to develop a commercially viable telephone repeater forced the Bell System to develop its own research community. After Vail became AT&T's president in 1907, he chose Carty as chief engineer, and the self-educated Carty championed the idea of assembling scientists to perform research, rather than relying exclusively on outsiders. Carty's assistant, Frank Jewett, who had become good friends with Professor Robert Millikan while obtaining his doctorate in physics at the University of Chicago, was in a better position than Carty to recruit top university talent. At Jewett's request, Millikan agreed to send two or three of his best students to Western Electric's engineering office in New York. These new recruits, beginning with Harold D. Arnold in 1911, formed the basis for the engineering department's research branch.[7]

The research branch made little progress toward the transcontinental goal until 1912. Then AT&T's engineering department learned of the invention by a onetime employee of Western Electric, Lee De Forest. His audion was a three-element vacuum tube that not only could send radio waves more effectively than existing devices but could amplify them. Western Electric's Arnold, the Jewett recruit who had the training in electron physics that De Forest lacked, quickly grasped the scientific principle. He turned the audion into a practical electrical amplifier, which is what Carty knew was needed. The result was the development of a "high-vacuum tube" for amplifying sound in telephone cable in April 1913 – and AT&T's purchase of the audion patent from De Forest.[8] It was this new tube which allowed the Bell System to span the continent. The circuit was completed in June 1914, tested on July 29, and history was made the following January.

Harold Arnold's breakthrough was symbolic of Western Electric's history: it was shaped by external forces yet acted as an agent of considerable social change. In a sense, Arnold's triumph marked the

4

beginning of a new electronic age. Development of the high-vacuum tube amplifier did more than make possible the transcontinental telephone line AT&T had promised. The high-vacuum tube revolutionized communications, leading to the creation of new industries including radio, television, and sound motion pictures. In the process, Western Electric was firmly integrated into the Bell System, and research and development programs became an essential feature of that integration.

This book is a history of a manufacturing company (the institution and its people) that was shaped by its parents (Western Union in the 1870s, and AT&T in the 1880s and thereafter), by the government, and by the communities in which it operated its plants. Conversely, Western Electric shaped the international telephone manufacturing industry. Western built telecommunications systems that helped redefine the world as a global village. The company played key roles in the birth of both electronics and microelectronics, in the rise of the total quality movement, and in industrial psychology's coming-of-age. In short, Western Electric helped shape the way people of the twentieth century lived.

Western Electric's story is also a tale of creative tension. On the one hand, relationships with its parent and the government circumscribed virtually all of its activities. Both parent and government pressured Western to focus on its primary task of domestic telephone equipment manufacture. Bell remained concerned that Western would draw upon Bell's resources to expand into other lines of work. On the other hand, Western appeared convinced that only by such diversification could it maintain high-quality production in the boom and bust cycles of a specialized business. Indeed, the company's creative forces offered perpetual temptations to expand its scope beyond the company's central mission, whether toward international manufacture or consumer products.

The most significant creative force was research innovation, which not only led to improvements in telephone equipment, but also pulled the company toward radio, television, motion pictures, and many other possibilities. The combination of these creative forces and Western's position as captive supplier to a regulated monopoly, meant that the company would confront, and then bypass or abandon, some of the most spectacular paths not taken in American business history.

WESTERN ELECTRIC AND ITS PARENTS

Americans are fond of personalizing events, even those involving wider forces. The civil rights movement, for instance, is Martin Luther King, Jr.'s; the American system of mass production is Henry Ford's. Following the same line of thinking, corporations are viewed as the extended shadows of charismatic individuals, and the accomplishments of those organizations reflect an individual's vision. Western Electric was unusual in that it was the lengthened shadow of two men: Enos Barton (from within the company), and Theodore Vail (from without). Both Barton and Vail were straitlaced, honest, and paternalistic – traits that became commonly associated with Western Electric and the Bell System.

The differences between Barton and Vail were more important, however, than their similarities. Their diverse visions provided Western with tension that helped shape the company. Barton sought a broad scope for his company, to allow it to become "the department store of electrical apparatus." Vail, on the other hand, envisioned Western as the telephone apparatus manufacturer that would help make "universal service" possible.

Vail was president of AT&T from 1885 to 1887, then left until J. P. Morgan convinced him to return in 1907.[9] Vail's presidency changed the leadership relationship between AT&T and Western Electric. Previously, the leadership of the two companies had represented two mutually exclusive groups. Enos Barton's relationship with AT&T as Western Electric's president from 1886 until 1908 involved simply reporting on how Western Electric matters were going; he was never invited to enter Bell's inner circle. That changed with Barton's successor. When Harry Thayer became Western Electric's president in 1908, he was also an AT&T vice president. When Vail retired in 1919, Thayer replaced him as head of AT&T. A flow of executives between AT&T and Western Electric became familiar: subsequent AT&T presidents Frederick Kappel and Haakon Romnes had previously headed Western Electric. Indeed, the most abrupt change in Western Electric's landscape during the first half of the century came after one of its own, former assistant secretary Walter Gifford, became AT&T's president in 1925.

During the first year he headed the Bell System, Gifford stunned Western Electric, decreeing that it focus on its core business of domestic telephone manufacture and supply. This marked the triumph of Theodore Vail's vision over Enos Barton's. Gifford's intention was to align the goals of Western with those of the Bell System. In so doing, he did what competitors such as General Electric and Westinghouse could not, eliminating Western Electric from the ranks of the largest distributors of electrical equipment in the world, which he did by setting up a separate corporation (Graybar) for that function. Gifford also sold Western's international business to ITT, ending a forty-three-year tradition of overseas manufacture. Gifford also inherited a major change from his predecessor, Harry Thayer. Just before Gifford took over, Bell Laboratories was established as a separate entity that assumed the work previously conducted by the research division of Frank Jewett and Harold Arnold in Western Electric's engineering department.[10]

The 1925 reorganization of the company established the Bell System's institutional responsibilities that lasted until the 1980s: Bell Laboratories designed the network; Western Electric manufactured the telephones, cable, transmission equipment, and switching equipment; the operating companies installed the phones, operated the local networks, and billed the customers; and AT&T long lines operated the long-distance network. And the federal government regulated the Bell System.

Although Western Electric's role in the Bell System became constricted in many ways, its position afforded the company significant opportunities. Whereas many manufacturers set out to reach a certain size in order to achieve economies of scale, Western Electric did not need to do so. As the manufacturing arm of the Bell System, Western's role was to fill the orders that it was given rather than to seek a certain level of work. Therefore, to adapt Malvolio's phrase, whereas some companies are born to great size (through an initial merger), and some companies achieve great size, Western Electric was the largest to have its great size thrust upon it.

A telephone company president once remarked, "Western Electric does big things in a big way; it also does small things in a big way."[11] One of the "small" things was quality. With little control over volume, the company sought control in other ways, such as cost accounting and efficiency. Because of the company's enormous scale, tiny incremental improvements in quality or reductions in cost could have a tremendous impact. A "gospel of efficiency" became a driving force at the company even before the turn of the century, beginning with the movement toward scientific management.[12]

Western Electric's scale, and its response to it, helped embody the great irony of twentieth-century quality control: whereas we associate nineteenth-century quality with the smallest-scale operations, the great twentieth-century quality revolution came from one of the world's largest-scale manufacturing operations. At the time of the company's founding, individual artisans at the myriad small-scale manufacturing operations in America checked their own work as, apparently, did Western Electric's nineteenth-century foremen. Mass production changed all that. Jobs were broken down into parts, with no one individual responsible for the entire product. The increase in telephone business resulting from competitive expansion after the expiration of Bell's fundamental patents pressured Western Electric to restructure its business and, under Bell's tutelage, to standardize its product line. By the turn of the century, like other companies, Western Electric was training individuals as inspectors to assure specification and quality standards, in order to avoid sending bad products to the customer. When this approach became unwieldy, the company sought a means to control quality other than by examining every product.

In the 1920s, Western Electric's Walter Shewhart took manufacturing quality to the next level by creating statistical "control charts," which plotted observations on processes over time to see if changes in output were random or reflected changes in process. Applying statistical techniques to quality assurance, control charts went beyond deficiencies of individual items to offer evidence regarding the stability of an entire process.[13] Subsequently, experts trained at Western Electric spread the gospel of quality throughout the world. The modern quality movement symbolically came home after the 1984 elimination of Western Electric as the Bell System's separate manufacturing entity. In 1994, AT&T Power Systems became the first U.S. manufacturer to win Japan's Deming Prize, which salutes companies for successful dedication to the concepts of total quality management.[14]

Another of Western Electric's attempts to improve efficiency had even wider-ranging implications. From 1924 until 1933, the Hawthorne plant was the site of a series of experiments conducted under the auspices of the National Research Council. The initial studies involved the impact of changes in lighting levels on the productivity of several groups of workers. The first two sets of tests showed that increased levels of supervision played a larger role in productivity increases than levels of illumination. Subsequent experiments yielded similar results.[15] The experiments raised the possibility that, as Thomas J. Peters and Robert Waterman put it, "it is the attention to employees, not work conditions per se, that has a dominant impact on productivity."[16]

The impact of these experiments has been felt worldwide and by many generations. The phrase "Hawthorne effect" came to mean unexpected outcomes from nonexperimental variables in the social or behavioral sciences. The Hawthorne experiments have been elevated to the position of a modern Rosetta Stone, unlocking secrets for various fields that study the workplace, from sociology to psychology to anthropology.

A final example of the Bell System's impact on Western is financial reporting. Independent companies, whose stock is traded on an exchange, make every effort to present a promising picture to their shareholders. Investors react so strongly, even to quarterly financial results, that companies pay excessive attention to immediate results rather than to managing for the long term. Western Electric's stock was not traded publicly, and the stock of its parent – as a regulated monopoly – fluctuated little. Western's management was free to pursue a long-term planning process that other firms could only dream about.

Not only did Western Electric not need to show Wall Street what substantial profits it was making, but its parent spent considerable energy in trying to demonstrate how *little* profit Western made. This was for the benefit, not of Wall Street, but of the government. Regulators were sensitive to the possibility that any Western Electric excesses might be passed on to customers in the form of increased rates. Therefore, it was important for the Bell System to demonstrate that Western did not make excessive profits at the consumers' expense. Financial-reporting peculiarities are but a small part of the impact of the federal government–Bell System relationship on Western Electric.

WESTERN ELECTRIC AND GOVERNMENT

In the twentieth century, the federal government was the second force that shaped much of what Western Electric did, even though Western Electric was not regulated. Instead, AT&T was regulated by the federal government, and the local phone companies were regulated by state governments. Grist for the regulatory mill were the various relationships of AT&T and the operating companies, including those with Western Electric. The federal government frequently made Western Electric–Bell System relationships the focus of investigation. Western Electric received perhaps more governmental attention than any non-regulated business enterprise in American history.

In 1913, the Interstate Commerce Commission investigated the role of Western Electric in the Bell System. In the 1930s, the Federal Communications Commission investigated the Western–AT&T relationship. In a 1949 antitrust suit, using the FCC's findings, the Justice Department sought to pry Western Electric loose from the Bell System. In the late 1970s, the Justice Department pursued a similar goal. Time after time, AT&T showed a willingness to do almost anything to hold onto Western Electric, from creating Cold War defense systems in the 1950s to agreeing to spin off the various local telephone companies in the 1980s.

As a pioneer in the electrical manufacturing business and as a technological leader, Western Electric, on the other hand, persistently presented itself with opportunities beyond its traditional role of supplying telephone equipment for the Bell System. Unlike most companies, for which movement in new directions is the result of strong innovative leadership, technological innovations at Western Electric provided opportunities at almost every turn. This tendency was accentuated at Western because the company's "research branch" represented the roots of Bell Labs, the largest private research institution in the world. The dominant role of research in the Bell System appears counterintuitive, because the Bell System was constricted by government regulation and shielded from competition. Yet if the Bell System did not continually modernize, it ran the risk of being viewed as a parasitic monopoly: research represented a public service and a public relations device. Bell Labs and its predecessors gave birth to numerous innovations that changed not only the way America – and the world – did business, but also the way people conducted their lives.

Western Electric's relationship with the government had substantial social ramifications. Corporations are often accused of sacrificing the well-being of employees and communities in order to amass increased profits. Western Electric's governmental relationships helped to imbue the company with a different set of priorities, aligned with those of the government. Civil rights is a good example. The company's record as an employer of African Americans was a poor one on the eve of World War II. Labor shortages during the war led the company's major northern plants to hire African Americans. The postwar era, a period of sustained government contracting for Western, saw a transformation in the company in this area. The company began to take a leading role in civil rights, insisting on integrated bathrooms and drinking facilities as conditions for constructing plants in southern towns. It became a leader in pursuing the principles behind the Civil Rights Act and the affirmative-action policies of its second largest customer. Vallmer Jordan, who began his Hawthorne career in 1952,

and then became one of the company's first African American supervisors in the mid-1960s, personally experienced the company's transformation: "They treated me like a stepson, but realized I was a wor-
thy son."[17]

The government's formal relationship with Western Electric involved more than just regulation of its parent. Two military companies
of Western Electric employees became the backbone of the telecommunications work in the European sector during World War I. Western Electric's size and ability to handle mass production, as well as its
long tradition of working with the government, made it an attractive
contractor. The company's size and economies of scale fit the needs of
"hot war," when the nation sought companies that could mass-
produce a limited number of designs. As the world's largest manufacturer of electrical devices, Western Electric played a crucial role in
supplying telecommunications equipment to the government during
World War I. During World War II, it was America's leading producer of radar. The percentage of the company's business dealing with
the government rose from less than 1 percent in 1939 to more than
80 percent in 1943 and 1944.[18]

The end of the war would have terminated Western Electric's role
as government contractor if the company had not been so adept at
short-run production. The requirements of the Cold War were sub-
stantially different from those of hot war, because the government
sought companies that could constantly produce new designs. Western
Electric was one such company. By mid-century it was producing
25,000 different designs per year, nearly two-thirds of which required
production of fewer than one hundred units per year.[19] Little wonder
that the 1956 "Final Judgment" provisions that prohibited the Bell
System from pursuing nontelephone activity contained one notable
exception: government contracting.[20] The federal government would
be Western's second largest customer (behind the Bell System) for the
duration of Western's existence.

In 1984, as part of a Modification to the Final Judgment (MFJ),
AT&T agreed to divest its twenty-two wholly owned local operating
companies. AT&T's restructuring, in response to its new competitive
position, included the elimination of Western Electric as a separate

entity. What had once been a centrifugal force now became a part of the core mission of AT&T manufacturing: going global. By 1993, AT&T had more than 50,000 (mostly manufacturing) employees abroad – including employees in America's onetime Cold War antagonists, the People's Republic of China and various independent republics of the old Soviet Union.[21] In 1996, most of those overseas employees became part of the new independent company, Lucent Technologies.

In this book, we use Western Electric's crucial relationships with parents and government to break the company's history into seven chronological parts. Chapter 1 includes the period from the company's 1869 founding until 1882, when Western Electric joined the Bell System. Chapter 2 outlines the period between 1882 and 1900, when Western Electric was a part of Bell but not yet integrated into Bell's system. Chapter 3 traces the process of defining Western Electric's place in the Bell System, culminating in 1925, when AT&T decided to sell Western Electric's overseas operations, to abandon its wholesale electrical supply business, and to establish Bell Labs as a separate research group. Chapter 4, ending in 1950, presents a paradoxical period for the company: after abandoning overseas manufacture, Western became increasingly influential around the world, through the impact of the Hawthorne experiments, the introduction of sound to motion pictures, the beginning of a worldwide revolution in manufacturing quality, and other activities. Chapter 5, ending in 1972, features Western's double life as producer of custom-made defense systems for the government and as mass producer of telephone apparatus for the Bell System. Chapter 6 ends with the 1984 breakup of the Bell System, the disappearance of Western Electric as a separate corporate entity, and the establishment of Network Systems as an AT&T manufacturing division. Chapter 7 concludes with the 1995 announcement of trivestiture, which meant that, after numerous attempts by the government to pry Western Electric loose from AT&T, the company unilaterally spun off its telecommunications manufacturing capability – essentially the old Western Electric – into Lucent Technologies.

BEFORE THE BELL: 1869–1882

HROUGHOUT 1969, ITS CENTENNIAL YEAR, the Western Electric Company used the slogan "100 Years of Progress." Traditional signs of progress were easy to see: Western Electric was America's eleventh largest industrial organization, with 184,000 employees. As the manufacturing arm of the Bell System, Western had produced the equipment that provided telephone service to more than 95 percent of American households, and through the Bell System each of those households could contact every other. The concept of "universal service" that AT&T president Theodore Vail had promoted during the first decade of the century had come to pass, and thus the primary mission of Western Electric and the Bell System had been accomplished.

Such measures, however, revealed little of where Western Electric had come from. Its original mission had nothing to do with the Bell System. Indeed, the company's history predated that of its AT&T "parent." Western did not spring from the brow of Bell Telephone, but had existed before Alexander Graham Bell made his invention. It was the telegraph, not the telephone, that planted the seeds of the Western Electric Company, providing Western's founders with gainful employment during their formative years, a network of contacts with which to start a business, and a product sufficiently in demand to sustain the business.

The thread connecting Western Electric, the behemoth electrical manufacturer of 1969, to Gray & Barton, the tiny startup of 1869, was the nature of their institutional relationships. Attempts to trace corporate roots do not always find a younger version of the same entity but often something entirely different that appears to bear no relation to the older corporation. Western Electric's 100-year backward glance revealed a company that looked far different, yet the relationships – first to the greatest telecommunications empire of the nineteenth century, then to the greatest telecommunications empire of the twentieth century – were strikingly similar. Gray & Barton was shaped by the dictates of Western Union, and Western Electric by the dictates of Bell Telephone. Indeed, Gray & Barton owed its creation to two policy decisions taken by Western Union in the late 1860s: one involving its manufacturing arrangements and the other its labor relations.

THE WORLD OF WESTERN UNION

The 1869 conception of Gray & Barton grew out of a world of telegraphers, inventors, and industry consolidation. The new company was just one of many attempting to improve on the telegraph, the greatest communications breakthrough of the first half of the nineteenth century. After its 1835 invention by Samuel Morse and others, the electric telegraph had contributed to the quickening pace of life, changing the ways in which people related to one another, how financial markets and business organizations worked, even the conduct of warfare. It made communication independent of transportation. It also created challenges for inventors, including how to transmit more than one message on any one line (multiplexing) and how to sustain a signal over long distances. Such efforts to improve the telegraph provided the nation with an early high-tech industry.

Once the American government had made the decision not to own and operate a national telegraph network, the U.S. telegraph industry spent about two decades dispersed among many companies. The realization that the success of the telegraph depended on creating a nationwide system led Western Union to acquire its competitors and to build the first transcontinental line in 1861, thereby becoming America's first private communications giant.

Western Union's east–west lines proved to be a competitive advantage during the Civil War, when the north–south lines of its principal competitor, the American Telegraph Company, were severed.[1] Subsequent consolidations with its principal competitors increased Western Union's capitalization from less than $400,000 in 1858 to more than $40 million less than a decade later. After an 1866 merger with American and the United States Telegraph Company, 90 percent of the nation's telegraph lines belonged to Western Union, and it became America's first nationwide multiunit business enterprise.[2]

This nationwide business offered unparalleled opportunities to its employees. In handling messages from distant places, telegraphers had the chance to observe a wider world. Telegraph operator was one of the first available jobs to engage its practitioners in issues that transcended the parochial interests of their local communities, thereby preparing them to seek wider opportunities. Some became industrial magnates. In the 1850s, future steel baron Andrew Carnegie learned to transmit and translate what he called "the miraculous tick, tick, tick of the tamed lightning."[3] In 1867, Carnegie helped organize the Keystone Telegraph Company (a Western Union competitor) as a prelude to a career of taming entire industries. Similarly, telegraph pioneer Alfred Vail's cousin Theodore parlayed his 1860s experience as an operator and his subsequent career in the railway mail service into the top telecommunications position in the world: the presidency of AT&T.[4]

There were also career opportunities within Western Union itself. A century before one of the mythical images of advancement to the executive suite became the rise from the mail room, corporate advancement truly meant rising from the telegraph office. The company employed what business later termed a "promote from within" strategy, choosing almost all of its managers from the ranks of its telegraphers rather than searching for talent elsewhere.[5] Future Western Union presidents Thomas Eckert and Robert Clowry rose from the ranks of operators, as did company electrician George Prescott and regional superintendents John Van Horne and Anson Stager.[6]

Stager, one of three cofounders of Gray & Barton, had a career that traced some of the major early developments in the American tele-

Figure 2. Anson Stager. A company founder, telegraph pioneer, and electrical industry venture capitalist

graph industry. Born in Ontario County, New York, in 1825, he served a telegraph apprenticeship in Rochester. Stager moved on to work as a full-time operator for the new Pittsburgh, Cincinnati & Louisville Telegraph Company in Lancaster, Pennsylvania, in 1846, then became the first operator in Pittsburgh, where his office boy was Andrew Carnegie.[7] In 1852, Stager resigned to become general superintendent of the Mississippi Valley Printing Telegraph Company, one of the firms that subsequently merged to form Western Union. Stager's relationship with Mississippi Valley and then Western Union would last nearly thirty years.[8]

As Stager's responsibilities expanded, stories began to proliferate around him. At a time of highly publicized contests between men (and animals) and machines, even the reputations of telegraphers grew up around physical accomplishments in an increasingly mechanized world. One example was the physical ability of some operators to receive messages by ear rather than by the slower method of reading Morse code from tape. Their ability to hear messages from the clicking of the receiving register led to a mechanical innovation. By the 1850s, "sounders," which increased the volume of clicking sound through the use of metal components, had replaced the original Morse register.[9]

But the accomplishments of other operators' ears paled in comparison to those of Anson Stager's tongue. In the late 1850s, Stager was traveling in Ohio on a train whose engine broke down far from the nearest station. Never one to wait patiently, Stager cut down nearby telegraph lines and tapped out a message requesting another engine. The trick was how to determine whether the response was yes or no. Stager knew that the tongue reacts much like a magnet in response to electrical current, extending and retracting in response to the opening and closing of the circuit. His tongue was long enough that he could "read" its response when placed in contact with the wire, and he soon announced to the other passengers that a relief engine was on its way.[10]

Stager's name reached to wider circles during the Civil War, when the telegraph revolutionized wartime communications. When George McClellan became head of the Army of the Potomac in November 1861, he named Stager superintendent of U.S. military telegraphs.[11] As an aide-de-camp to War Secretary Edward M. Stanton, Stager was present during President Lincoln's 6:00 A.M. visits to the War Department telegraph office to learn what had happened the night before.[12] In August 1862, Stager convinced War Secretary Stanton to issue an order that, "the use of the telegraph lines being required for military purposes, all persons actually employed in constructing and operating telegraph lines . . . be exempt from military duty so long as they remain in such service."[13] In 1865, Stager was breveted a brigadier general before returning to civilian life, a further indication of how important the telegraph operation was to the United States Army.[14] After the war, Stager became Western Union's central region superintendent.

Whereas for some operators, such as Anson Stager, working as one of the "Knights of the Key" led to lofty advancement in the corporate ranks, for others it was a formative experience in a life of invention. Because most offices were staffed by only one or two operators, telegraphers needed mechanical skills to fix problems with the machines.

Many went further, seeking to understand the technology behind the apparatus.[15] Consequently, many technical advances in telegraphy came from the operators. Thomas Edison, one of the itinerant telegraphers who had learned their trade during the Civil War, was one example of how the telegraph community of the 1850s and 1860s brought together the worlds of the operator and the mechanic.[16] Little wonder that many tinkerers among America's youth dreamed of becoming telegraph operators.

Industry restructuring changed that. Western Union's consolidation, like twentieth-century mergers, eliminated redundant managerial positions, promising fewer promotional opportunities for telegraphers. Many peeled off to join electrical manufacturing shops or to set up their own. Edison was one example: in late 1868, he moved to Boston, the country's leading center of light engineering. There Edison would fit in with the numerous skilled artisans (from clockmakers to opticians) who now saw their main chance in electrical invention. In January 1869, The *Telegrapher* reported that Edison "would hereafter devote his full time to bringing out his inventions." Actually, in addition to his work in the shop of Charles Williams Jr. in the daytime, Edison continued as a Western Union operator at night.[17] The Williams shop produced some of America's first fire-alarm telegraphs, but would become better known as the host for Alexander Graham Bell's experiments and as the first manufacturer of Bell's telephones.

Other Western Union telegraphers stayed but pursued collective bargaining, joining the National Telegraphic Union or the Telegrapher's Protective League.[18] This was the situation another Gray & Barton cofounder faced in 1868. It turned him into an entrepreneur. Enos Barton was born and raised in Jefferson County, New York, in 1842. Barton was uninterested in farming, and by the age of twelve was a messenger in the telegraph office of Watertown, the county seat. During the next fifteen years he moved up in the telegraph hierarchy, progressing from messenger to part-time operator, to full-time operator, to main-line operator, to press-wire operator. Barton was one of the Civil War telegraph operators exempted from battle by Stager's influence. Based in New York City, Barton ensured that telegraph

Figure 3. Enos Barton. A company founder, he served for forty-seven years as secretary, president, then chairman of Western Electric.

messages from the front reached the newspapers. After the war, he became chief operator at Western Union headquarters in Rochester, with a staff of five.

Throughout his career, Enos Barton had witnessed Western Union's periodic price reductions aimed at driving new competitors out of the market. These reductions were usually accompanied by reductions in wages for telegraphers.[19] Such was the case in late 1868, when Western Union announced that it would reduce all operator salaries beginning January 1. At the same time as management opportunities at Western Union appeared to be diminishing, Barton's current prospects also looked dim: his salary was scheduled to fall from $100 to $90 a month.

Rather than either becoming part of a collective response or taking a reduction in pay, Barton began to consider other options. He even went so far as to make an offer on a farm, only to be turned down.[20] He then began to develop transferable business skills, taking a course in bookkeeping. So, when George Shawk came to Rochester looking for someone to handle the administrative aspect of his business, Barton was already thinking along those lines.

Shawk owned a six-man shop in Cleveland, a twenty-five-foot-wide loft on the fourth floor of a building at 93 St. Clair Street, which had once been one of Western Union's four manufacturing shops.[21] In the wake of its 1866 consolidation, Western Union had two shops in Anson Stager's central region – one at Ottawa, Illinois, and the other in Cleveland – making working models of inventions and manufacturing telegraph instruments.[22] In 1867, Stager consolidated the region's manufacture of equipment at the Ottawa shop. In addition to closer proximity to future Central Division headquarters in Chicago, the Ottawa shop provided considerably more capacity than the one in Cleveland.[23]

George Shawk had worked at the Cleveland shop since 1855, had been superintendent for the last four years, and wished to remain in Cleveland.[24] So, in 1867, he paid about $1,500 for the tools and equipment he needed in order to sustain a jobbing and model shop. In late 1868, Shawk wanted to convince Rochester, New York, to install the same sort of fire-alarm system he had sold to the city of Cleveland. Realizing that officials of the city of Rochester were unlikely to know about his system, Shawk sought local help. He called on Enos Barton, with the thought that Barton might have an idea of whom Shawk should see there.[25]

Seeking a contract, Shawk found a partner. When Shawk moaned about his poor sales skills, Barton offered his. Barton later recalled, modestly, that Shawk "had a number of offers from parties who desired to go into partnership with him, but perhaps because he was better acquainted with the other parties," he chose Barton.[26] Having sized up Barton as a promoter to match his own craftsmanship, Shawk offered him a half-interest for $1,500. Barton agreed, on the condition that he could visit the shop first.

SHAWK & BARTON

In early January 1869, Barton took the train to Cleveland. George Shawk's tiny fourth-floor shop seemed to be engaged in the manufacture of everything electrical: bells, annunciators, telegraph equipment, and fire and burglar alarms. The annunciators had found a place in the homes of the wealthy as a means of communication with servants. Various rooms were equipped with push buttons for the master or mistress. The button would ring a bell in a cabinet in the kitchen or butler's pantry, where an arrow would indicate the location of the summons. The shop's burglar and fire alarms operated on a similar principle. If a door or window was raised, the alarm went off in the annunciator cabinet, where an arrow indicated the location of the open door or window. The fire alarm used thermometers to similar effect. If the temperature in a particular room rose quickly, the annunicator cabinet would register the location of the fire.[27]

Barton quickly recognized that business was good. He saw a business with more demand than it could supply and in great need of organization. He learned of the inventions being hatched there, the most promising of which was a device that would print a telegraph message as it was received. After browsing through the shop's books and talking to various businessmen and telegraph operators in Cleveland, Barton met with the resident inventor, Elisha Gray. Gray was a perpetual presence at George Shawk's shop; he seemed constantly to need models for his electrical inventions.[28]

Gray's arrival as high-tech inventor in telegraphy parallels the sudden successes we see in today's computer industry. The personal computer is described as "the triumph of the nerds," the odd (predominantly male) figures for whom concern about practical matters such as personal grooming sometimes just does not fit into schedules that can be described as erratic at best. When one of these figures, such as Bill Gates, succeeds in creating a huge empire, or another, such as Steve Wozniak, becomes a cult figure, many wonder what such unusual individuals did before the twentieth century's electronics revolution. The life of Elisha Gray provides one answer.

Gray was born on an Ohio farm in 1835, but realized quite young that his interests lay elsewhere: "When I saw a piece of machinery of any character whatsoever, I usually attempted to reproduce it." Electricity captured Gray's imagination. He recalled, "I read whatever I could find relating to this subject, with the same energy and interest

Figure 4. Elisha Gray, a company founder and inventor. His laboratory was "wherever he happened to be."

that most boys would read Robinson Crusoe or the Arabian Nights." Most significantly, Gray built his own Morse telegraph register.[29]

From then on, Gray's mind seemed always to be on his inventions – often to the exclusion of practical matters. Gray's wife told a story about how once, when he was putting his pants on in the morning, she informed him his breakfast was ready. Fifteen to twenty minutes later, she went upstairs and found him in the same position, with his pants half on. He had been thinking about his latest invention the entire time.[30] As one of his assistants later pointed out, Elisha Gray's laboratory was "wherever he happened to be."[31]

Supporting himself as a carpenter, Gray attended Oberlin from 1857 until 1861. He was peddling milk when Oberlin College physics professor C. H. Churchill met him, discovered his interest in electricity, and offered him the use of his lab. Gray conducted experiments in Churchill's Oberlin laboratory, then began to make a living through inventions.[32]

In the 1860s and 1870s, Western Union was the principal sponsor of electrical research in the United States. The company subsidized young inventors – including Thomas Edison – in exchange for control of the products and patents their work produced.[33] That world of invention was an extremely competitive one, requiring both skill and self-promotion. Western Union officials not only had the luxury of a buyer's market but, with a virtual monopoly, had no sense of urgency about technical advances that a competitive situation might create. The company electrician was therefore more gatekeeper than talent scout: he "had to act as a barrier to a flood of capricious inventors which have swarmed upon us and demanded attention."[34] In such an environment, inventors needed connections, and living in Oberlin, Gray had them. The advisory board of Oberlin's school of telegraphy included Western Union's president, Jeptha Wade. Between Wade and the school director Chester Pond, Gray found ample connections to gain a hearing in Cleveland.[35]

Elisha Gray's first patent (of one hundred) in October 1867, for a self-adjusting relay, separated him from a large crowd. The self-adjusting relay was a device that contributed to making effective long-distance telegraphy more reliable. For years, one of the industry's obsessions was how to send messages over long distances without the signal weakening. In 1858, George Hicks, a Cincinnati operator, invented an "automatic repeater," which transferred a weakening signal to a new circuit and battery.[36] Repeaters required relays, which switched a signal from the incoming line to a local circuit. Various conditions required operators continually to adjust the relays in order to receive messages – until the advent of self-adjusting relays, simultaneously invented by Gray and Edison in 1867.[37]

Gray's self-adjusting relay captured the attention of Anson Stager. Gray could not contain the excitement he felt when describing that initial demonstration in a letter to his wife: "We had our machines on exhibition today and created quite a sensation among the 'authorities.' Pres. Wade [of Western Union] and Gen. Stager were present besides other lesser lights. They acknowledged the machine to be novel and useful and could see no reason why it should not do all that was claimed. They immediately offered me a room in their building with facilities for using all their lines in order to give it a fair test." Stager encouraged Gray to do his work at the Western Union shop run by George Shawk and provided him with wire and other supplies at cost.[38] Gray now had the three things coveted by all telegraph inventors: in Shawk's shop he had machinists who could build and modify his models, and through Western Union he had both access to lines on which to conduct experiments and a possible source of capital.

Elisha Gray convinced Enos Barton that George Shawk's workers were better versed in electricity than any group in the country and were therefore prepared to grow with the coming revolution in equipment manufacture. Barton was sold: he made a token down payment on the partnership. The stickler was that Barton had saved no more than $200 as a telegraph operator, well short of the $1,500 Shawk asked for. In a gesture symbolic of America forsaking its agricultural roots for the new machine age, Barton's mother mortgaged the family farm to raise money for his business venture.[39]

Settling into the shop on St. Clair Avenue, Barton learned the ropes, "doing everything from tidying up the office and keeping the books to handling correspondence and outside sales and helping the 'hands' operate the foot lathes."[40] Barton was also the company's marketing department. He called on his old boss from Rochester, James D. Reid, who was now editor of the *Journal of the Telegraph*.[41] The April 1, 1869, edition carried an advertisement for Shawk & Barton that set the tone for what would become Western Electric's balance of custom work and mass production: "Having purchased the Stock and Tools of the Western Union Company's Cleveland Shop, [we] will manufacture to order and keep on hand all articles of Telegraph Machinery and Supplies." They promised to "continue to manufacture Instruments after the favorite Western Union standard patterns, and shall keep up with the times in all valuable improvements." They provided not just manufacture, but "the construction and equipment of telegraph lines of any required length, in any part of the United States, for individuals or corporations."[42]

Barton soon realized that he was in the right line of business but with the wrong partner. Although George Shawk was known as an "ingenious, careful, prompt business man," his temperament did not seem well suited to the changing fortunes of the business world.[43] Like many start-ups, Shawk & Barton had cash-flow problems and diffi-culty meeting payroll.[44] Such problems precipitated "mercurial" mood swings in Shawk: "If an order or two came in he was enthusiastic about the prospects of the business. If money got scarce and a few days passed without new orders or if reclamations were made by cus-tomers, he was easily discouraged."[45] Barton's aggressive pursuit of business and his willingness to sponsor inventors – including Elisha Gray – did not always sit well with his partner.

Shawk soon wanted out, and in May 1869 Enos Barton was more than willing to take on Elisha Gray as his partner.[46] In addition to Barton's observation of Gray's work at the Cleveland shop, the two had also developed a close friendship after Barton moved into the Perry Street boardinghouse where Gray lived.[47] Above all, Barton en-visioned the possibility of establishing a manufacturing plant to meet the needs of the new electrical era and saw Gray's inventions – and the market potential they represented – as a means toward that end. Barton's recognition of the positive value of Gray's inventions began a tradition of manufacturing innovation that was to characterize the subsequent development of the Western Electric Company.

GRAY & BARTON

Elisha Gray's reputation had grown more quickly than his resources. He would need help raising the money he needed to buy out George Shawk. One hundred years later, Gray, like his high-tech successors in Silicon Valley, might have enlisted the assistance of a venture capital-ist. In contrast, a Hollywood version of the story might have hinged on the willingness of the richest man in town to help Gray out. Gray essentially found both in the person of Cleveland's Anson Stager.

Stager's mansion on Euclid Avenue – which later became Cleve-land's University Club – was testament to one of America's most successful careers in telegraphy. As one of the world's foremost au-thorities on electrical communications and a man of considerable means, Anson Stager was a likely prospect to become an early high-tech venture capitalist. Best of all, he was already familiar with Gray's work.[48]

Gray's opportunity came in May 1869, when Stager asked him about the progress of his latest project. Gray was working on a private-line printer, something Western Union needed for an important new market segment. In the 1850s and 1860s, Western Union had focused on long-distance (city-to-city) telegraphy. Although this emphasis responded to the needs of the railroads, it ignored a growing need in other corners of the business world for intracity communication. Financial and commodity markets employed squads of messenger boys to run between exchanges and brokers. Such intracity communication took longer than long-distance transmission between cities. A necessary development accompanying the proliferation of private lines was a device that allowed an individual to strike the appropriate keys and create a message that could offer users immediate information, such as stock or commodity quotations, thus eliminating the need for an operator to translate Morse code.

After a brief discussion with Gray, Stager decided to visit the shop to see the new apparatus. On the way there, Gray explained to Stager that progress was handicapped by Shawk's hesitance and told him about Shawk's offer to sell Gray his interest in the shop. After Stager had met with Barton and the three had inspected Gray's model, Stager suggested that they meet again the next day. He needed to solicit the advice of his lawyer.

The next day, an optimistic Gray and Barton arrived at Stager's office and waited in an anteroom while Stager consulted with attorney Norman Williams of the Chicago firm Williams and Thompson.[49] Although he knew neither Gray nor Barton, Williams was quite familiar with their line of work: his father-in-law, Judge J. D. Caton, had been president of the Illinois & Mississippi Telegraph Company until he sold out to Western Union in 1866.[50] Caton claimed to have been the first to combine telegraphy and the law in one unusual respect: he had conducted a trial by telegraph in 1849.[51] For the new enterprise, the combination of telegraphy and the law appeared to hold less promise. When Stager finished with Williams, the high hopes of Gray and Barton were quickly dashed when Stager announced: "I got a bad reaction from my lawyer. He has recommended that I keep out of the proposition." The reason? "You haven't enough security."[52]

Just as Gray and Barton were excusing themselves to leave, Stager smiled and repeated what he had told Williams: "No man could have greater security than faith in the character and abilities of the men with whom he proposed to do business."[53] The upshot was that Stager agreed to provide Gray with the $1,500 in exchange for an interest in Gray's patent for the printer telegraph Stager liked so much. Thus Gray & Barton, the predecessor company to Western Electric, was born in 1869, but not through the act of a solo founder. The fledgling company needed technical expertise (Gray), a source of capital with an expansive vision (Stager), and a promoter with administrative expertise (Barton).

Shortly afterward, a Cleveland tax man arrived at 93 St. Clair Avenue to collect $5.64 in property tax, which Gray & Barton had accrued based on an 1869 assessed valuation of $182, to find the fourth-floor shop occupied by Moses A. Buell Telegraph Supply.[54] To the tax man the scene was all too familiar. Opposite "Gray & Barton," he wrote, "Busted up, left for parts unknown." Despite appearances, Gray & Barton had neither skipped town to avoid paying taxes nor gone bankrupt:[55] Gray and Barton had moved to Chicago.

Anson Stager had acceded to Western Union's "suggestion" to relocate from Cleveland to Chicago. The rapid population increase in the West called for a "strong executive authority to control the present and prospective vast interests which center there." Cleveland was deemed "too far east for such a control."[56] Therefore, Stager convinced Gray and Barton to move too, and in November 1869 they visited Chicago "to reconnoiter and feel the enemy's position."[57]

In Chicago, the two partners agreed to buy out the repair and model shop of another onetime Western Union operator, L. C. Springer. There, Gray and Barton faced the difficulty that cash-poor founders of many a new business confront: hesitation to trust someone without a proven track record. They offered a note to Springer for the $500 purchase price, but he held out for cash until he learned that

General Stager would endorse a $500 note. To the new company, Stager's name was as good as gold.[58]

Stager added more than his endorsement to the enterprise, buying a one-third share for $2,500. In its new home, the company rapidly earned a reputation for high-quality workmanship, which would become a hallmark of Western Electric as well. Consequently, during its first year in Chicago, the shop grew to house seventeen workers. Gray & Barton soon needed larger quarters; in May 1870, it moved to 479 State Street in time to witness a watershed event in Chicago history.[59]

In October 1871 a fire destroyed one-third of the city, including most of the business district. Western Union's new Central Region headquarters and most of its lines were destroyed. The fates were kind to Gray & Barton, however: the fire was extinguished two blocks from its State Street building. Meanwhile, its original Chicago neighborhood on South Water Street was destroyed.[60]

Although the human and financial cost of such disasters is enormous, catastrophes can provide a macabre boost to certain segments of the economy engaged in various facets of rebuilding. Gray & Barton was not only fortunate to avoid the former but reaped the benefits of the latter. Demand rocketed for fire-alarm apparatus (naturally), for hotel annunciators and house calls, and for Morse instruments. The company's relationship with one customer in particular, Western Union, deepened in the wake of the fire. While Gray & Barton helped Western Union reconstruct, Western Union helped Gray & Barton restructure.

THE FORMATION OF WESTERN ELECTRIC

In March 1872, the executive committee of Western Union approved a motion "for consolidating the Machine Shop of this company at Ottawa and the establishment of Gray & Barton at Chicago into an independent manufacturing company."[61] Anson Stager, who was both a Western Union executive and part owner of Gray & Barton, brought an apparent conflict of interest to the issue. Nevertheless, he convinced

Western Union president William Orton that the new combination could meet most of Western Union's needs for telegraph manufacture, and Western Union sold the Ottawa shop to Gray & Barton.

So, in April 1872, Gray & Barton became the Western Electric Manufacturing Company, thereby strengthening its ties to Western Union. Despite the new company's diminutive stature, Western Union paid it attention well out of proportion to its size. Western Electric was capitalized at $150,000 ($50,000 of which came from Western Union in exchange for one-third ownership). This represented a mere drop in the bucket compared to Western Union's capitalization of $40 million. Gray & Barton's sales had averaged about $3,000 a month in 1871, whereas Western Union's exceeded $600,000. Gray & Barton's profits had just begun to exceed $500 a month, whereas Western Union averaged more than $200,000.[62]

Western Union was well represented among the upper echelons of the new company, contributing three of Western Electric's five directors.[63] In addition to Stager, they included Western Union treasurer Stafford Lynch (a onetime telegrapher who subsequently served in Stager's military telegraph during the war) and Western Union supplies manager Thomas Orton. As a concession to General Stager's proprietary interest in Western Electric, Western Union granted him its proxy at Western Electric shareholder meetings.[64] Anson Stager was elected president of the new company, Stafford Lynch vice president, and Enos Barton secretary/treasurer.

Barton handled all the hiring, made sure the workers were paid on time, did all the accounting, and handled most of the relationships with customers.[65] Although Stager was president, he had less and less to do with the day-to-day operations of the shop as time went on. Little wonder: more than any other individual, Stager helped to introduce and organize electrical industry in Chicago. He would serve as president of the Chicago Telephone Company (Illinois Bell's predecessor), president of the Chicago Edison Company, president of Western Electric, and vice president of Western Union – all at the same time. As a representative of the Vanderbilt interests in the West, Stager also served as director of four railroads, director of Northwest National

Bank, and organizer of the Chicago Chamber of Commerce, and held many other positions.

Elisha Gray, although nominally superintendent, was a mysterious figure to many of the workers. Western Electric's research department was a ten-by-ten-foot second-floor loft that served as Gray's laboratory.[66] In addition to being part owner, Gray held the title of Company Electrician, as did other electrical inventor/scientists of the day. His staff was modest: by running errands and carrying things around for Elisha Gray (in addition to his other tasks) Charles Hobart *was* the staff.

Charles Hobart's experiences provide a window into life at Western Electric during its early years. He had been part of the University of Illinois cadet corps, which was brought in to prevent looting after the Chicago fire. Hobart spotted, and later remembered, Gray & Barton's sign near the edge of the burned-out area, because "electrical" carried the same sort of cachet as the Internet does today. Prior to the establishment of an employment department at the turn of the century, Western relied on its employees to recruit relatives and friends. Hobart had grown up with the Bartons and the Kelloggs in Adams, New York, where Hobart's father was pastor of the church Enos Barton attended.

Hobart was paid one dollar a day, and it was a long day: he left Downer's Grove at six in the morning to catch a Chicago Burlington & Quincy train, arriving at the plant by seven, where he remained until six in the evening. His days were not only long, but busy: indicative of the company's modest size – there were only twenty-five employees – was the fact that Hobart did all of the company's packing, shipping, and billing. Like the others in the shop, he worked six days a week, ten hours a day.[67]

Hobart was working so hard that he asked for help and received permission to hire an assistant. He chose Arthur Stanley, with whom he played baseball and shot prairie chickens at Downer's Grove and would now share the early morning train ride. Stanley became assistant packer, shipper, and billing clerk.[68] So both Hobart's hiring and his recruitment of an assistant remained within the circle of family and

Figure 5. Western Electric's main Chicago shop, 1877

friends rather than being done through posting a public announcement of an opening. By the time Stanley joined him, Hobart had
already seen a number of new faces – from Ottawa.

It was July before the new company took over the business and
property of Gray & Barton. The big problem was locating building
space, because the period after the great fire was a time of building
scarcity. Stager's solution was to build new quarters on Kinzie Street

near State, which would remain the company's manufacturing center until 1884. The company leased parts of the basement and first floors, as well as the entire second and third floors.[69] There they moved the employees and equipment from the Ottawa plant to Chicago. Among the newcomers was James C. "Pop" Warner, a telegraph pioneer who made instruments for Samuel Morse's early experiments.[70]

Barely a year after Western Electric moved to Kinzie Street – and only two years after the Chicago fire – the new company and partially rebuilt city had a chance to show off. The fall of 1873 brought the Chicago Inter-State Industrial Exposition, where Western Electric's display included Gray's printer telegraph, hotel annunciator, electric fire alarm, and Sholes & Glidden's typewriter.[71] The typewriter's presence in Western Electric's exhibit reveals one of the advantages to Western Electric of the Western Union connection: exposure to a steady stream of inventive talent. Anson Stager, of course, was the key intermediary between Western Electric and its primary customer, Western Union. His position as general manager of Western Union put him in contact with numerous inventors who were trying to sell the communications giant on their work. If Western Union had no direct use for an invention, Stager would often send it along to Enos Barton. Such was the case with the typewriter.

At numerous public exhibitions, inventors C. Latham Sholes and Carlos Glidden had been trying to find takers for their "writing machine." Stager at first turned them down because they had failed to develop a means of producing duplicate copies. Stager did, however, propose that, considering Western Electric's experience with manufacturing Gray's printing telegrapher, the company might be able to improve the machine. They ultimately negotiated a deal in which Western Electric pursued those improvements in exchange for the exclusive rights to manufacture and sell the typewriters.

At this point a promoter named George Washington Napoleon Yost entered the picture; he convinced Sholes and Glidden that the thinly capitalized Western Electric was not the right outfit to handle their invention. Barton, realizing this, visited E. Remington & Sons at Ilion, New York. Remington's factory, which had produced rifles, had been virtually idle since the end of the Franco-Prussian War. Barton

33

negotiated a contract with William Smoot, Remington's head of production, whereby Remington would manufacture the typewriters and
Western Electric would have exclusive selling rights in the Midwest.[72]

By mid-1874, Remington had the first Western Electric Series 1
typewriters ready for distribution. Within a year, however, Yost had
convinced Remington that they should do their own selling; so Remington paid Western Electric for those rights. This pattern – Western
Electric developing a product then having a supplier manufacture it
for sale under the Western Electric trademark – was to become quite
common once the company entered the electrical appliance business
in the 1880s.[73] But before addressing that marketing challenge, the
company would face a big change in research.

GRAY, BELL, AND THE TELEPHONE

Elisha Gray's primary goal at Western Electric was similar to that of
many of his contemporaries: to create a system of transmitting multiple messages over telegraph wires simultaneously ("multiplexing"). In
1872, Western Union had adopted Joseph B. Stearns's modification
of the Morse system, "duplexing," which provided for simultaneous
transmission of messages on a wire in opposite directions.[74] Theoretically, the Stearns modification doubled the capacity of Western
Union's system; inventing a multiplex (which Edison would do in
1874) could be a real gold mine, for which Western Union would pay
handsomely.

One possible approach, featuring a variety of musical tones as the
multiple messages in a single direction, occurred to Gray serendipi-
tously. In early 1874, while observing his nephew " 'taking shocks' for
the amusement of the smaller children" in a bathtub, Gray "noticed a
sound proceeding from under his hand at the point of contact," which
reproduced a sound emanating from another source in the bathroom.[75] Gray was subsequently able to create a similar effect, which
he called "vibratory currents," in a series of public demonstrations
using a violin. Gray was so impressed with the discovery that he decided to pursue a practical "harmonic telegraph" on a full-time, inde-

pendent basis after finding a new source of capital: Samuel S. White, a manufacturer of dental equipment from Philadelphia.[76] Ironically, Gray's work was just beginning to head toward Western Electric's long-term future (the manufacture of telephone equipment) when he gave up his day-to-day position as the company's superintendent in May 1874. He retained the title of superintendent for a year, and for a few years after that his name appeared on the company letterhead as "electrician." Gray's resignation did not, however, limit his relationship with Western Electric to absentee owner with nominal title. In fact, some of his most significant demonstrations took place at Western Electric.[77] The first, in May 1874, was an attempt to transmit sound over telegraph lines (the "harmonic telegraph"). The transmitter was placed in one of the company's small experimental rooms and the receiver in an office – on the same floor – about fifty to seventy-five feet distant.[78]

In July 1874, Gray demonstrated an apparatus for the transmission of musical tones. The transmitter was placed at Western Electric's shop, and the receiver at Anson Stager's second-story offices in the Merchant's Insurance Building at Washington and LaSalle Streets.[79] Stager assembled a distinguished group in his spacious office to witness the demonstration, including Civil War hero Phil Sheridan, Charles Haskins of the Northwestern Telegraph Company, and C. H. Summers, assistant electrician of the Western Union Telegraph Company. Stager's office was close enough to the street that the quiet was periodically disturbed by horse-drawn wagons, but Stager recalled that during periods of quiet he "could always distinguish the tune." Stager then went to the Western Electric shop (less than a mile away) to witness the transmission by Gray's assistant, William Goodridge.[80]

For much of the next year and a half, Gray toured (including an overseas trip in August and September 1874), demonstrating his discoveries. He was aware that vibratory currents could apply equally to the transmission of music, messages, or the human voice. He chose not to pursue the last – much to his later regret.[81]

Given a choice of exploration in multiplex, musical, or voice transmission, the path of greatest challenge for investigators was voice, for the human voice produces the most complex wave forms of the three.

Furthermore, the most obvious practical applications would be to the telegraph, and the deepest pockets available to sponsor such research belonged to Western Union. What Gray or Bell needed, then, was a compelling reason not to do the obvious thing. They also needed some backbone, since advisors of both steered them away from the telephone. In the final analysis, Gray's extensive work with the telegraph may have blinded him to a host of creative options, just as his nearly ten-year relationship with Western Union likely prevented him from seizing the possibilities he could see.

Alexander Graham Bell did not have that institutional handicap, so he could focus more easily on the issue of voice. He was, as John Brooks puts it, "as steeped in the physiology of human speech as a man could be."[82] His grandfather had run a London elocution school and may have been the model for Henry Higgins in George Bernard Shaw's play *Pygmalion*. Bell's father had also had a career in elocution, including the creation of "Visible Speech," a version of lipreading used to teach deaf people to communicate. Bell began his career as a partner of his father. After the family moved to North America, Bell pursued vocal physiology in Boston. He also began to tutor the deaf, including the son of merchant Thomas Sanders and Gardiner Hubbard's daughter, Mabel.

Bell's relationship with the telegraph – and Western Union – was indirect, through his partner and future father-in-law, Gardiner Hubbard. As early as 1869, Hubbard had joined the hue and cry against Western Union's telegraph "monopoly," delivering an address to the Philadelphia Board of Trade endorsing the popular notion that the telegraph be nationalized, like mail delivery, in the form of a "postal telegraph" (telegraph services offered at post offices).[83] Hubbard's obsession with the telegraph influenced the way in which he viewed Bell's work. Whenever he sensed Bell veering toward voice applications, Hubbard expressed disapproval, even threatening to stand between Mabel and Bell.

Bell, like Gray, was intrigued by Western Union's 1872 adoption of Joseph Stearns's method of duplex telegraph. If Stearns could make a fortune off the duplex, what might Bell do with a multiplex? In October, Hubbard, thinking along the same lines, offered to fund Bell's work developing the multiplex.

Such assistance turned out to be a mixed bag. In the summer of 1875, Bell reached the same conclusion that Gray had arrived at earlier in the year: that he could transmit speech. Hubbard was not interested in this possibility and insisted that Bell stay focused on the telegraph, pursuing the multiplex. Gray received similar advice from both his lawyer, George Willey, and his financial backer, Samuel White. The difference is that whereas Bell rejected that advice, Gray accepted it. Gray commented: "Bell seems to be spending all his energies in [the] talking telegraph. While this is very interesting scientifically it has no commercial value at present, for [the telegraph industry] can do more business over a line by methods already in use than by that system."

Nevertheless, opportunity continued to beckon Gray, and he continued to recognize scientific, if not commercial, possibilities in his observations. In October 1875, he watched two boys playing with what was known as a "lover's telegraph," two cans connected by string. Gray recognized how the same principle of voice transmission could be applied using an electrical device. However, he shelved the idea for three months while pursuing the multiplex telegraph, until finally filing a caveat – not a patent – for voice transmission on February 14, 1876, the same day upon which Gardiner Hubbard filed a patent in Bell's name for "an improvement in telegraphy."

A caveat is typically filed for work in an early stage, giving notice of a possibly patent-bearing concept. Gray's attorney, George Willey, alert to this distinction, wrote to financier Samuel White that Gray could file a patent the next day, in time to contest the issuance of a patent to Bell, but he advised against his doing so. Gray was with White when the letter arrived, and the two discussed it. White suggested that Gray concentrate on the multiplex, and Gray agreed – leaving the telephone field to Bell, whose patent was approved on March 7, 1876. Just as, in 1867, Gray had triumphantly reported to his wife Willey's prediction that Gray was "bound to be rich and celebrated," in 1876, shortly after filing his patent application, Bell wrote to his father, "the whole thing is mine – and I am sure of fame, fortune and success."[84]

In June of 1876, at the Centennial Exposition in Philadelphia, one of the great attractions was a demonstration of Bell's telephone. Gray was unimpressed and assessed the telephone much as he had previously: "As to Bell's talking telephone, it only creates interest in scientific circles. [Its] commercial value will be limited."[85] The cofounder of what became Western Electric would later realize his grave mistake and spend much of the rest of his life trying to claim credit for the invention of the telephone himself.

Gray died in 1901 a broken man. Among his papers was found a scrawled summation of his final twenty-five years: "The history of the telephone will never be fully written. It is partly hidden away in 20 or 30 thousand pages of testimony and partly lying on the hearts and consciences of a few whose lips are Sealed, – Some in death and others by a golden clasp whose grip is even tighter."[86] This elegy to the truth sparked inaccurate portrayals of Gray as an innocent who had lacked both sufficient financial resources and the killer instinct to wage a fair fight with Bell's deep pockets. In fact, Bell's backers had fewer financial resources than Gray's, but the Bell company's subsequent growth into a corporate behemoth led many to engage in sympathetic support of Gray as an ex post facto underdog.

WESTERN UNION VERSUS BELL

The invention of the telephone represented a missed opportunity not only for one of America's great inventors but for the nation's largest communications company. The early 1870s were a heady time for Western Union, which had about 10,000 employees in 7,500 offices generating annual revenues of about $10 million.[87] The well-capitalized giant had established a network of wires and offices connecting every city or town of consequence from coast to coast and was poised to reap the fruits of a monopoly on transmission of news to America's newspapers. As so often happens in the business world, Western Union was most vulnerable at the peak of its power. It was more concerned with protecting the empire it had erected on one technology than with pursuing the technology that would create a far greater empire.

In the fall of 1876, less than a year after the patent of the cash-

38

strapped Bell was approved, Gardiner Hubbard offered to sell the telephone patent to Western Union for $100,000 – and William Orton turned him down.[88] Orton saw little future in the telephone. A year later, Orton changed his mind, and Western Union established the American Speaking Telephone Company, a Bell competitor. Western Union approached development of the telephone much as it had approached the telegraph. Because Western Union was unable to use Bell's research, it rounded up the patents of the usual suspects: leading telegraphic inventors Thomas Edison, George Phelps Jr., and Elisha Gray (plus Amos Dolbear), all of whom were working on the transmission of voice.[89] A battle for control of the telephone erupted between the deep pockets of Western Union and the thinly capitalized Bell company.

In September 1878, Bell Telephone Company sued Peter A. Dowd of Massachusetts to protect Alexander Graham Bell's patents from infringement by Dowd's employer, Western Union.[90] Western Union's lawyers chose to erect a defense around the work of Elisha Gray. By the time of the settlement, Western Union's telephone system, operating in fifty-five cities, had more phones in operation than Bell did.[91] The telephone business increased so quickly for Western Union that it turned over its New York Church Street shop to Western Electric for manufacturing capacity.[92]

The introduction of the telephone presented manufacturers of telegraphic and other electrical equipment with an opportunity rather than a threat. On Kinzie Street, Western Electric seemed well placed to capitalize on the telegraph's position on the cutting edge of communications.[93] The technology involved in producing telegraph equipment was sufficiently similar to that of telephone equipment to make for a smooth transition from one to the other. Any company that successfully produced batteries (for power), wire, or switchboards for the telegraph was well prepared for telephone manufacture. Indeed, the telephone instrument itself was the most radical departure from what Western Electric and its competitors were already making. Western Union, which had been a customer and source of financing for Western Electric's telegraphic manufacturing, played the same roles for its telephone manufacturing.

Western Electric brought divided allegiances to its Western Union telephone arrangement because it had already become a distributor of telephone equipment for Bell. Anson Stager had pursued – and received – a license from Bell to develop private-line service.[94] For some time, Western Electric had skillfully (and in the minds of some Bell people, unethically) straddled the fence, acting as distributor for Bell and as captive supplier to Bell's competitor. Finally, Western Electric loosened its ties with Bell and cast its lot with Western Union. The result was a catastrophe that shaped the company's strategy for decades afterward.

The battle between the communications empire of the nineteenth century and the communications empire of the twentieth century lasted just over a year. Its brief duration surprised few observers. The outcome, however, surprised many: the upstart Bell won. At the apex of the "Gilded Age," the period of American history most frequently likened to laissez-faire capitalism, when money could seemingly buy anything, the company with deep pockets lost. The Federal Communications Commission later referred to the "surprising capitulation of the powerful Western Union to the diminutive Bell Company." How did David slay Goliath in such an environment?

Shortly after the testimony in the patent suit was complete, another struggle was beginning among Gilded Age captains of industry whose Olympian battles shaped the economic landscape below. This battle pitted Titan against Titan for control of Bell's antagonist. Angling to take over Western Union from William Vanderbilt, Jay Gould started the American Union Telegraph Company, in the hope that the competition would reduce the value of Western Union stock. At the same time, he approached Bell's general manager, Theodore Vail, with the intent of combining interests. Although Western Union was frightened by the proposed Gould–Bell alliance, its greatest concern was with threats to its core telegraph business.

In November 1879, Western Union abandoned telephone rights and patents to Bell. In exchange, Bell agreed to transfer all telegraph messages to Western Union, to pay a 20 percent royalty on any telephone rental income it received in the United States for the life of Bell's patents, and not to use the telephone business for "transmission of general business messages, market quotations, or news for sale or publication in competition with the business of Western Union."

Both Bell and Western Union viewed the agreement as a victory. Although the royalty Bell agreed to pay was a stiff one, it had secured rights to the great communications medium of the future. Although Western Union had abandoned a promising market, it succeeded in protecting the core business of the world's greatest private communications company. Both companies achieved a measure of what businesses seek: control of their own environment.

That is precisely what Western Electric lost. The agreement between Western Union and Bell left Western Electric in a vulnerable position – namely, closed out of telephone manufacture, a business with an apparently bright future. In November 1879, only a year after the installation of the first commercial telephone exchange, a telecommunications manufacturer left out of the telephone business was in trouble. Enos Barton recalled the dark autumn of that year: "Our business seemed to have a very poor prospect."[95]

WESTERN ELECTRIC JOINS THE BELL SYSTEM

When Western Union abandoned the telephone business, Western Electric was disappointed but not surprised. In July 1879, Anson Stager had predicted that the telephone – which had made his pet project, the printer telegraph, obsolete – would be controlled by "the Bell Co. or parties outside Western Union."[96] Reading the handwriting on the wall, Stager shifted his interest to the telephone, becoming president of telephone companies in Illinois, Indiana, and Iowa. Meanwhile, Stager's Western Electric made concerted efforts – both direct and indirect – to hook up with Bell.

Although its manufacturing capacity was quite an enticement, Western Electric had many detractors at Bell. Its conflict with Western Union had left sufficient scars to make Bell view with suspicion any entity (such as Western Electric) that had been on the other side. Certainly, the Western Union–Bell agreement did not change Thomas Watson's opinion that Stager and Barton were "a set of men capable of almost any game."[97] And Watson's opinion mattered; aside from his role in the creation of the company, he now reported directly to Bell's general manager, Theodore Vail, and was a major stockholder.[98]

Despite such misgivings, in May 1880 Vail met with Enos Barton on a yacht near Boston. One reason Vail was willing to speak with Barton was Western Electric's January 1880 acquisition of the rights to the patents for the telephonic inventions of John Irwin and William Voelker (owned by Irwin). The most significant of the Irwin–Voelker patents posed a threat to Bell's telephone transmitter, so Vail had offered to buy the patents outright, but nothing had come of that. Now Vail recommended that Western Electric join forces with those of Charles Williams Jr.[99]

Williams needed help. Since 1877, the manufacture of telephones for Bell had been done in Williams's Boston shop, the site of Bell's early experiments and where the young Thomas Edison had cut his teeth. Within two years, increasing volume had overwhelmed the Williams shop, and in 1879 Bell licensed additional manufacturers in Baltimore, Chicago, Cincinnati, and Indianapolis.

The most important of Bell's four manufacturing licensees was the E. T. Gilliland Company, and Western Electric's indirect approach to a relationship with Bell was through Gilliland. Ezra T. Gilliland was one of the experienced telegraphers who made the transition into the telephone manufacturing business. He had established the Indianapolis Telephone Company in February 1879, a most propitious moment. Until 1878, phone users could only make connections with two or three others. Then a workable exchange with a switchboard was established in New Haven, Connecticut, to connect twenty-one subscribers, and the demand for those who could make workable switchboards took off.[100] Gilliland designed telephone instruments and switchboards at the Indianapolis Telephone Company beginning in early 1879 and installed the first telephone exchange in Indianapolis.

In May 1879, Bell traveling agent Oscar Madden reported that Gilliland had established "facilities for turning out work which sets anything and everything which Williams has completely in the shade." Madden advised: "I look upon G. as an exceedingly bright and ingenious mechanic, one who can aid or hurt us very materially, and for that reason should be kept in our service."[101]

Gilliland seemed to be just what Bell was looking for. Bell expected a rapid increase in demand, Thomas Watson wrote Gilliland in June 1879, so his share of Bell's business would "only be limited by the capacity of your factory." Watson added that Theodore Vail expected Gilliland's plant "to rush things and turn out instruments rapidly."[102] Even with Gilliland in the fold, however, one of Bell's old problems recurred: the difficulty of arranging for sufficient manufacturing to keep up with demand. By late 1880 Gilliland had fallen "far behind."

In December, Gilliland told Vail that he needed to expand his plant in order to keep up with orders but the terms of his license prevented him from doing so. Gilliland's financial backers refused him the necessary funds unless he secured a waiver of Bell's option to terminate at six months' notice. Vail was accommodating, because he believed that since the inception of the license Gilliland had "done more towards developing the apparatus used in connection with Exchanges than any man" except Bell employees. Bell's president, W. H. Forbes, promptly approved Vail's request that Gilliland's license be extended to five years.[103]

Gilliland's "backers" were from Western Electric. Realizing how important Gilliland was to Bell, Stager and Barton had begun to accumulate ownership of the Gilliland Company for Western Electric. They kept a low profile because they realized that factions at Bell wished to avoid an alliance with them. But once Gilliland had secured a five-year license, such secrecy was unnecessary, and in March 1881 Western acquired 61 percent of Gilliland's company.[104] Western still had no agreement with Bell, but it had a majority interest in Bell's most valued manufacturer. Now Bell was vulnerable: Western Electric had the right to cancel the license of Bell's favorite manufacturer on six month's notice.[105] Reaching an agreement had become as important to Bell as it was to Western Electric.

There was one possible obstacle to their working relationship: Western Union, which owned a large chunk of Western Electric stock and was well represented on its board of directors. Fate intervened in the late spring, however, when Jay Gould took over Western Union. Gould quickly replaced Western Union's top people – including Anson Stager – with his own. This intensified Stager's desire to work out an agreement between Western Electric and Bell.[106] Western Union president Norvin Green, sensing the hostility of Stager and others at Western Electric, sold Western Union's one-third share in Western Electric to Bell for $150,000 (three times what the company had originally paid).[107] By November, the efforts of Vail, Forbes, and Stager resulted in Bell's acquisition of a majority interest in Western Electric.

In February 1882, Western Electric and Bell signed an agreement making Western Electric Bell's exclusive manufacturer of telephones in the United States. Western agreed to sell only to the American Bell Telephone Company (which in 1899 became American Telephone & Telegraph, AT&T), which then leased the phones to regional "operating" companies, which in turn leased the phones to end users.[108] The Western Electric contract combined with AT&T's agreements with its licensees to form the three pillars of the nascent Bell system and provided the system's organizing principle for the next century: long-distance service was handled by the parent company, local service by the operating companies, and manufacture by Western Electric.

2

IN BELL'S WORLD, BUT
NOT OF IT: 1882–1900

N MAY 1907, THEODORE VAIL BECAME THE
head of Western Electric's parent. One of the ways in which Vail
put his stamp on the company was by inserting an essay into
AT&T's 1907 annual report describing his vision for telephony.
Vail's magisterial essay introduced the public to the concept of "universal service," in which all telephones would be interconnected as
part of what Vail called the "Bell System." In that seminal annual
report, he also maintained that universal service "could not be furnished by disassociated companies."[1] When Vail penned that essay, it
had been twenty-five years since Bell had acquired Western Electric.
Nevertheless, one would be hard pressed to argue that since the acquisition Western had behaved as if it belonged to any system.

Just a few years prior to Vail's return, in June 1901, AT&T's acting
president, Alexander Cochrane, had written to Western Electric's president, Enos Barton: "It has seemed to me at times as though we might
be brought into closer touch with the operations and plans of your
Company."[2] Cochrane's term as AT&T's president was going to expire at the end of the month, so this was not an executive's mandate
for change; rather, it was a wistful hint at how things might have been
different during the first two decades of Western Electric's affiliation
with Bell. Although Bell owned about 60 percent of Western's stock
during that period, it had exercised little control over its captive manufacturer.

The following year, Cochrane's successor, Frederick Fish, ordered
the compilation of a history of the first quarter-century (1877–1902)

Figure 6. Theodore Vail, president of AT&T, whose concept of "universal service" shaped Western Electric's mission

of the Bell Telephone Company. By 1903, Fish's staff had produced more than one hundred and fifty manuscript pages. The history was never published, but was noteworthy in two respects. First, the section written by statistician Walter S. Allen makes the first recorded reference to "universal service," foreshadowing Vail's embrace of the idea.[3] Second, despite having acted as Bell's captive manufacturer from 1882 to 1902, Western Electric was never once mentioned in the entire manuscript. Until Western Electric was effectively integrated into the system, Theodore Vail's alternative to "disassociated companies" would be more a blueprint for the future than a celebration of the past.

A necessary condition for the establishment of the system Vail envisioned was the combination of mass production with mass distribution (vertical integration). Effective integration of Western Electric and AT&T's affiliated local phone companies ("operating companies") appeared to promise many efficiencies. Putting local service and manufacturing under the same umbrella as long distance would reduce transaction costs (marketing, purchasing, and other administration), making them lower than those of "disassociated" companies that dealt with one another in the marketplace. Standardization of equipment would make possible manufacturing economies of scale. Using a captive supplier promised better control over proprietary technology. Finally, a reliable source of supply would prevent the whims of a sometimes capricious marketplace from causing a breakdown of service.

The integration of Western Electric into the Bell System was to involve two stages. The first, which lasted about twenty years, was a struggle for control. Bell's acquisition of Western did not immediately change Western's behavior because the goals of the two enterprises were not aligned and each company pursued its own agenda. The second stage, from about 1900 to 1925, involved the actual process of integration – the true establishment of a Bell System and the delineation of Western Electric's role within it. In this latter period, Western's agenda, which had been separate from – and sometimes in conflict with – that of its parent, shifted into alignment with that of the Bell System.

The 1880s and 1890s were a yeasty time for electrical manufacturers. Bell acquired Western Electric only a few years after the inventions of the telephone and the electric light, when possibilities in the electrical industries seemed to be growing at a geometric rate. Having started as a manufacturer for the telegraph business, Western already produced a full line of nontelephone apparatus and spent the next twenty-five years expanding on that. In addition to making telephone equipment, the company was an early manufacturer of electric power machinery, electric lights, and machines for computing. From the February day in 1882 when Western agreed to direct its telephone equipment manufacture toward meeting Bell's needs, the two companies argued about what else – if anything – Western should do. Upon Theodore Vail's 1907 return that question remained unresolved.

INTERNATIONAL EXPANSION

The value of international business was one issue upon which Bell and Western Electric agreed. On July 16, 1881, only eleven days after Bell bought Western Union's one-third interest in Western Electric, Enos Barton reported to superintendent Milo Kellogg from Boston that "Mr. Vail is very emphatic and explicit now in regard to the export of telephones."[4] In 1880 Bell had established an export operation, the International Bell Telephone Company, headquartered in Antwerp. Bell imported telephone apparatus there from the American Bell Telephone Company of Boston and from E. T. Gilliland's Indianapolis plant.

Western Electric had already ventured overseas, but not out of any grand design. Rather, it had done so out of desperation. Western's 1879 exclusion from the American telephone business, when Bell's patents appeared to exclude it from domestic telephone manufacture, had first catalyzed the firm to seek foreign business. Enos Barton traveled to Europe and in February 1880 reported back: "I am well assured that by organizing a good shop here a good business can be made."[5]

Because transportation and tariff costs for the Antwerp operation were quite high, Bell considered establishing its own factory there. In October 1881, Gilliland, negotiating for Western Electric, convinced Bell to invest in a 45 percent interest in a new manufacturing company in Antwerp, the Bell Telephone Manufacturing Company, with Western Electric owning the remaining 55 percent. The sole problem Barton saw was "the only way we can get any good out of the European telephone business is to have some of us who know the business . . . come here to live." Barton, however, did not want to be that person.[6] Therefore he was relieved when Gilliland agreed to act as European plant superintendent and to supervise the construction of the plant in Antwerp.[7]

Gilliland returned to America shortly after completion of the Antwerp plant. Not long afterward, however, a fire destroyed the plant, and Gilliland refused to return to Europe to rebuild it. Instead, it was rebuilt under the direction of F. R. Welles, who had taken over man-

Figure 7. F. R. Welles, who took Western Electric abroad in 1880, then ran its overseas operations for thirty years

agement of the European operation.[8] Welles was Western Electric's first college graduate. At a time when less than 10 percent of Americans had high school diplomas, a college grad was a curiosity in the business world. Many companies venturing overseas learned that becoming an international company was not the same thing as being cosmopolitan. Therefore college men, who presumably could better navigate the shoals of language and custom, became desirable overseas representatives.

The son of a maker and distributor of agricultural implements, Welles had graduated from the University of Rochester (the school where Enos Barton matriculated but never graduated). There he met Barton's brother George, a connection that led to Welles's joining the company in 1876 and becoming the company's first stenographer, having taught himself shorthand and typewriting to qualify for the job. Welles also did extensive letter writing, an important skill for a man who would spend nearly thirty years of his career overseas.

Antwerp was just the beginning of Western's overseas manufacture. The company sought new markets and responded to foreign governments' preference for locally produced equipment by setting up other manufacturing facilities overseas.[9] Such was the case in 1883, when Western Electric built a plant in London. Bell soon lost its taste for manufacturing and in July 1890 agreed to sell its 45 percent interest in the Bell Manufacturing Company to Western Electric. By 1900, Western Electric was manufacturing in some of the capitals of world commerce: London, Berlin, Paris, Tokyo, Antwerp, and Milan. It was well on its way to developing America's most far-flung empire of overseas manufacture.[10]

DOMESTIC CONSOLIDATION

During the early 1880s, Western Electric simultaneously pursued expansion abroad and consolidation at home. Consolidation promised to reduce duplication of management and other expenses. In short, it would achieve economies of scale.[11] Telephone manufacturing, which had grown out of a world of small shops, was becoming big business.

Upon his return from Europe, Gilliland was appointed to a committee to look into the consolidation of shops. The committee's first decision involved consolidation of Western's Midwest manufacturing operations, either in Indianapolis or Chicago. The committee included two veterans of Western's Chicago shop (Vice President Enos Barton and Superintendent Milo Kellogg) and one from Indianapolis (Gilliland). It must have been awkward for Barton and Gilliland to serve together on the committee. Onetime competitors for Chicago's telephone manufacturing business, now they had to decide whose plant would survive and expand, and whose would disappear.

Barton's Kinzie Street plant in Chicago had a spotty track record, partly because of the difficulties that stemmed from sharing their building with others. Western only had the top floor, fifty feet of the basement and second floor, and twenty-five feet of the first floor.[12] The production of cable, for instance, was more in the style of Rube Goldberg than that of Henry Ford. During the process of production, the core went from the second floor to the basement to the roof. Once the core was joined to the outer sheaf, the cable was passed down the stairs to the basement, then up the stairs for wiring. W. R. Patterson, who would later become superintendent, explained: "There was an elevator to the shipping room, but the finished cable was too heavy for it; so it was passed out the window and down to the shipping reel set up on a wagon. Then the reel was lagged and hauled to the freight house." Patterson added (as if he needed to!): "I think this was the only cable made in just the way described."[13]

Nevertheless, Chicago was the fastest-growing major city in the United States and had already become one of the nation's two communications centers (along with New York). The committee also concluded that Chicago had a better labor market: "by moving away from [Chicago] or its immediate vicinity we should also in great measure lose the work of years in building up and holding together a body of workmen in our line which are in many respects unequaled." The committee recommended erection of a larger plant in Chicago. The Clinton Street plant, at the corner of Clinton and Van Buren Streets, represented a new world for Western Electric – its own four-story building.

That meant closing Gilliland's plant, although Indianapolis offered cheaper labor, fuel, and real estate as well as lower taxes.[14] It was as if once the Indianapolis shop had served its purpose – to entice Bell into acquiring Western Electric – it had become dispensable. Charles Williams's old shop in Boston became dispensable too, as Western consolidated its East Coast manufacturing in New York.

After serving as juror during his plant's death sentence, Gilliland moved to Boston and opened an experimental shop for Bell in December 1883 (which he renamed the mechanical department in June 1884). By relocating to Boston, Gilliland became the first individual to move between Western Electric and Bell. Although that became a fairly common occurrence in the twentieth century (most notably when Harry Thayer moved from the Western Electric's presidency to AT&T's presidency), it was quite rare early on. The experimental shop had three specific functions: assessing the promise of inventions submitted to the company, inspection of Western Electric products manufactured for Bell, and the designing of new products.[15] Reflecting the attitude of his new boss, Theodore Vail, Gilliland saw the shop's general charter as "the establishment of uniformity in methods employed by different exchanges looking to the adoption of one universal telephone system."[16] The shop was the kernel that sprouted into both Bell Laboratories and Bell's vaunted quality-control system. It also provided Gilliland a forum in which to critique his onetime competitor, Enos Barton.

ENOS BARTON'S COMPANY

The first four years after Western joined the Bell System was a period of general economic downturn in the United States. Western Electric's sales fell steadily and profits evaporated. Although Anson Stager was president, Enos Barton essentially ran the company and shouldered the blame for its poor performance. Bell's general manager, John Hudson, and AT&T's president, Theodore Vail, agreed on the need to fire or at least demote him.[17]

Barton's style no doubt compounded their assessments of his substance. He lacked the verbal dexterity and polish necessary to make a strong first impression on either higher-ups or subordinates. "He was then slower and more deliberate of speech than in later years," according to Welles, his onetime stenographer. "He sought long for the right word to express his exact meaning." Charles Fay, general manager of the Chicago Telephone Company, viewed Barton as "a slow man, [who] needs spurring." Barton's foreman in Chicago, Charles Lewis, was more blunt: Barton "did not, in the beginning, impress any of us as being very smart."[18]

Therefore, after Anson Stager resigned as president in January 1885 (he died in March), Western's board replaced him with William Smoot, the longtime superintendent of the E. Remington & Sons works, with whom Barton had negotiated typewriter production a decade earlier. Whereas Stager had been a "hands-off" president, Smoot was very hands-on, taking over some of Barton's responsibilities. For Enos Barton, this was not only a promotion denied, but effectively a demotion.

The selection of Smoot seemed to seal Barton's fate never to head the company he had helped to found. Smoot was only thirty-nine

Figure 8. Western Electric's New York office staff, 1883. Enos Barton occupies the central position in the second row; his successor as Western president, and Theodore Vail's successor as AT&T president, H. B. Thayer, is in white hat in the back row.

(three years younger than Barton) when he took office. Therefore, Barton could not reasonably expect to succeed him – until Smoot died from typhoid fever in February 1886, after barely a year as president. Faced with choosing a president for the second time in little more than a year, Western's board again balked at offering the job to Enos Barton.

The board selected a search committee of three: Bell's general manager, John Hudson, Vice President Charles Bowditch, and Western Electric's legal counsel, Norman Williams.[19] After months of discussion, the committee offered the presidency to Charles Fay, citing his superior organizational skills. Williams realized one of the consequences to their decision: Barton would resign, ending his Western Electric career.

Fay, who lacked manufacturing experience, did not want Barton to

53

leave and offered Barton the presidency in two years if he would stay on. Barton declined. Fay then offered to become vice president if Barton would assume the presidency. Fay's judgment planted doubts in the search committee. Bowditch doubted that "putting a watchdog" on Barton was "the true way to get the best out of any man."[20]

The committee did not wish to show disrespect to the company founder. The slim 53 percent majority of Western Electric shares Bell controlled made it injudicious to antagonize the other 47 percent, and Williams noted the substantial "following of stock [Barton] represents."[21] Therefore, the committee offered Barton the chance to sell a "plan for a better organization" at the next board meeting. He agreed, made his presentation, and was given a "probationary" year more befitting a new hire than a founder. Barton never forgot how he was treated by the Bell people, and thereafter wariness of the company's parent became a way of life at Western Electric.

In October 1886, Enos Barton finally became president. It was worth the wait. He guided the company for the next twenty-two years. By the time of his death in 1916, Barton had become a Western Electric icon. As founder, president, and chairman, he devoted nearly fifty years to shaping this company. Western Electric had two other founders (Elisha Gray and Anson Stager) and thirteen other presidents, but Enos Barton stands alone – so much so that it is difficult to imagine how the company would have developed if he had not become president.

Subsequent to his presidency, if Western Electric employees had looked back at Enos Barton he would have seemed familiar to them. Although Western changed dramatically after Barton's departure, the company had absorbed many of his values and personal traits – including paternalism, humility, and loyalty. Enos Barton treated his company as an extended family. In a sense, it was. Most of his key early recruits were family or friends, and the company never completely abandoned such hiring practices. In the 1880s, for instance, the Clinton Street insulating department employed many women from Alsace-Lorraine because they were family or friends of their expatriate foreman, Frank DuPlain. Similarly, in the 1960s and 1970s,

Iron Curtain and Latin American refugees found jobs at the Hawthorne plant through family and friends.

Barton's paternalism could exasperate or exhilarate. Well into the 1890s – when the company employed thousands – the head of Western's New York operation, Harry Thayer, could neither hire nor increase the salaries of his staff without Barton's approval. Yet Barton could also offer aid to a member of the Western Electric "family." In 1901, for instance, he arranged – and helped pay for – an operation for a onetime employee. In Barton's spirit of corporate responsibility sprouted the roots of Western Electric's system of welfare capitalism.

Barton would never have taken the credit for creating that system, or just about anything else. In a nation whose defining character traits included self-promotion, Enos Barton expended little energy in promoting himself. In 1905, on the occasion of the hundredth anniversary of Jefferson County, New York, as one of the county's most illustrious native sons he could have told how he had risen from a local farm to the presidency of the world's largest manufacturer of electrical equipment. Instead, Barton spoke at length about the county, never mentioning himself. Titles also meant little to him. He was content to sign himself as "secretary," and did so until President Stager insisted he use the title "vice president." Enos Barton held his ego in check, whether he was dealing with business associates or speaking to his onetime neighbors.

Barton preferred to promote his company and its products. One member of his staff, Charles DuBois, recalled that "Mr. Barton made it somehow impossible for us – at least in his presence – to talk or think about our personal importance. We could exalt 'the Company' as much as we chose, but his inscrutable composure and silence when a man showed any trace of egotism was generally sufficient to change the conversation." DuBois, who later became one of Barton's successors as president, explained: "This was not because he was unsympathetic, but because he felt strongly the danger to a young man of a 'swelled head,' and further, he wanted us to feel as he felt: that whoever might be the immediate agent in a successful transaction it was the Company that really did things."[22]

His subdued temperament appeared to make Enos Barton the right man to head a captive manufacturer. Indeed, Western Electric's subsequent executives tended to be "company men." In the post–World War II era, for instance, most of the company's executives entrusted their careers to higher-ups rather than lobbying for particular promotions. Long before the era of "the organization man," the Bell System appeared to have found in Enos Barton a man who would assuage its worries about executives who pursue their own interests rather than those of the organization. The organization Barton would look out for, however, was Western Electric, not Bell Telephone.

Enos Barton inspired loyalty to himself and valued loyalty to Western Electric. An 1898 eulogy he delivered for one of his subordinates reveals as much about Barton as about its subject: "Perhaps the predominant spirit which characterized his intercourse with others might be described as a certain *loyalty*. He was loyal to the interest which he represented."[23] From Enos Barton, that was the highest praise, just as it became for Western Electric. Employees' long service became the source of praise, parties, promotions – and job security.

Barton valued loyalty to Western Electric rather than to Bell. This is no surprise with respect to the employees whose service predated Western's inclusion in the Bell System. Yet up to the day Western Electric disappeared as a separate entity – more than one hundred years later – Western's employees identified themselves more with the company Enos Barton founded than with the system Theodore Vail envisioned.

Such loyalty to Western Electric presented a particular problem in the decades immediately following its acquisition by Bell because Western's agenda differed from Bell's. Bell wanted a reliable manufacturer of telephone equipment. Western sought profitability and growth, but also sufficient diversification to avoid dramatic swings in performance.

Philosopher Isaiah Berlin once compared the individual who attempts to do many things to a fox, and the individual focused on one thing to a hedgehog. Enos Barton was a fox, but he headed a captive supplier whose parent wanted a hedgehog. Ever prepared for a downturn in his main line of business, Barton's inclination was to expand the company's scope and find willing buyers for various new product lines. He was more of an entrepreneur than an organization man in a system that so imbued its people with institutional ways that they were later said to have "Bell-shaped heads." Therefore, Barton was the right choice from Western's perspective, but the wrong one from Bell's.

INTEGRATION BY CONFERENCE

Enos Barton's early years as Western Electric's president featured the first formal steps toward a vertically integrated Bell system. Those first steps involved a series of conferences of executives and prominent technical representatives of Bell, its licensees, and Western Electric. At the first conference of Bell and its affiliates in October 1886, Bell's general manager, Theodore Vail, also represented another entity: the American Telephone and Telegraph Company (AT&T), which was established in 1885 to handle long-distance telephony for Bell.

Although the 1886 conference was the only one Vail attended – he left Bell in September 1887 – the conferences reflected his vision. Vail saw the new company's mission as vital. He realized that the expiration of Bell's key patents in 1894 would usher in a dangerous period of competition and saw the establishment of an efficient long-distance network as an excellent defense against that competition. Industry newcomers in the 1890s would have to take years to establish such a network, hence Vail's sense of urgency in 1885. He believed that Bell should act as if the "competitive" period had begun well before the expiration of the patents.[24]

The switchboard was a linchpin of Vail's growth strategy. His strategy involved expansion both in depth and breadth: depth by amassing more subscribers in each town or city, and breadth by developing the ability to connect subscribers from distant towns and cities to one another. State-of-the-art switchboard technology, which had been Western Electric's principal innovative strength since the late 1870s, was crucial to the strategy's success. Therefore, an entire set of later conferences was devoted to switchboard issues from 1887 to 1891.

The initial telephone switchboard of the 1870s was hardly a labor-saving device. A call would go through a call register clerk, who then sent a ticket, naming the party, to the operator, who then made the connection. Upon completion of the call, both parties signaled "telephone through" on their call boxes and the register clerk advised the operator to disconnect. As the number of lines increased, the operators moved to a separate room from the call-box clerks, and another go-between was added: runners between the call-box clerks and the operators.

Not surprisingly, one of the limiting factors in attracting new telephone subscribers was the time required to get a connection. In the late 1870s, customers waited an average of three to five minutes for a connection to be made. In 1879, General Manager Leroy Firman of the Chicago exchange of the American District Telephone Company (ADTC) developed a switchboard that allowed a single operator to complete the entire call connection. Firman's "multiple" switchboard increased the capacity of the exchange and improved service. Each connection, however, required operators to perform a series of time-consuming motions, but they only had one hand free to do so because the other was occupied holding their telephone receiver. Western Electric's innovations helped make the process more efficient. Frank Shaw invented a telephone headset, thereby freeing the operator's second hand. Charles Scribner's "click" test allowed operators to more quickly hear a busy signal before connecting a call.[25] These innovations to Firman's multiple switchboard reduced average connect time to about forty-five seconds in Chicago and well under twenty seconds on the faster boards in New Orleans and Nashville.[26] Telephone use became much more attractive, and subscriptions increased.

Consequently, the size of telephone exchanges grew tremendously, and designers struggled to increase the capacity of switchboards. This presented challenges to technical staff. Conditions at large exchanges could not be replicated in a laboratory, so Western Electric and other manufacturers did their experimenting at the exchange itself. Because each exchange was unique, Western Electric could not achieve standardization. Even when standard components could be used, local operating companies frequently requested that they be modified to include an innovation developed by one of their own "experts." Western Electric felt bound by its contract with Bell to provide such instruments regardless of their merits.

Such experimentation was the nineteenth-century equivalent of installing a computer before it had been debugged; it could put an exchange out of order. Chicago Bell's general manager, B. E. Sunny, recalled that in late 1887, when Western Electric installed a switchboard of special make at the Chicago exchange, the operators could "[barely] make any connection at all." Bell vice president John Hudson therefore suggested a conference to discuss how to reduce the annoyance to subscribers to a minimum.[27]

The first switchboard conference was convened on December 19, 1887, in New York City. Even in his absence, Theodore Vail cast a long shadow. The main topic discussed was how to achieve Vail's goal of standardization of equipment and methods throughout the affiliated companies.[28] Standardization was a timely issue, because switching still offered "diseconomies" of scale: the larger boards cost more *per line* than the small ones. Whereas a 50-line "standard" board cost $150 in 1880, a 2,700-line multiple board in Boston cost $40,000 three years later.[29] At times, Enos Barton became defensive, as conference attendees focused on Western Electric's practice of building switchboards to the specifications of those setting up the exchange rather than insisting on a more standard approach.

Western Electric and Bell could not even agree on the fundamental issue of who was "the customer." At an 1891 conference, Western's Charles Scribner offered one conception of the customer: someone at the operating company to which Western supplied equipment, the telephone exchange managers. According to Scribner, "the people who use the apparatus and people who know what it is that they require . . . those who are handling switchboards and using them are the best ones to consider the question."[30] To AT&T's Angus Hibbard, in contrast, the customer was the person using the service, "a business man who needed a telephone. It is what he wants; it is his problem of what he wants to be done for him, and for which he will pay his money."[31] In other words, the operating companies should standardize around what the ultimate customer wanted. That was something over which Bell had more control than Western Electric did.

By 1893, when Bell's first major patent expired, the company had not yet succeeded in integrating its system of operating companies, much less integrated manufacturing into its operations. Engineers from AT&T, Bell, Western Electric, and the major operating companies did not succeed in setting standards. Yet one message conveyed at the switchboard meetings was that Bell was not going to control Western Electric's "excessive" innovation until the operating companies agreed to move toward standard equipment.

The end of Bell's patent monopoly, and its failure to integrate its operating companies during that patent monopoly, made future developments in the industry uncertain. Not limited by Western Electric's switchboard patents, other companies' systems quickly challenged the multiple switchboard at the very time when the termination of Bell's telephone patents ended its monopoly. Although Western would control the fundamental multiple switchboard patent until 1899, alternative switchboards for large cities represented a significant threat.

One example was the 1893 installation of an "express" switchboard in San Francisco. The express was based on groups of small exchanges in which calls could be "transferred" from one exchange to another, just like long-distance calls. It worked well in large communities where most phone calls would remain within an exchange. But it also sped up the transfer of calls through the use of automatic signals, which notified the operator both when the hand set was lifted off its hook and again when the phones were hung up. Another competitor introduced a completely automatic switchboard, eliminating the need for operators on local calls.

As the technology behind telephony became less visible, users could focus more on their application of the device – an important prerequisite for a mass market. In addition, the onset of competition created a market attractive enough to dramatically increase the number of subscribers. With the end of Bell's patents and the advent of viable competition for Western Electric's switchboards, the two companies faced a period of doubt about Western's identity and its relations with its parent just when they both were about to enter the world stage – at the World's Columbian Exposition in Chicago.

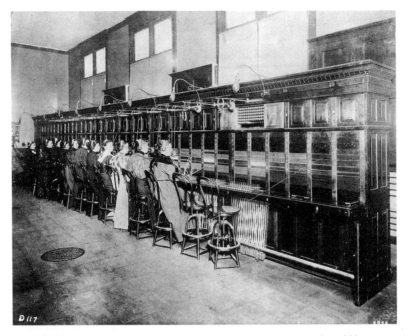

Figure 9. First multiple switchboard equipped with automatic signals, in Worcester, Massachusetts (1896)

THE FUTURE ON DISPLAY

In the summer of 1893, the philosopher William James wrote to his brother Henry about big doings in Chicago: "*Everyone* says one ought to sell all one has and mortgage one's soul to go there. . . . People cast away all sin and baseness, burst into tears and grow religious etc., under the influence!"[32] James was writing about the Columbian Exposition, the last big world's fair of the nineteenth century. The most stunning aspect of the Exposition was its use of electricity and light. Using ninety thousand incandescent lights and five thousand arc lights, the Exposition featured more lighting than any American city, leading people to call the fairgrounds the "White City."[33] Originally scheduled for 1892, four hundred years after Columbus first landed in the New World, the event actually opened in May 1893 and attracted roughly thirty million people (at a time when America's population was just over sixty million).[34]

Chicago's fair reflected the evolution that had taken place in the business world since Philadelphia's Centennial Exposition seventeen years earlier, where Alexander Graham Bell had demonstrated the telephone. Whereas for Bell and other makers of electrical devices involved in the field of electricity the 1876 exposition had presented an opportunity for virtuoso display, the 1893 exposition felt more institutional. Whereas the electrical gadgetry on display in 1876 had come either from individuals or small firms, larger firms like Western Electric (whose Clinton Street plant was just a few miles north of the White City) sent displays in 1893. The business of exposition display, like that of electrical manufacture and much of the U.S. economy, had gone corporate. The writer Edward Bellamy found it distasteful: "The underlying motive of the whole exhibition, under a sham pretense of patriotism, is business, advertising with a view to individual money-making."[35]

Bellamy was right to notice that the fair represented institutional advertising to its many participants. Before the concept of institutional advertising in print caught on in the twentieth century, Western Electric and other electrical manufacturers relied on two methods of getting the word out about their companies that are similar to those which high-tech firms use today: hawking individual products in trade journals and at trade shows. Even a poor promoter like George Shawk advertised in trade journals such as the *Telegrapher* and the *Journal of the Telegraph*. Under Enos Barton, the company continued to do so in the *Electrical Review*, *Electrical World*, and *Western Electrician*, nineteenth-century versions of today's computer journals.

Western Electric presented displays at two types of shows, industry events and world's fairs. Its decision to display or not was – just as Bellamy suggested – a business decision, weighing costs and benefits, with an emphasis on audience. One of Enos Barton's first moves after becoming president in 1886 was to inform Bell's general manager, John Hudson, of his opinion regarding the advisability of a Western Electric display at the 1887 Electrical Exhibition in Brussels: "Our experience with electrical exhibitions of late years is that they are attended more by our competitors than by our customers, and that a public exhibition of our very best work helps our competitors and imitators more than it helps ourselves."[36]

The costs and benefits to Western Electric of the Columbian Exposition surpassed those of trade shows. The company spent more than $100,000 – roughly 20 percent of its annual profits – on its Chicago display. For that kind of money it could have built a new factory. This was a triumph of marketing over manufacturing.

The White City's celebration of electricity and light provides a useful lens through which to view Western Electric's strategy, and its relations with its parent. The central questions raised by the Exposition were crucial to Western Electric: what would the future look like, and how would it come about?[37] As Western considered how to present itself, it faced questions of self-definition, such as which opportunities to pursue and which to let go.

The divergent missions of Bell and Western Electric were evident at the Columbian Exposition. Prior to 1893, the manufacture of telephone apparatus had increased, but not at the same pace as the growth of electric light and power, Western's two greatest distractions from the manufacture of telephone apparatus. In 1885, William Smoot argued that "the Electric Lighting field is now by far the largest electrical work in sight, and is worth trying for to a reasonable extent." Smoot also saw the running of electric power plants as "necessary in order to introduce the system [of electrical lighting]."[38] Western Electric stayed in the business of electric lights and power machinery, establishing a separate department for the development of power apparatus in 1891. As we have seen, at the time of the Chicago Exposition, Bell's two most important telephone patents were about to expire, opening the telephone business to competition. Furthermore, Western faced increasing switchboard competition. Consequently, Enos Barton chose to emphasize Western's developments in electrical light and power.

Bell and Western, which were having such difficulties integrating into one operation, did not show a unified face to the public. They exhibited separately. Bell's greatest promotion for the Columbian Exposition was the opening of the first long-distance service between

New York and Chicago on October 18, 1892 (with Alexander Graham Bell manning the New York end of the connection) well before the Exposition opened. The following summer, at the fair, the Bell Company offered the public a chance to make similar calls from a long-distance phone booth at the rear of the temple in the electricity building. Thus visitors could test for themselves the quality of a connection with a New York operator.

By contrast, Western's most widely discussed exhibit had nothing to do with the telephone. Rather, it involved incandescent lighting, in an attempt to "reproduce in as realistic manner as possible the natural transitions of light during a period of twenty-four consecutive hours of night and day." By showing a series of painted scenes onstage in various types of light, the exhibit acted as a very slow-motion picture a year before the coming of commercial motion pictures. J. P. Barrett, author of a book on the Exposition, considered it "by all odds the most attractive and popular exhibit in the Electrical Building, and one of the most interesting at the Exposition."[39] More than three thousand people viewed this exhibit each day.[40]

Western also displayed an "electrical reminder," a clock that could be set for an alarm bell to ring at any quarter-hour interval.[41] That alarm clock was a reminder of a time when bells and alarms were an integral part of the company's business, rather than the scant 1 percent they represented in 1893. Similarly, although telegraph apparatus had never amounted to more than 10 percent of the company's business after Bell acquired control of it, Western exhibited state-of-the-art keys, sounders, relays, and repeaters.[42] It also compared contemporary telegraph switchboards to telephone switchboards. Western Electric and the German firm Siemens and Halske were the largest firms that could display both as part of their history, having successfully made the leap from telegraph to telephone equipment manufacture.

Barrett noted that "in one corner of the space allotted to the Western Electric Company was shown almost every instrument or piece of apparatus used in telephone work."[43] This included a historical exhibit showing the evolution of switchboards since 1883. Switchboards older than that "ancient date in this recently developed business" had not been preserved. Western also displayed insulated wire and cable, which had comprised substantial chunks of its business since the industry's "ancient" times.

Western Electric won ten awards at the Exposition, only two of which were for telephone equipment (telephone cables and multiple switchboards). It also garnered prizes for its old standbys, from telegraph apparatus to annunciators and signaling apparatus.[44] It won for electrical lights, from Columbian street lampposts to the application of electrical lights for the creation of scenic effects in theaters. It also won for dynamos.[45] Clearly this was not just a manufacturer of telephone equipment.

THE DEPARTMENT STORE OF ELECTRICAL APPARATUS

The Columbian Exposition not only provided Western Electric a forum in which to showcase its products but the opportunity to observe a possible corporate role model. The dominant company at the Exposition was General Electric (GE), Thomas Edison's corporate legacy. Just one year after the Edison General Electric Company merged with Thomson-Houston to form General Electric, the new company won more than thirty awards at the Exposition in a variety of fields – more than twice as many as any other firm.[46] Looking toward the new century, Western concerned itself with how well it would compete with companies like General Electric, and to what extent it wanted to be like GE.

In 1895, Enos Barton instructed the company treasurer, J. M. Jackson, to draw up a financial comparison of Western Electric with General Electric and with the nine-year-old Westinghouse. General Electric was the most profitable; Western and Westinghouse were roughly comparable. Barton ordered similar comparisons in subsequent years. In pursuit of more control over his business, his profits, and his work force, Barton sought to expand the scope of Western Electric's business. In scrutinizing what other prominent electrical manufacturers were doing, he found that they also were diversifying.

Barton had always kept an eye out for a wider range of business, but not until the mid-1890s did he pursue it in earnest. As he put it, "We are reducing prices on our patented apparatus, spending more than ever in experiments." Consequently, the company's competitive product lines had increased. He concluded that "we are becoming a department store for electrical apparatus."[47]

The department store analogy came naturally to Barton. With the exception of telephone and telegraph companies, Western Electric's closest relationship was with a department store. Chicago department store pioneer Marshall Field had been a close friend of Anson Stager and served as pallbearer at his funeral. Field was a longtime customer of Western Electric, in a wide range of products. From fire alarms to elevator annunciators to watch clocks to electric lighting, if Western Electric made it, Marshall Field bought it.[48] If Western Electric wanted to display it, Field would help: he donated one million dollars to help make the Columbian Exposition possible.[49]

Barton voiced a philosophy about the scope of Western Electric's business that clashed with Bell's conception of Western's role: "The question naturally arises whether room and facilities for our possible demands for telephone exchange apparatus might not be provided by discontinuing some other lines of work." Barton's solution fit his expansive temperament: "Manufacturers that depend for an outlet for their products upon some one line of business, as for instance railroads, telephone or telegraph companies, or makers of muskets, must expect extremes of dullness and briskness." Diversification, he insisted, was a means of avoiding such extremes and a way to keep his key workers busy.

While Barton wanted to build up his dynamo business, Hudson objected to the potential effect on telephone manufacturing. Why could Western Electric not give up the dynamo work and focus on telephone work? In so doing, it could delay expenditures for plant construction. If little profit was to be had in manufacturing dynamos, Hudson suggested, would not shutting off that branch of work make "room for the pressure that is coming in telephone work?"[50] While Bell remained concerned about Western Electric's devotion to non-telephone business, Barton declared it "advantageous to have more than one kind of work on hand to be ready to do a general electric manufacturing business."[51]

At its two American manufacturing locations (Chicago and New York), the company employed different approaches to expanding the scope of its business. In Chicago, Enos Barton focused on the two new glamorous lines of electrical manufacturing: electric lights and electric power equipment. Beyond these lines, one of Chicago's most notable ventures was the experimental work Charles Scribner did on x-rays. In 1896, the first x-ray experiment in North America was performed at Western Electric. As in the case of many other opportunities, Western abandoned the field, and General Electric became America's top producer.

Harry Thayer's New York factory is where the company tried most of its wider-ranging possibilities. In the late 1880s, telephone apparatus volume was insufficient to keep Thayer's factory busy enough to maintain his skilled workers. One job he took on was building a huge (six-by-twenty-foot) annunciator. The device used electrical current to highlight particular numbers (like the floor indicators in elevators). In this case, the annunciator was to be used for the game of Keno by miners in Leadville, Colorado. The purpose of its manufacture was cloaked in secrecy because of Enos Barton's distaste for gambling.[52]

Word got out anyway. Six months later, Thayer received a letter from Mobile, Alabama: "I understand that you are manufacturers of gambling machines. If so, I would like to have you make me a table with a magnetized top, so that when the dice are rolled, a secret push button will so magnetize the table, that the loaded dice can be manipulated in favor of the dealer." At that point, Thayer put an end to Western Electric's involvement in the gambling business.[53]

The most promising lines of ancillary business involved inventors who made devices useful to the U.S. government. By 1890, Thayer had developed a relationship with a naval lieutenant (and inventor) named Bradley A. Fiske. Fiske's experiments at Thayer's shop during the next two decades led to the semaphore range finder and other signaling devices that were widely used during World War I. Another relationship Thayer cultivated was with Herman Hollerith, whose tabulating machine represents one of the company's most significant paths abandoned.

Many computers prior to the 1980s employed punch cards as "software," a technology developed by Herman Hollerith nearly one hundred years earlier.[54] Hollerith established a system of punched cards and created a machine that sensed the perforations and tallied results. He first used his equipment in Baltimore to compile mortality statistics in 1886; then for the U.S. surgeon general in 1889; then, most significantly, for the U.S. census in 1890.[55] Hollerith had worked for the United States Census Bureau in the 1880s, when the 1880 census count had taken seven years to complete. With the benefit of Hollerith's equipment, the 1890 census took only two years to yield results.[56]

The keypunches for the 1890 census were made by Pratt & Whitney, the electrical card readers ($25–30,000 worth) by Western Electric.[57] This was no great leap for Western. After all, the technology for Hollerith's machines was similar to that employed by printing telegraph machines, which had been a marquee product for Western beginning in the 1870s. The printing telegraph employed a moving tape with perforations corresponding to dots and dashes, and electrical contacts made or broken by the perforations transmitted the information. The machines Western built for Hollerith were different only in that, instead of transmitting information, they counted it. Western also built the first tabulating equipment for the insurance industry in 1891, and the first such equipment for railroads in the 1890s.[58]

Western Electric was an important connection for Hollerith. America was not the only country performing census work, and Western's worldwide offices offered important connections with foreign governments. Western's Columbian Exposition exhibit advertised the company's presence in Antwerp, Berlin, Paris, and London – to which the company added Tokyo and St. Petersburg before the end of the decade. Western's affiliated St. Petersburg plant built the machines for Russia's census in 1897, and the Berlin plant built machines for the Austrian census.

The key point of decision for this relationship came in 1896, when Hollerith tried to convince Western Electric officials to buy him out, then hire him as manager.[59] When Western Electric chose not to buy him out, Hollerith chartered the Tabulating Machine Company in December 1896, issuing stock valued at $100,000.[60] After receiving the contract for the 1900 census, Hollerith began to build machines in his own shop rather than having Pratt & Whitney and Western Electric do so.

In 1911, Hollerith sold the Tabulating Machine Company and its patents as part of a three-way merger to form the Computing-Tabulating-Recording Company (CTR). Three years later, Thomas Watson became CTR's general manager, and in 1915 he became president. In 1924, Watson renamed the company International Business Machines Corporation (IBM). Accepting Hollerith's offer in 1896 might have changed the course of Western Electric's history, and indeed the history of the computing industry.

The mid-1890s appeared to offer ample grounds for Barton's fears of losing telephone business, as Western had in 1879. Bell's second major telephone patent expired in 1894, a year when America was in the grip of an economic downturn of epic proportion. Despite Enos Barton's deepest fears about "dullness" in telephone work, Western Electric experienced a phenomenal spurt in growth the last five years of the nineteenth century – and most of that growth was in the telephone business. The end of Bell's monopoly engendered a variety of local competition; and Bell's licensees, in response to this vigorous competition, expanded at an unprecedented rate. While Bell's share of the American telephone business (and Western's share of telephone equipment manufacture) shrank to 50 percent, the market took off. In the decade 1885–1895, the number of telephones in the United States had increased from about 155,000 to nearly 340,000 – barely doubling. But during the next five years (1895–1900), the number of phones quadrupled (to 1,355 million), and Western Electric's sales to Bell more than quadrupled.[61]

Western Electric, although still the monopolistic supplier to the Bell licensees, became a limiting factor in Bell's expansion. It had to struggle to provide telephone equipment at the increased rate demanded by the licensees. By 1899 Western Electric was frequently six months to a year behind in supplying switchboards and major components. Unable adequately to service the rapid increase in new customers, several licensees, even when faced with growing competition, had to stop canvassing operations for new business. By May 1899, Bell's general manager, C. J. French, fretted that "the growth of the telephone business of our licensees of the whole country today seems measured by the amount of apparatus which the Western Electric Co. is able to supply and no more."[62]

Under the 1882 contract, Bell could have sought out alternative manufacturers until Western Electric was equipped to supply sufficient material at a quality Bell required. But though French and other Bell officials continued to worry about Western Electric's ability to provide telephonic equipment, there is no indication that they seriously considered seeking alternative manufacturers. At the same time, Barton certainly did not offer to immediately drop Western's other lines; in fact, Western was just gearing up to become a distributor of consumer electrical apparatus.

In the 1890s Bell began moving toward integrating the operating companies. By granting permanent licenses in return for stock in licensee firms, Bell gradually increased its stock holdings in licensee firms, thus gaining operating control of many, if not most, licensees by 1900. The integration of Western Electric, however, still remained to be accomplished as the twentieth century dawned.

3

SYSTEMS OF MANAGING AND MANAGING OF SYSTEMS: 1900–1925

I N July 1900, three of Enos Barton's most trusted lieutenants concluded that his management style was not suited to Western Electric's twentieth-century needs. Harry Thayer, the New York plant manager, Charles DuBois, the corporate secretary, and William Patterson, the Chicago plant manager, wrote to Barton: "We believe that the necessity exists for a more definite organization plan for the Western Electric Company. . . . Every employee should know for what work he is responsible and to whom he is responsible. This is not the case now."[1] The three executives proposed an organization based on functions such as engineering, purchasing, manufacturing, selling, accounting, and finance.[2] Thayer, DuBois, and Patterson acknowledged the risks in their proposal, such as "the danger of relying on system to take the place of personal energy and enthusiasm." Yet they considered the dangers of doing nothing were greater, because "the organization is every day becoming more definitely formed but whether correctly or not we do not know."[3]

Indeed, some areas of Western Electric's business had been assigned to no particular department, and responsibility for the success or failure of some projects was unclear. Similar functions reported to different departments. Electric-light construction, for example, reported to the sales department, but switchboard erection reported to engineering. Many managers were overworked because they took on duties not specific to their jobs. Thayer, DuBois, and Patterson wanted to avoid confusion in correspondence, duplication of work, and situations with "no one having authority." Lack of authority might mean chaos, an-

Figure 10. President Enos Barton with Western Electric executives. Barton's successor, H. B. Thayer, is seated to his left. Thayer's successor, C. G. DuBois, is seated to Barton's right.

archy – or worse. Therefore, they described their proposal as a "well directed effort over mob violence."[4]

In the absence of other evidence, one might believe that the Western Electric Company was on the brink of ruin. This was not the case. Rather, it was the company's success that precipitated the crisis. During a decade that included four years of national economic depression, Western's work force had tripled, its revenues had grown sixfold, and its profits had grown even faster. The organization's structure and procedures simply had not kept up with its expansion. Enos Barton still ran the company as an entrepreneurial enterprise rather than one to be managed. Barton kept organization, policies, and procedures in his head rather than in any document published and distributed to employees. Western Electric's cult of personality surrounding its founder was about to give way to a new class of managers: stewards of the bottom line, armed with systems and standards.

This was the future speaking, not just through the message, but through the messengers. Successful big business requires a healthy relationship between owners and their agents, and that is what Thayer and DuBois offered (Patterson retired before their proposal was implemented). Whereas Barton the entrepreneur had been more comfortable running the company as if it were an independent entity, Thayer and DuBois more easily adapted to life in the Bell System.

The Bell System was also more comfortable with Thayer and DuBois. Thayer was a Dartmouth graduate (class of 1879), which no doubt endeared him to the more snobbish culture of AT&T. During Barton's thirty years as Western Electric's president and then chairman, he was never part of the parent company's inner circle. By contrast, within a year of becoming Western's president, Thayer became a vice president of AT&T. When Theodore Vail stepped down ten years later as AT&T's president, Thayer replaced him – and Charles DuBois became the president of Western.

DuBois, like Thayer, was a Dartmouth graduate (class of 1891), and his philosophy of business was similar to Thayer's. He began a talk to the Telephone Society of New York with the words: "The burden of proof rests on every man every day to show that he is positively efficient."[5] DuBois followed a financial path toward that end. In 1898, he became Western Electric's corporate secretary and established a shop cost system, the first step toward enabling management to pinpoint problems in manufacturing processes. In 1907, he became AT&T's controller and developed and installed a comprehensive accounting system for all the Bell telephone companies.[6]

Thayer's gift was his ability to run Western to AT&T's satisfaction; DuBois's was in translating a business into numbers that indicated how it ran. Both skills were crucial to making the idea of the Bell System become a reality. The need for such skills was reinforced by the financial panic of 1907. In February of that year, Western Electric reported that 1906 had been the most profitable year in its history. In the late spring, a financial crisis swept world markets. Among other results, this crisis allowed J. P. Morgan to install Theodore Vail as head of AT&T. At Western, orders began to dry up. As late as December 19, the company had reported to Vail a projected profit for 1907 of more than $3.5 million.[7] It turned out that Western *lost* money in 1907, something that had not happened to the company since Barton became president in 1886. Some stockholders claimed Barton "cooked up the figures."[8] Vail was as outraged by Western's apparent lack of control as he was by the results.[9] In late 1908, Thayer succeeded Barton as president.

By the time of Barton's death in May 1916, the company had been transformed. The creation of the *Western Electric News* in 1912 was evidence of the change. The *News* periodically ran stories about how a particular department worked and displayed organization charts showing how individual jobs and departments fit in with the rest of the company. The month after Barton's death, the *News* devoted virtually an entire issue to Barton's memory. Thayer wrote in that issue that Barton "gave the business a spirit of progress, striving always for better methods and greater efficiency."[10] Thayer's tribute was as much a reflection of his own sensitivities as it was of Enos Barton's. From the vantage point of 1916, when most of the day-to-day decisions of American big business were made by middle managers, Enos Barton's ad hoc management style seemed quaint. The way the company went about its business under Thayer and DuBois had changed sufficiently that the *Western Electric News* frequently ran stories reminding everyone how inefficient the old ways had been.

The 1900 memorandum that Thayer, DuBois, and Patterson had sent to Barton was essentially a manifesto for managerial capitalism's overthrow of personal capitalism. Harry Thayer and Charles DuBois completed that transition, as well as Western Electric's integration into the Bell System. Thayer and DuBois would run the company from 1908 until 1926, and their organization proposal was an indication of how they wanted to do it. A functional organizational structure, more sophisticated financial reporting, and a closer relationship with AT&T characterized Western Electric for most of the twentieth century.

SCIENTIFIC ENGINEERING

The rise of Thayer and DuBois coincided with American industry's embrace of a new "science" of management. The number of engineers in the United States increased from 7,000 to 135,000 in the years 1880–1920, and engineers were the first to systematically apply methods of science to business management.[11] "As scientifically trained people became managers," noted an observer, "management became more scientific."[12] Literature of the management movement at the turn of the century is found in engineering journals more often than anywhere else, and technology-based companies such as Western Electric were among the first to try new management techniques.

The professionalization of management principles in America was shepherded by relatively few hands. Prominent among the few were Magnus Alexander of General Electric, Channing Dooley of Westinghouse, and Walter Dietz of Western Electric. Dietz was trained in engineering at Purdue, where Dooley was his fraternity brother (and they both dated the woman who would become Mrs. Dietz).[13] A few years after his 1902 arrival at Western Electric, Dietz moved from engineering to education, and spent the rest of his career in personnel and training. In 1913, the National Association of Corporation Schools (NACS) was created – an organization "dominated by representatives from the electrical industry," including Alexander, Dooley, and Dietz. In 1917, Dietz served as NACS president. Programs of corporate education and management science converged: within a decade, the NACS had evolved into the American Management Association.[14]

"Scientific management" meant many things to manufacturers, including systematic analysis of each operation and wage incentives to promote workers' adherence to detailed instruction.[15] Time-and-motion studies became a hallmark of scientific management; the stopwatch was its symbol. The overriding concept behind these methods was the separation of planning from execution. Practitioners believed that less educated workers (in many cases, immigrants) could not be trusted to think for themselves, so separate groups of planners determined how work should be done and how much work should be expected.

Frederick Winslow Taylor popularized such a division of labor: "In our scheme, we do not ask the initiative of our men. We do not want any initiative. All we want of them is to obey the orders we give them, do what we say, and do it quick."[16] A Western Electric example of this separation of labor – and expertise – was conveyed by Amos Dixon. His first job, in 1902, was in drafting, and Dixon inquired about the purpose of certain circuit elements. His supervisor told him that only the engineers were supposed to know what "even the condenser in a subscriber's set was for."[17]

Scientific management at Western Electric and other manufacturers elsewhere involved an attack on foremen's power. In the 1890s, many skilled craftsmen at Western became foremen as their departments expanded, and they controlled how the factory operated. These foremen contracted with Western Electric to manufacture at a set price and took responsibility for inspection and quality. The company furnished the materials and equipment and, on longer contracts, advanced the foremen funds to pay wages. The foremen, in turn, hired the workers and set their wages. The foreman's own income consisted of the amount left over at the end of the contract.

Most foremen had to cut costs in order to turn a profit, leading to Bell complaints about "cheap" workmanship at Western Electric.[18] The foremen considered themselves accountable to Western Electric rather than to the ultimate customer: once the product left their department, they felt absolved of responsibility. Western left foremen largely autonomous, except when Enos Barton personally intervened. When production delays elicited Barton's intervention, products would go out on time, but frequently with reduced quality.[19]

Barton eliminated the contract system in 1897 and took further steps to limit the autonomy of shop foremen over the next few years. The approach of foremen acting as contractors gave way to personnel departments handling employment policies and planning departments that determined what it should take – in time and material – to get the product out the door. The way was clear at Western for scientific management.

Before employing the time-and-motion studies we now associate with scientific management, Western made an intermediate step. "Scientific engineering" focused more on the efficiency of machines than of people. Such an approach matched the needs of an urban manufacturer: skilled labor was abundant but space was scarce. Concocting creative ways to squeeze maximum productive space out of a building was a valued skill.

Western Electric's champion of scientific engineering was Henry Fleetwood Albright.[20] Albright was ideal for the job. He was serious and formal, more concerned with solving production problems than human ones. Albright had already worked at America's other two leading electrical manufacturers (Thomson-Houston and Westinghouse) when he came to Western Electric in 1892. In 1898, Thayer promoted him from salesman to the company's first factory engineer, based in New York.

Thayer had authorized a two-million-dollar plant expansion for rapid telephone construction. Increased production demands resulted from the newly competitive phone business after expiration of Bell's patents. One of Albright's first contributions in his new job was to show that expansion was unnecessary and that the increased production capacity could fit into the current plant. Western Electric need not spend the two million dollars. Albright had demonstrated that scientific engineering was more than just a theory: it could bolster company profits. He was promoted to superintendent in 1901.[21]

With its increased volume and commitment to scientific engineering, Western Electric seemed poised to use assembly-line production techniques and to realize the economies of scale of a vertically integrated operation. Western did not, however, set up an assembly-line operation until 1928. One reason was the company's difficulty in achieving standardization. Thayer was aware that the company's products offered a range of possibilities toward that end. In a 1905 speech he gave before the Telephone Society of New York, Thayer pointed out that his company both made items that left the factory as a standard product, such as subscriber telephones, and made items to order, such as switchboards.

A 1902 agreement between AT&T and the operating companies reduced variations to four basic switchboards. However, switchboards did not lend themselves to assembly-line production, because customers could order them with capacities ranging from fewer than 300 lines to more than 1,500. No attempt was made to standardize the size of the main frames except for small switchboards, where the main frame had units of 100 phone lines. Nor was there any attempt, due to "varying local conditions," to standardize the relay, service meter, and coil racks or the power plants. It took four months to construct an average switchboard comprised of 450 thousand pieces made from about 3.8 million parts requiring some 15 million operations. Because Western worked on several switchboards at a time, preliminary scheduling for construction had to be initiated four months prior to receipt of specifications.[22] A process taking so much time also required high levels of investment in inventory.

In 1904 Western Electric manufactured 550,000 telephones; such numbers suggest that an assembly-line process was possible. It was not. That year Western Electric produced 154 varieties out of 354 standard sets potentially available to its customers. Many of those sets were used by only one operating company. Demand for a particular set frequently arose after Western had "almost come to the conclusion that the demand never will come"; obsolescent apparatus might be ordered after the demand had "entirely stopped." Yet, under its contract with Bell, Western still had to supply these goods.[23] And AT&T had its own systematization problems: getting the operating companies to standardize their operations and equipment. So while Western's relationship with Bell guaranteed a large-scale business, the same relationship stifled assembly-line economies.

An assembly line requires the arrangement of machines in sequential order, to minimize the amount of time each product passes through the line. It is quite expensive to modify such an arrangement periodically, so the assembly line, or "product" approach, is best suited to companies or plants with limited product lines (such as Ford with the Model T).

Henry Albright provided an alternative that fit Western's broad product line: functional manufacturing. His approach in New York was to place all similar machines together; therefore, this was called the "colony" system. Functional manufacturing went beyond space conservation. Albright's experience convinced him that a separate de-

78

Figure 11. H. F. Albright was the company's leading proponent of scientific management, which Western Electric helped export to Japan.

partment would operate all punch presses better than if they were scattered among several departments. Another department would operate drill presses most efficiently, and so on.

By arranging the equipment according to function, theoretically the most efficient department would handle the entire output of the factory, reducing both equipment and labor costs.[24] With a functional approach to manufacturing, Western Electric improved quality by placing each function under the control of the most skilled workers who specialized in a particular operation. This conserved equipment costs and allowed for easy shifting from one product line to another without completely restructuring the factory.

Albright argued that the duplication of tools in various departments was inefficient. Western maintained specialized equipment at either the New York or the Chicago factories, but not at both. Keys, spring jacks, lamps, cords, and cables were shipped from Chicago to New York, while desk stands, protectors, relays, and plugs were shipped from New York to Chicago for final assembly into switchboards.

Albright caught Enos Barton's attention with this approach. His functional manufacturing became the centerpiece of Western Electric's factories all over the world, those in Paris, London, Berlin, Rome, Vienna, and Milan early in the twentieth century. Later, Albright produced similar designs for Kearny, New Jersey, and for Nippon Electric's new factory in Tokyo.

Albright's most significant work was close to home, where Barton asked him for an efficient arrangement of Hawthorne's machine shop.[25] In 1908, Albright became the company's general superintendent and moved to Chicago. At the growing Hawthorne works, he presided over the consolidation of the company's domestic manufacturing.[26]

HAWTHORNE

On March 9, 1904, C. W. Houger arrived at Twenty-second Street and Forty-eighth Avenue in Cicero, Illinois, as the first employee at Western Electric's new Hawthorne plant. He was the contact man with the architects and contractors who were already erecting powerhouse buildings and a water tower where acres of farmland used to be. As Houger strolled toward the entrance, he asked himself, "What possible use could the Western Electric company have for a big piece of prairie land?"[27]

The dramatic growth in demand for telephones in the last decade of the nineteenth century and the first decade of the twentieth placed pressures on the Bell System to develop procedures to supply a rapidly growing market. Bell licensees could, according to Bell's 1882 manufacturing contract with Western Electric, turn to other manufacturers; but, practically speaking, Western had no competition for its services to the operating companies. The Bell System crisis of capacity became a Western Electric crisis of capacity.

Executives at both Western and AT&T received numerous complaints from local phone companies about delayed deliveries of telephone equipment. A letter that AT&T president Frederick Fish received from the Chicago Telephone Company was typical: "There has always been more or less delay in getting even . . . *standard* articles." Furthermore, "the Western Electric Company is not in a position to even name us a date when they may be delivered." The solution appeared to be "the establishing of several other factories."[28]

Western had at first responded to the capacity crisis by renting additional space and by operating around the clock – when workers were available.[29] A company in such need of labor is vulnerable to a labor stoppage, particularly if its situation becomes public knowledge. Western's did. The Boston News Bureau reported in 1899 that, although "the company's plants are being run night and day, it has been unable to meet the demand for telephone apparatus." Enos Barton was concerned that any publicity for Western's night work and overtime "advertises our vulnerability."[30] Therefore, Western considered spending more than one million dollars on new buildings in Chicago and New York.[31]

For its first thirty-four years, Western had manufactured in cities because of the availability of skilled labor and easy access to transportation and communication. After the fact, Western Electric vice president Howard Halligan gave another reason for staying in Chicago so long: "During this period the future of the business was judged to be sufficiently uncertain so that its property ought to be easily salable."[32] In 1902, the company's future seemed more secure, and it chose a different path – to build on the outskirts of Chicago, where land was cheap and the company had more room to grow.[33]

Halligan did not mention another reason to abandon the downtown: labor relations, which had been a recent concern for Chicago employers. At the time, only London could compete with Chicago as the world's trade-union capital.[34] In March 1900, Enos Barton informed his sister that "we have been having a part in Great Events. The Labor Question has come right up against us."[35] The previous month, two hundred and fourteen Western Electric machinists had walked out, part of a wider strike of about six thousand machinists in

Chicago.[36] The machinists sought recognition of their union, but Harry Thayer summarized the company line: "The recognition of unions as the unions are nowadays operated is so far from our principles and policy that I can not imagine such an event."[37]

Although the timing of the strike was not good for Barton and Western Electric, Barton did have some recourse: manufacturing in New York. Western's Chicago workers were affiliated with the American Federation of Labor (AF of L), while the New York workers affiliated with the Knights of Labor. Enos Barton felt confident that "we are not likely to have trouble in New York and Chicago both at once," because of the poor relations between the AF of L and the Knights of Labor.[38]

The machinists' strike of 1900 no doubt reminded company veterans of the circumstances surrounding Western's reduction from a ten-hour to a nine-and-one-half-hour day in 1886. In May of that year, a strike on behalf of the eight-hour day at the McCormick Harvester works was accompanied by shootings and a bombing. The Haymarket Riot resulted in thirteen deaths and the subsequent execution of four German American anarchists. Haymarket Square, where the events occurred, was just down the street from Western's Clinton Street plant (which employed numerous German Americans).

The 1900 strike was settled, however, without the same level of violence. Among the demands of strikers at other establishments had been the nine-hour day. Thayer's pragmatic philosophy of labor relations was evident in his advice to Barton: "I do not believe there is any other way in which we can so strengthen our position on the labor question with so little sacrifice."[39] In May, Western Electric adopted the nine-hour day.

Although the machinists' strike was settled in May, the building trades presented a more prolonged problem, not reaching an agreement until February 1901.[40] In April 1900, Enos Barton wrote that "the condition of the building trades is such in Chicago that the building of new structures is not worth while for us. . . . We have not proposed to erect any buildings in the present condition of the labor market in Chicago."[41] Therefore, Barton sought a solution to the company's capacity problems by proposing purchase of a large plot of land *just outside of Chicago.*[42] The move reflected the belief that, left to their own devices, Western's workers would neither unionize nor strike. If the company were going to incur the risk of concentrating so much production capacity in one plant, it was going to do so at a safe distance from the volatility of downtown and the extreme elements of the labor movement Thayer termed "agitators and idlers."

So the Hawthorne plant was built on two hundred acres of land abutting the west side of Chicago, in the town of Cicero. Although the new location was virtually on the prairie, it had some of the conveniences of an urban location: two railroad crossings and a right-of-way to the river.[43] When Hawthorne's Cable Plant opened in February 1905 with a group of thirteen women transferred from the Clinton Street plant, the population of Cicero was forty-five hundred.[44] Within fifteen years, this boom town's population reflected the tremendous expansion at the Hawthorne plant, increasing tenfold.[45]

With the move to Hawthorne, Western Electric got the stable work force it wanted in 1902. By 1920, 86 percent of Cicero residents were of foreign birth or parentage (predominantly Czech and Polish, groups without a history of labor activism).[46] Cicero had achieved a higher percentage of single-family home ownership by the 1920s than any community in Illinois. People making mortgage payments (especially through the company's Building and Loan) had less incentive to strike than other workers.[47] Not surprisingly, Hawthorne unionized later than many large manufacturing establishments.

Paradoxically, at the same time Western Electric moved away from downtown, the company's story increasingly became a *Chicago* story: Hawthorne's enormous size allowed the company not only to move its Chicago operations there from Clinton Street, but to consolidate its domestic operations there from 1905 to 1913. This meant closing the New York plant: the decrease in production costs at Hawthorne overrode any savings in shipping to eastern destinations.[48] Hawthorne joined the ranks of giant "works" in American industry, including the Cambria Steel factory in Johnstown, Pennsylvania, with 20,000 people; General Electric's Schenectady plant with 15,000 people; and the

Ford plant at Highland Park, with more than 10,000.[49] When the consolidation was completed in 1913, Hawthorne – with 14,000 workers – was the single biggest employment site in the Chicago area.

The difference between Hawthorne and the Clinton Street plant was noted by Thayer in late 1904, after his first visit to Hawthorne, before the new plant was operational: "The machinery building is big enough for a world's fair building . . . the whole outfit has been laid out on a grand scale."[50] If anything, Thayer's assessment underestimated the contrast in size between Western's operations at Hawthorne and those at Clinton Street. At the turn of the century, Clinton Street housed about 3,000 workers. By the 1920s, Hawthorne's work force was more than *thirteen times* that. The language at Western Electric reflected the difference in size. Hawthorne, and its one hundred buildings, became known as a "works," in contrast to the Clinton Street "plant" and the company's earlier "shops." These differential labels based on size remained throughout the twentieth century as the company built elsewhere: from works to plants to shops.

Hawthorne became quite a works, employing more than 40,000 workers in the 1920s. By then, it had become a virtual city unto itself, complete with restaurant, hospital, library, credit union, powerhouse, ballpark, gymnasium, news media (the *Hawthorne Microphone*), band shell, and a band in blue uniforms and brass braid. Hawthorne also had its own railroad, Manufacturer's Junction Railway, to move raw materials into the plant, finished products out, and all kinds of materials from one part of the plant to another. At Hawthorne, one could pursue the arts (from dancing to photography) or education (from English to circuits). Hawthorne even offered the sort of groups and rituals a society uses to convey membership and to recognize passages. Elections for offices in employee organizations featured parades and rallies, and service anniversaries and retirements called for parties. The plant also ran beauty contests, and sponsored *forty* employee bowling leagues. For Western Electric, Hawthorne represented a departure, not just from Chicago, but from the way the company once did business.

A SHIFT IN EMPHASIS

The construction of Hawthorne finally brought debates with AT&T regarding Western's scope of operation to one resolution: departure from the electrical power business. The electrical power question contributed to the mixed feelings AT&T expressed about Hawthorne from the start. In 1902, when Enos Barton first broached the idea of building Hawthorne to AT&T's executives, President Frederick Fish gave the project a qualified blessing: "I think [Barton] needs the land for his heavy work, but have been afraid that he had the intention of branching out extensively into the manufacture of the larger types of electric and power apparatus, which I should regard as unwise." Barton assured him that this was not his intent.[51]

Fish had good reason for his concern about unbridled expansion. At the same time he proposed construction of Hawthorne, Enos Barton was unsuccessfully negotiating for the acquisition of several other independent telephone manufacturers and pushing for expansion of Western Electric's nontelephone work. Barton may also have considered the acquisition of independent phone manufacturing plants as a means to free up his Chicago plant facilities for nontelephone manufacturing.

The year Hawthorne opened, Fish wrote to Barton that "the telephone business of the Western Electric Company and the interests of the Bell operating companies [would] suffer to a substantial amount" unless Western "were able to devote all their time to the telephone business and not be distracted by outside matters."[52]

Within two years, Fish concluded: "I cannot help thinking that the time has come when we should deal definitely and decidedly with this question, and my own belief is that we should dispose of the [electrical lighting and power] business absolutely."[53] This was not completely disinterested advice. Prior to becoming AT&T president, he had been principal in the law firm Fish, Richardson, and Storrow (to which he would return). One of the firm's most valued clients was General Electric. Fish was essentially advising one client to abandon a market in which it competed with another client.

That conflict of interest was resolved when Theodore Vail replaced

Fish in 1907. By then, Western Electric faced not only a clash of institutional goals with AT&T but intimidating market conditions. Although the demand for power machinery was growing rapidly, Western's principal American competitors in that business (General Electric, Westinghouse, and Allis-Chalmers) were able to meet demand with prices below Western's costs. The construction of the Hawthorne plant left Western with a dilemma: should it run that huge plant at partial capacity, or attempt to fill it with a potentially losing business that would require heavy investment in engineering and tool-making?[54]

In 1909 Western resolved its dilemma, selling its power-generation manufacturing business to General Electric.[55] Western would continue to sell such equipment, but as a jobber rather than a producer. Western's solution to that problem continued a trend: between 1882 and 1900 Western Electric had created an independent supply department that distributed a variety of electrical goods under the Western Electric name. In 1890 Western began distributing Edwards bells and annunciators, and added Bryant wiring devices the same year. The following year it began distributing Phillip's wire, and in 1892 added Cutter's street-lighting fixtures. In 1897 Western added Sunbeam lamps and Goodyear lamp cord to the jobbing supplies it distributed.[56] By the turn of the century, many of Bell's operating companies had turned to Western for additional supplies.

The 1882 contract between the American Bell Company and Western Electric had dealt only with telephone apparatus developed by Western. It did not include commercial supplies such as cross-arms, pole-line hardware, and insulators. In 1901, at the suggestion of Theodore Spencer, the general manager of the Bell Telephone Company of Philadelphia, Western Electric became the supply agent for that company. In June, Western negotiated a similar supply contract with the Bell Telephone Company of Missouri. The idea behind the supply contracts was the elimination of duplication of purchases and warehousing of supplies, helping to both lower the cost and standardize the product line within the Bell companies. By 1913, all of the operating companies had signed supply contracts with Western Electric.

Western Electric was becoming the world's largest electrical distributor. As early as 1906 some 50 percent of Western Electric sales came through the supply department, and the number of Western's distributing houses had increased from two to fifteen (and would reach forty-four by 1919).[57] When the company established the *Western Electric News* in 1912, the new publication featured full-page ads of merchandise such as sewing machines, vacuum cleaners, electrical ranges, and washing machines. At the same time, Western advertised in newspapers, magazines, and technical journals with combined circulation of nearly 100 million.[58] More and more, Western Electric's name was associated in the popular consciousness with products it did not manufacture.

Western Electric's abandonment of the manufacture of electrical power equipment had other ramifications: it freed up much-needed research manpower for telephone work at a time when Theodore Vail advocated universal service. This brought a clear shift in AT&T and Western Electric research. Previously, while Western Electric's principal lines of development had been largely limited to switchboard and cable design, American Bell and AT&T had focused on transmission technology. Following a 1907 restructuring, most of Bell System research was consolidated in New York – under Western Electric. Over the next few years Western Electric would increasingly be called upon to solve both technological and economic problems facing AT&T.

PROGRESSIVISM COMES TO WESTERN ELECTRIC

In April 1913, Western Electric's president, Harry Thayer, convened a conference of Bell System executives at Hot Springs, Virginia, to discuss Western's role in the Bell System. Present were two dozen of Thayer's Western Electric colleagues, a half-dozen executives from Western's parent, AT&T, and fourteen representatives of Bell's local phone companies. The occurrence of such a conference was perhaps as significant as the subject matter discussed. The Western Electric of Enos Barton had been far too independent to take the lead in such a conference.

Thayer was a natural person to call the meeting because he was also a vice president of AT&T (which owned 96 percent of Western Electric's stock) and an architect of the modified supply contracts, which had helped make the idea of the Bell System become a reality. More than anything, this conference suggests that by 1913 Western Electric saw itself as firmly ensconced in the Bell System. Indeed, earlier that month, Thayer had reported: "Our relations with the Associated Bell Companies have never been as good as they are today and we are receiving better and earlier information in regard to their requirements, thereby enabling us to give them better service."[59]

AT&T must have felt the same way about Western Electric. Not only had Western Electric's performance improved over the previous five years (1912 brought record sales), but so had its financial reporting. Estimated and actual profits ($4.85 million vs. $4.65 million) were virtually identical, as opposed to 1907's $3 million difference.

The Hot Springs attendees realized that this was a pivotal time for AT&T, Western Electric, and the Bell System. J. P. Morgan, the man who had installed Theodore Vail as head of AT&T, had died a month before the Hot Springs meeting. Morgan's passing symbolized the beginning of a power shift from the financiers in New York to the government in Washington, and Hot Springs attendees acknowledged the new reality of an activist government. The antitrust activities of the Roosevelt and Taft administrations had reflected the Progressive movement's eagerness to tame big business, and there was no telling what the incoming Wilson administration (which also called itself Progressive) might do. The Bell System should be prepared for attention from Washington.

Some attention had already been paid. Three months before the Hot Springs meeting, Attorney General George Wickersham had warned AT&T that its planned acquisition of independent telephone companies in the Midwest violated the Sherman Antitrust Act. Vail had refused to connect Bell facilities with those of the independents. This had been part of a strategy of communications monopoly that included AT&T's acquisition of a controlling interest in Western Union in 1909. Following Wickersham's warning, the Interstate Commerce Commission had begun an investigation of the Bell System. T. J. Perkins, an AT&T attorney at the Hot Springs meeting, reported to his colleagues that the U.S. Supreme Court concurred with the commission's assertion of authority to investigate the "collateral business of a common carrier." At the same time, an antitrust suit had been filed against the Bell System in federal district court in Portland, Oregon.

Vail's response was to reverse his strategy. In December 1913, AT&T vice president Nathan Kingsbury wrote to James McReynolds (Wickersham's successor) that AT&T would sell Western Union, would stop its movement to acquire independent phone companies, and would allow noncompeting independents to connect to Bell's lines. The "Kingsbury Commitment" also was a major step toward standardization of equipment.[60] Western Electric, which handled 97 percent of Bell's equipment business and 59 percent of the world's, would develop its business from increased telephone use rather than through Bell's acquisitions.

This was not the only way in which Western felt the influence of AT&T. On the eve of World War I, American companies were attempting to resolve the relationship between their enterprises and society. The Progressive movement, which featured antitrust sentiment, also emphasized efficiency, faith in experts, and the welfare of the individual.

In that spirit, in August 1912, Magnus Alexander of GE sent Theodore Vail the text of an address Alexander had delivered to the American Academy of Political and Social Science. Alexander's cover letter called "particular attention" to his suggestion for the creation of a "Department of Applied Economics, which might more properly be called a Department of Applied Psychology." Such a department would "apply the same scientific, calculated and sagacious study to the human needs in industry that are now applied everywhere to the engineering, selling, financial and purchasing requirements."[61]

Alexander's idea was well timed. The Bell System had come together in many ways by 1912, but the associated companies had not done so "systematically" with respect to human needs. Vail's associate, Walter Allen, noted another advantage of such efforts: they would "benefit the companies in their general public relations by convincing the public that the management has really at heart the human side of the business and is striving to better conditions in industry."[62] The following year, AT&T announced the establishment of the Bell System benefit and insurance plan. Few could have anticipated how soon the plan would be put to a severe test.

THE COMING OF WELFARE CAPITALISM

On Saturday, July 24, 1915, nearly seven thousand Western Electric employees, family members, and friends lined up for a steamship ride to Michigan City, Indiana. The occasion was Hawthorne's fifth annual picnic. The plant, which normally ran six days a week, had closed for the festivities. The company's annual picnics dated back to 1881, but did not achieve enormous scale until the advent of the Hawthorne affairs.

This year, Western Electric chartered five steamers with the Indiana Transportation Company, including the *Eastland*.[63] Prior to its scheduled departure, however, tragedy struck: the *Eastland* capsized a few feet from its dock on the Chicago River, killing approximately nine hundred Western Electric employees, family members, and friends. This was far more than a company tragedy: it represented the largest loss of life from disaster in Chicago history, even greater than that caused by the great Chicago fire of 1871.[64]

The *Eastland* did not claim the famous and wealthy, as did the *Titanic*. Nor were any of Western Electric's executives killed. Rather, this was a tragedy of the working class, engaged in what President Thayer called "their innocent pleasures."[65] Indeed, although the disaster occurred downtown in a major city, it was largely a neighborhood affair. Most of the victims were from the communities near the Hawthorne plant, Berwyn and Cicero. Most were of Polish, Bohemian, or Hungarian descent; more than half were women, most of whom were single and worked in the factory.

In the days following the tragedy, the company made little effort to operate the plant. Attendance was voluntary, and only a hundred workers showed up on Monday, and a thousand on Tuesday. On those two days, Western turned away eight hundred local residents

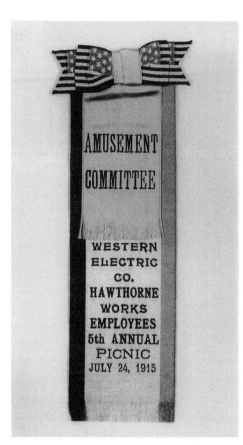

Figure 12. The 1915 Hawthorne picnic (advertised here) never took place. The cruise ship *Eastland* capsized, killing approximately nine hundred Western Electric employees, family members, and friends.

who were offering to fill the jobs of the victims.[66] Instead, the company gave preference to relatives of victims.[67] Wednesday, the day of the greatest number of funerals, was declared an official day of mourning, and the plant was draped in black.[68]

The *Eastland* disaster put the Bell System's new benefit and insurance plan to a severe test. Established in 1913, the plan included death benefits to families of employees with more than five years of company service.[69] The standard death benefit was six months' salary to survivors of those with more than five years' service, and one year's salary

Figure 13. The gates of Hawthorne draped in mourning in honor of the *Eastland* victims

to survivors of those with more than ten years.[70] Of the 465 employees who died in the accident, however, only 121 had five years' service.[71] The magnitude of the disaster forced the company to improvise, allocating an additional $100,000 for relief. That was not enough: a Chicago citizen's committee, headed by representatives of local companies, raised an additional $350,000 for the families of victims.[72]

The *Eastland* disaster – and the company's response to it – showed how Western Electric had embraced Progressive Era principles. Between 1910 and 1915, in addition to the benefit and insurance plan, the company convinced the Chicago Public Library to locate a branch at Hawthorne, created the *Western Electric News*, and established the Hawthorne Club to handle concerts, dances, parties, and sports – including the annual picnic.[73]

The Hawthorne Club also oversaw education. By 1915, the Hawthorne Evening School (called "Hawthorne University") was offering nine different subjects, segregated by gender. Men could study elec-

Figure 14. The Western Electric Grays of the Chicago Commercial League, 1907. The squad's pitcher, Clarence Stoll (*front row, right*) became Western Electric president in 1940.

tricity and magnetism, telephone practice, practical mathematics, shop practices, mechanical drawing, business English, and mechanical principles. Women could study business English or typewriting. Enrollment for the 1914/1915 year was 891 men and 174 women.

The establishment of the Hawthorne Evening School brought within the company's walls services that previously had come from without. At Clinton Street, some of the acculturation and education of immigrants took place at Jane Addams's Hull House, a settlement house where social workers came to live in an attempt to provide educational opportunity for, and to act as advocates on behalf of, working people. An important function that settlement houses performed was teaching English. America was receiving an influx of immigrants that differed from the last big group from the early 1880s, which had come from northern Europe and 97 percent of whom spoke English. This latest wave of workers was from central and southern Europe, and more than one-third spoke no English.[74] Settlement

Figure 15. At the 1913 Hawthorne picnic, women of the cable plant wore sashes that read "Votes for Women," celebrating the achievement of women's suffrage in Illinois.

houses in major cities such as Boston, New York, and Chicago received financial support from the business community and in turn influenced some business policies.

Hull House was established in 1889 only a few blocks from Western's Clinton Street plant. Less than a year after it opened, Addams wrote to her sister: "We saw a number of girls at the Western Electric Works last week, and they are all so pleased and enthusiastic over coming, we mean to have a general social time for them every Friday evening."[75] Women had been employed in various occupations at Clinton Street since the plant's 1884 completion. Much of the women's work there differed little from traditional women's work in the household, particularly the more repetitive tasks such as the winding, braiding, and sewing of wire. Indeed, Western's first female employee, Sarah Adlum, wound magnets at the old Kinzie Street plant.[76] Addams expressed hopes of forming classes – presumably to teach English, among other subjects – for the Western Electric women.[77]

It is not clear how the subsequent relationship between Hull House and Western Electric developed, but by 1896 Addams was submitting to Enos Barton monthly "accounts," which were kept more in the style of a social worker than an accountant. Addams's records indicated how long each resident had lived at Hull House, how much stipend each resident received, what each resident paid for board, and

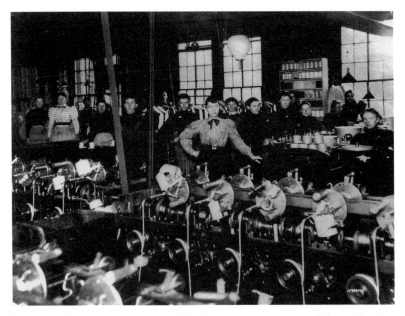

Figure 16. Cotton-binding unit of Chicago cable department, 1890. At the time, numerous women worked in the shop, but few had office jobs.

total "general expenses."[78] This was a primitive form of welfare capitalism.

Hull House's residential staff included unpaid teachers, some of whom worked at Western Electric during the day and taught in the evening. The most notable example was future vice president Gerard Swope. Swope joined Western Electric in the fall of 1895, after completing a degree in electrical engineering at MIT. The following year, a friend introduced Swope to Hull House, where he joined the staff as an unpaid teacher. By day, he designed power apparatus; by night, he taught algebra and electricity to workmen – and foremen – from the same plant.[79] Swope lived at Hull House (and met his wife, social worker Mary Hill) from 1897 to 1899 while he began to ascend the corporate ladder at Western Electric. Western Electric's abandonment of Clinton Street for Hawthorne meant the end of such Hull House involvement. But the company replaced Hull House's classes for its workers with its own extensive program at Hawthorne.

Western Electric's provident funds and the Hawthorne Club's educational and recreational programs essentially institutionalized the paternalism of Enos Barton, particularly at Hawthorne. Where special favors had once been granted on an individual basis, company or plantwide policies were established to provide guidance for both manager and employee, and were administered out of newly created personnel departments.

Proponents of welfare capitalism sought an antidote not just to the threat of unionization but to high worker turnover rates. Semiskilled workers, whose numbers proliferated with the rise of industrial big business, were both the most likely to leave their jobs and the most costly to replace.[80] Using contemporary estimates, it would have cost about *one million dollars* to replace Western's work force. If everyone left in the same year, replacement costs alone (never mind profits forgone from decreased production) would have reduced the company's profits by 20 percent. Loyalty, therefore, was a valuable asset, and the Bell System cultivated it.

Management's concern with loyalty was demonstrated on the weekend of October 17–18, 1913, when the Telephone Pioneers of America held their third annual convention in Chicago. Western's chairman, Enos Barton, and its president, Harry Thayer, attended, as did AT&T's president, Theodore Vail, Alexander Graham Bell's associate Thomas Watson, and more than four hundred others.[81] This was part of Western's growing attachment to the Bell System. The Pioneers invited anyone from the parent, Western, or the operating companies who had worked in the Bell System for at least twenty-one years to join the organization. In 1915, the company began to award service pins to men and women who had qualified for the Pioneers. Rewards for output had been supplemented with rewards for loyalty.

Western Electric's participation in the Pioneers, combined with inauguration of the Bell System pension and insurance programs in 1913, signaled the beginning of an informal cradle-to-grave covenant between employer and employee. The company offered something beyond a paycheck: steady employment for some, rotational training and advancement for others, and a welfare system to support the employee's family and retirement. In exchange, the employee pledged loyalty to the company for the duration of his or her career.

In establishing such programs of welfare capitalism, Western Electric was not alone.[82] At the turn of the century, the Western world was coming to grips with the impact of industrialization and urbanization on the individual and society. In Europe, the state became involved, pooling the risks of its citizens with government unemployment, sickness, and old-age security programs. In the United States, government programs did not arrive until the 1930s and the New Deal. Up to then, social stability and security were provided more by the business enterprise than by the government or trade unions. Indeed, one goal of welfare programs was to stem the tide of unionization – and they appear to have succeeded to an extent. At the same time as American companies were creating programs of welfare capitalism, the United States had the lowest unionization rate among industrialized countries.[83]

Although welfare capitalism was not a universal phenomenon (many small firms could not afford such programs), by 1926, 80 percent of America's 1,500 largest firms had at least one aspect of it, and half had a comprehensive program.[84] Not all welfare programs were created equal. Programs in science-based firms, such as those in the electrical manufacturing industry, received particular attention from the press, from academia, and from industry peers. The industry's influence, therefore, was out of proportion to its size, giving these programs "the aura of technological inevitability," according to Sanford Jacoby. "Welfare capitalism," writes Jacoby, "came to be seen as America's future."[85]

PATHS TO SUCCESS

When E. W. Rockafellow left Western Electric in 1923 to accept a vice presidency at National Pole Company (Western's supplier of telephone poles), the *Western Electric News* summed up his career as "From Office Boy to Vice President: [testimony to] how far energy and ambition, coupled with foresight and judgment, will carry a man in the business world."[86] The Rockafellow legend included reference to how the office boy had learned shorthand on his own time in 1888 to prepare for a job as Thayer's stenographer. The same energy and ambition that had qualified Rockafellow for the stenographer's job led him to abandon the position for one in the stock department after a very brief tenure. He then became a purchasing agent and a traveling salesman before rising to the position of general supply sales manager. As Western Electric and other manufacturers began to employ tens of thousands of workers, establish bureaucratic, hierarchical organizations, and publish organization charts, it was imperative to show that upward mobility loomed as a reward for those with loyalty and skill.

This was particularly important because Western Electric was developing a hierarchical organization that Ronald Pook compared to "the Old World of Europe – master and peon – stratified in well-defined layers, disciplined and well ordered." Pook, an Englishman who began his Western Electric career at Hawthorne in 1919 and later rose to the position of assistant works manager there, saw "power and privilege on the one hand, submission on the other." He believed that one reason such a class system could exist in an American manufacturer without much protest from the underlings was that so many of Hawthorne's work force were European immigrants, who already knew their place.[87] Such hierarchy and paternalism were not limited to Western Electric but appeared in many other "modern manors."[88]

Rank at Western indeed had its privilege, including, at the highest levels, limousines and country club memberships. In addition to the opportunity for higher rates of pay, advancement meant greater responsibilities for hiring, firing, and allocation of work, increased limits of expenditure, and more seating space and furniture. A shop worker had no desk – not even a drawer – and might share a locker with another worker. The works manager at Hawthorne, by contrast, occupied an entire suite of offices in the building 27 tower. The suite included a fireplace, private dining room, kitchen, and shower.[89]

Henry F. Albright, the first occupant of these offices after the tower's completion in 1919, set the tone for Hawthorne's hierarchy. Carrying a gold cane, Albright was chauffeured to Hawthorne in a Cadillac, where a guard saluted him at gate 8. When he entered building 27, the first elevator to arrive was emptied of its occupants so that Albright could ride alone to the sixth floor, which offered the only

98

direct access to the tower. Albright then ascended to the tower by private elevator or marble staircase.

The company attempted to avoid resentment in the ranks by showing that rising from the bottom to the top could – and did – happen at Western Electric. From its 1912 inception, the *Western Electric News* fostered the belief in Horatio Alger tales. At the same time, the *News* reminded its readers that Western Electric did not need to go outside to fill important positions. It compared the company's "promote-from-within" policy to those of other companies, "particularly in railroads, [where] it is often the practice to offer important vacancies to men who are holding similar positions in rival companies instead of giving the opportunity to the man down the line." The *News* proudly referred to Western Electric as the "Young Man's Company."[90]

The May 1914 issue was titled "The Office Boys' Number," in which the editors speculated that "it is doubtful if ever before has there been gathered together in any publication so comprehensive a record of the rise of so large a group of individuals from the foot of the ladder to places of standing and responsibility at the top. Indeed, it is extremely doubtful if there is another business organization in existence that can show such a remarkable record of former office boys and junior clerks now filling important positions in management." The company took the May 1914 number seriously: at forty pages, it was the largest issue of the *News* yet published. Similarly, at 30,000, it reached its widest distribution to date.[91]

The May 1914 issue profiled numerous company officials who had begun their careers as office boys, including Hawthorne's assistant general superintendent James Bancker, vice president Albert L. Salt, and Eddie Rockafellow.[92] The issue also featured two striking photographs. One was of "Chicago's Old Time Office Boys," sixteen Western Electric men who had started as such with the company from 1887 until 1910. On the opposite page was "Chicago's Hopes for the future," twenty-one current office boys, each holding a sign designating their hoped-for rise – from "Salesman 1921" to "Shop Foreman 1928" to "Assistant Treasurer 1938" to "Superintendent 1943."[93] The editors concluded: "With like ability and like application there seems to be no good reason why the Banckers, the Rockafellows and the Salts of the future will not grow up from the office boys of the present."[94]

The *Western Electric News* did not, however, record this bottom-to-top phenomenon at its peak but caught it in a downward slope. A cartoon in the "Office Boys' Number" suggested why. Titled "The Office Boy and His University," it showed a young man with his "ABC's" book leaving "The Experience Company, Hardnox and Hustle Proprietors."[95] The rise of Eddie Rockafellow and other graduates of the school of "hardnox" represented Western Electric's past more than its future. Rockafellow advanced without the benefit of any college education at a time when college graduates were assuming the key positions of responsibility in the company.

Western Electric was among the first companies actively to recruit college graduates. In 1898, engineering head Charles Scribner took advantage of the departure of Western's original switchboard installer to institute a policy of having college graduates in electrical engineering do switchboard engineering work before they moved into the engineering department.[96] Not long after, the company established a training program for engineering graduates.

Frank Jewett, who headed research in the Bell System for many years, noted that this was an industry-wide phenomenon: "With the growth of the technical industries, the engineering side of the business was the first to wake up to the necessity of taking college, university and technical school trained men into the business. The engineers were the first ones to organize college recruiting on a consistent basis."[97] When engineering recruits arrived at Western, a training program awaited them that involved rotational work among many departments, classroom training, and tests.[98]

The program gained tremendous visibility. On Mondays, department heads or officials of Western's suppliers addressed the students in the educational department lecture room. College graduates from England, Japan, China, and other countries came to Hawthorne for these education courses. Western Electric's international influence extended beyond its overseas manufacture and distribution.[99]

When Joseph Juran, an engineer from the University of Minnesota recruited in 1924, arrived at the company, he noticed that Western had two tracks for promotion. The "fast track" was limited to college graduates. Promotions were based on merit and could lead to high managerial jobs. "Slow track" promotions were based heavily on seniority and were limited to positions of shop foreman, general foreman, or other lower management jobs.[100]

So, by the second decade of the twentieth century, portraying an egalitarian past made the carrot of promotion appear more attainable than it really was. Of the generation that yielded Western's executives of the immediate post-Barton era – those born between 1860 and 1880 – less than 2 percent had attended college.[101] Yet, by the time of the first issue of the *Western Electric News*, executive positions had been closed off to all but the select few – men with college degrees.

Western Electric was not alone. In 1920, a *New York Times* editor noted that "in the past we have cited it as a triumph of free institutions and a prime cause of our industrial efficiency that so many of our corporation presidents have risen from the ranks."[102] Yet the *Times* editor observed, "that past is closing behind us."[103]

The future was easy to see. Western's executive ranks filled with individuals, from Harry Thayer to Charles DuBois to Gerard Swope, who had started with the company before the turn of the century as ten-dollar-a-week clerks. Such jobs achieved an ex post facto humble status that allowed for the continuation of Western's commitment to the myth of Horatio Alger. Yet a ten-dollar-a-week clerk ranked well above the office boy on the corporate ladder. More important, higher-ups kept a closer eye on the progress of these clerks, who were being groomed for greater things. Higher-ups looked for reflections of themselves, which created a cultural as well as an educational divide for a work force of ethnic immigrants. The secret to success, according to one cynic, was: "be born a WASP, get a college degree, and don't be born a woman."[104]

Indeed, opportunities for women were more limited. The contrast between their opportunities and those of men is demonstrated in the way New York manager (and Dartmouth graduate) Harry Thayer handled stenographers. Having realized that it was difficult to keep qualified men as stenographers for long periods of time, in May 1888

Thayer chose to replace Eddie Rockafellow with Florence Trigge, who became only the second woman in New York's office force.[105]

By 1897, New York's contingent of women in the office had grown to seventy-five, and Florence Trigge was still Thayer's stenographer. Thayer had discovered, as had so many other companies of the time, the advantages of hiring middle-class women: they were well educated and adept at language, did not demand as high pay as men, did not leave for higher-ranking positions, and were from a class less sympathetic to the cause of organized labor than were working-class men.[106] The only risk in hiring women was captured in a salute to stenographers by AT&T's magazine in 1923: "and pray she will not marry for a long, long time!"

Florence Trigge answered Western's prayers. As the *Western Electric News* put it, she gave her work "the best years of her life." In 1899, she became the first head stenographer in the New York office and was responsible for hiring all stenographers, clerks, and typists there. By the time she retired in 1915, Trigge had employed more than two thousand women, after interviewing about fifty thousand.[107]

Florence Trigge's contributions to the welfare, discipline, and morale of the women in New York were not unlike those Jane Addams had wanted for Western's factory workers in Chicago. Trigge enlarged and improved the lunchroom at the New York office. She created a rest room for the women that included magazines and a circulating library. She also added steamer chairs to the northeast wing of the building and opened a balcony with rocking chairs and window boxes on the south side so women could enjoy a rest in fresh air.[108] What she did *not* do was important as well: she did not push for higher wages or for unionization of the women. In many ways, Florence Trigge confirmed Western Electric's belief that a woman could better employ and supervise other women than a man could.

One of Trigge's contemporaries was Mary Richardson. She began as a stenographer in the Clinton Street office in 1899, and by 1902 had become assistant to the head stenographer there. As the *Western Electric News* put it, "this position demonstrated her executive ability." Eddie Rockafellow also was perceived as having "executive ability," but his options were less limited. Instead of pursuing the path toward

Figure 17. On the job training at Western Electric (1919)

chief stenographer, as Florence Trigge did, Richardson became secretary to the corporate secretary, C. G. DuBois. She finally became secretary to the company president, H. B. Thayer, and when he replaced Theodore Vail as head of AT&T, she moved with him. For a woman, then, demonstration of executive ability allowed her the opportunity either to supervise other women, as Florence Trigge did, or to toil in the reflected glory of a corporate executive, as did Mary Richardson.[109]

Shortly after Florence Trigge's retirement, the nature of opportunities for women at Western Electric changed, albeit temporarily. America's entry into World War I drew many company men into the military, and they had to be replaced. This not only brought more women to Hawthorne but led President Thayer to suspend his preference "that the women employed by us should be unmarried and likely to be permanently employed." Thayer not only wished to offer employment to wives of Western employees who were in military service but acknowledged that he might consider other married women if need be.[110]

EUROPEAN WAR AND INTERNATIONAL BUSINESS

In the summer of 1914, vice president and general sales manager Gerard Swope visited Western Electric's European plants and offices. This was his first visit since assuming responsibility for Western Electric's far-flung empire with its thousands of overseas employees. Elsewhere in the world, telephone service was provided by governments rather than regulated private concerns like AT&T. Host governments restricted supply to domestic producers, limiting Western Electric's export options. Therefore, the company manufactured in London, Paris, Milan, and Vienna, and had joint ventures in Canada (the forerunner of Northern Telecom), Russia, Japan (the forerunner of NEC), and China. On the eve of World War I, Western Electric was manufacturing in more countries than any other American company.[111]

Swope was about to learn a lesson in the risks of international business. He was in Berlin on July 28, 1914, negotiating a contract with Siemens-Halske, when Archduke Ferdinand of Austria-Hungary was assassinated in Sarajevo, triggering the start of World War I. Upon finishing with Siemens in Berlin, Swope traveled to Switzerland, Italy, France, and Belgium while European armies mobilized. When he arrived in Antwerp, Swope discovered that five hundred Belgian troops were stationed at Western Electric's factory. Many of the factory's workers, who belonged to the reserves, had already left their jobs and joined the army.[112]

Swope found business difficult to conduct in Antwerp, with constant interruptions from trumpet blasts and announcements of arriving military officers. Swope did manage to arrange to meet company officials from St. Petersburg and Berlin in London. Then Germany invaded Belgium on Saturday, August 1, and Swope fled to England. England declared war on Germany the following Tuesday, the day on which Swope was scheduled to meet with his European associates. The managers from Germany and Russia never showed up.[113]

Clarence Stoll, the American manager at Antwerp, fled with many of his employees to London. By early 1915, purchasing agent J. R. Oastler was the only member of the Antwerp's factory staff remaining on the Continent (in Paris). The others transferred to London or New York.[114] Several European managers made extended visits to or were reassigned to positions in the United States.[115]

As the Antwerp factory closed, employees buried plant records underneath the floor of the research department.[116] They also smuggled factory equipment and essential equipment plans back to Hawthorne, where surplus equipment was reserved for shipment as soon as Antwerp could be returned to Allied hands.[117] All this was done with the expectation that the war would end quickly, but the Germans did not evacuate the city for another three years. Only then were the records recovered, the surplus equipment from Hawthorne returned, and the Antwerp factory put back into operation.[118]

England's entrance into the war meant that all of Western Electric's European houses were involved in the war effort. Consequently, the company confronted the question that faces many multinationals: what policy do you pursue when war breaks out and you have affiliates on both sides? At the outset of the war, as the United States maintained a policy of neutrality, Western Electric avoided editorial comment on the war. The company's policy had not only patriotic but also business reasons: Western wished to avoid alienating any country where it had offices. In October 1914 Swope published an open letter in the *Western Electric News* ordering the omission from all letters written on behalf of the company or on company stationery of "expressions of opinion in regard to the war."[119] The *News* reported regularly on the war's effects on its European offices, but steadfastly avoided expressing preferences as to the outcome of the war.[120] That did not, however, mean that Western behaved in a neutral manner.

At the same time as the company espoused a policy of neutrality, its London affiliate actively supported the British war effort. London was the base of "the mysterious Mr. Nash," whom the English weekly

Passing Show credited with doing "more than any other man alive to conquer the U-boat." Throughout the early part of World War I, German U-boats had been the bane of the British war effort, and the *Passing Show* moaned that Britain would "have to take a much heavier toll of the U-boat pirates, before the menace is conquered." The mysterious Mr. Nash, conqueror of the U-boat, was the chief engineer of Western Electric Limited in London.

George Nash was a native Englishman, having worked for England's General Post Office and the National Telephone Company prior to joining Western Electric. He had been chief engineer of Western's London branch since 1911, but the onset of war changed engineering activities at Western Electric in London.[121] In 1915 the British discovered that a German listening post, using a little-known "valve detector" or vacuum-tube detector, was intercepting frontline communications. Under Nash's direction, Western Electric's London engineers developed a "sound barrage" to jam reception at German listening posts. The same year – as Western Electric pledged neutrality – Nash's engineers developed a mining detector, a series of listening devices set up along the trench perimeter, allowing Allied troops to determine the location of German subterranean encroachments.[122] By 1916, Western Electric engineers in London had also developed a sound barrage to prevent enemy listening posts from hearing Allied telephone communications in the front trenches.

But it was the "Nash Fish" that promised a solution to the U-boat problem. Like the mining detector, the Nash Fish grew out of Western Electric's prewar work on vacuum tubes for sound amplification. The Fish comprised two specially designed hydrophones fixed in a torpedo-shaped body filled with water to limit interference from water noises outside the device. A ship towed the device at a fixed depth, where the Fish detected a submarine and determined its position.

The British Admiralty established a training school and equipped two hundred trawlers and destroyers with the Nash Fish and depth charges. The admiralty established three patrols of "submarine hunters," who inflicted heavy losses on German U-boats. Nash's invention helped end the blockade of England. It also inspired King George to confer the Commander of the Order of the British Empire Medal on Nash.[123]

After Western Electric abandoned its public claim of neutrality in 1916, its American engineering department also dealt with the submarine problem, developing an early form of sonar.[124] Western Electric's new technology, if put in place, would have provided an early-warning system for submarines operating off the east coast of the United States.

During World War I, Western Electric advanced the state of the art not only in submarine detection, but also in airplane detection, fire-control systems, and gunfire detection and ranging. Moreover, the demands of war led Western Electric to speed up and expand its research arising out of the development of the vacuum-tube amplifier, and to solidify its relations with the government, particularly the army and navy. Its leadership in military technology would be revived in World War II and would place Western Electric in a strategic position to protect the Bell System at the beginning of the Cold War.

FROM DEPARTMENT STORE TO DEPARTMENT

In 1919, Gerard Swope left Western Electric for a vice presidency at General Electric. Swope's departure was hardly a surprise. Ten years earlier, he had negotiated the sale of Western's power apparatus business to GE and had impressed GE vice president Anson Burchard. Burchard asked Harry Thayer to add Swope as part of the deal. "I am not chattel," Swope protested, and refused to accompany the power business to GE.[125] Burchard renewed his efforts in 1916, offering Swope the chance to head GE's foreign business.[126] When the war ended in late 1918, Burchard tried again. Swope this time agreed and joined GE as president of its new international subsidiary.[127]

This appeared to be a lateral move, rather than a promotion, for someone who had headed Western's international operations. Yet Swope's future at GE offered more promise; President Charles Coffin was going to retire soon. At Western, President Harry Thayer was the heir apparent to Theodore Vail at AT&T, but Charles DuBois – a protégé of Thayer – was more likely to succeed his mentor than Swope, who was a protégé of Enos Barton.

Gerard Swope's departure symbolized Western Electric's abandonment of the title "Department Store of Electrical Apparatus" to General Electric. At GE, Swope became president in 1922 and remade the company in the image Enos Barton had wanted for Western Electric. One of Barton's goals had been to offer a broad product line, so his skilled workers had something to do when the main product (telephone apparatus) hit a "dull" period. Swope did the same at GE, expanding the role of consumer appliances relative to the company's manufacture of lighting and power products. Swope consciously diversified from the "vicious" cycle of a single product line to what he called the "virtuous" cycle of many product lines. Indeed, during the depression years of 1930–1935 the diversified GE would reduce its work force by only about 20 percent. During the same period, Western Electric – focused on the telephone business – would be forced to reduce its work force by more than two-thirds.[128]

Swope's departure also came as the Western Electric attitude toward AT&T was undergoing a transformation. Beginning in 1913, Western Electric executives (including Swope) published numerous articles and delivered many speeches about the company's role in the Bell System. Some of the early pronouncements were insistent enough to suggest that Western's full integration into the Bell System was still more goal than reality. Even within Western Electric consensus was difficult to reach. In 1915, Western devoted a conference to resolving whether the company's engineering department ought to manage product engineering from AT&T's perspective or from Western Electric's. Feeling ran high on the matter, particularly between E. B. Craft (Western's development engineer) and William Hendry (technical superintendent at Hawthorne). Craft took the AT&T view, while Hendry argued that manufacturing *was* Western Electric. Their argument escalated to a fistfight. Hendry won the fight, but Craft eventually won the war.

In 1922, Charles DuBois wrote an article for the *Western Electric*

News called "Our Place in the Sun: An Exposition of the Western Electric–Bell System Relationship." DuBois had earned the right to pen the article, having spent half of the previous twenty-four years as an AT&T executive and half as a Western Electric executive. He wrote: "Our patents are under control of the American Telephone and Telegraph Company and 97 percent of our capital stock is owned by it. Our programs and policies are all subject to review and censorship of the American Telephone and Telegraph Company." Attempting to lay to rest any lingering AT&T suspicions about Western's motivations, DuBois continued: "We have no secrets from [AT&T's] officials and no aims or ambitions except to do our part for the Bell System." Not only had GE taken on the role of department store of electricity, but, according to DuBois, Western Electric had willingly given it up. Western's new role was clear to DuBois: "we are, in all but legal status, a department of the Bell System."[129]

Western Electric's fate as a manufacturer of radio equipment supports DuBois's conclusion. In the 1920s, radio and telephone loomed as the two big growth markets in communications, and Western appeared poised to dominate manufacture in radio as it did in telephony. During the war, Western and General Electric had been the government's primary source of vacuum tubes. While GE developed the tungsten vacuum tube, Western Electric developed the "coated filament tube." Western had greater success bringing the tubes to production than GE, which had problems with its tungsten filament tube design. Therefore, the navy and the Army Signal Service standardized tube production around Western Electric's coated filament tubes. Western transferred vacuum-tube production from the New York engineering shops to Hawthorne, where it expanded its production from 100 to 15,000 tubes per week.

After the war, radio evolved from the domain of hobbyists to a commercial broadcast medium. No department store of electricity would be complete without a supply of vacuum tubes, and nobody was in a better position to dominate the vacuum tube market than Western Electric. Western was the only manufacturer that had moved vacuum-tube production out of the specialty shops and into a manufacturing plant. But Western made no move to monopolize the market for vacuum tubes, which would remain the coin of the electronic realm until after mid-century.

Patent infringement concerns and Western's subservient role in the Bell System overshadowed the company's manufacturing capabilities. The government had insisted on coordination of vacuum-tube development during the war to avoid the distraction of patent infringement litigation. That led to a patent war afterward. The key combatants were AT&T and GE, who had a history of conflict over patent rights. After years of litigation, GE patents threatened AT&T's telephone transmission capability, and AT&T's patents threatened GE's future in radio.

In July 1920, less than a year after GE formed the Radio Corporation of America (RCA) as a sales agency for its radio equipment, AT&T and GE negotiated a cross-licensing agreement involving radio and vacuum-tube production. The agreement between the GE-led "radio group" and the AT&T-led "telephone group" did not last. AT&T's concerns about the threat of radio increased when it recognized the potential growth of network radio. Network radio relied upon cable transmission of radio signals among the various affiliated broadcast stations. Any network which had its own cable lines for transmission between stations in the network would have the rudiments of a communications network that would parallel (and possibly compete with) AT&T's.

AT&T defended its telephone turf by trespassing on radio's. AT&T's strategy led to the creation of Western Electric's radio station WEAF in 1922 to compete with RCA's WJZ in the New York area. The competition lasted four years, during which WJZ inaugurated broadcasts of the New York Opera and WEAF used a long-distance feed to carry a football game from Chicago.

The radio–telephone battle ended with a July 1926 agreement. AT&T and Western Electric abandoned the broadcasting field, selling WEAF to a nationwide broadcasting service. When the National Broadcasting Company (NBC) formed the next month, WEAF became the network's flagship station. As part of the agreement, NBC transmitted between stations on AT&T's lines. The threat of an alternative to the Bell System's network of lines abated.

The main cost the agreement imposed on Western Electric was its surrender of a strong competitive position in the manufacture of radio equipment. The agreement limited Western to annual royalty-free manufacture of $3,500,000 worth of radio receivers and $1,500,000 in vacuum tubes for replacement purposes. Royalties of 50 percent would apply to any additional sales.[130] AT&T had chosen to protect its core business rather than extend Western's manufacturing capabilities with large-scale production of radio equipment.

The radio episode was evidence that Western Electric was far from an independent company and would sacrifice its own interests in order to serve the interests of the Bell System. Western behaved more like a department of AT&T by willingly abandoning a business (broadcasting) peripheral to its core, as well as a business (radio equipment manufacture) close to its core. By the time of the radio settlement, AT&T had further circumscribed Western Electric's potentials, and Charles DuBois had reason to reconsider his thoughts about Western Electric's place in the Bell System.

4

HEARD ROUND THE
WORLD: 1925–1950

N JUNE 4, 1924, WESTERN ELECTRIC'S
president, Charles DuBois, addressed a festive crowd at Hawthorne. There was much to celebrate: Western's sales for the
year would be more than twice those of 1919, when DuBois
succeeded Harry Thayer. Demand for telephones was so great that
Western Electric employed more than 60,000 people (also more than
twice the 1919 level). Furthermore, Western had begun construction
of a new plant at Kearny, New Jersey (patterned after Hawthorne,
including a tower suite of offices for the works manager). DuBois
could have been forgiven if he had shouted from the rooftops, but he
did not need to. He was dedicating the first permanent public address
system at any industrial site, a system that allowed many people to
hear what conventional telephone receivers had limited to an audience
of one.

Western Electric's development of the "loud-speaking telephone"
(loudspeaker) was a by-product of H. D. Arnold's high-vacuum tube.
Western Electric public address systems had been used at the 1920
presidential conventions and at Warren Harding's 1921 inauguration.
On Armistice Day (November 11) that year, Harding dedicated the
Tomb of the Unknown Soldier before 100,000 people at Arlington
Cemetery. His address was sent by telephone lines to New York, and
cross-country to San Francisco. In both cities, loudspeaker systems
broadcast Harding's speech. Nearly three years later, with his voice
amplified ten thousand times, DuBois demonstrated to 40,000 employees the system they had helped design and build.[1]

Figure 18. The Western Electric public-address system in Public Square, Cleveland, during the 1924 Republican National Convention

During the dozen years prior to DuBois's speech, Western's top executives – from Gerard Swope to Harry Thayer to DuBois – had addressed the issue of "Western Electric's role in the Bell System" in speeches and the *Western Electric News*.[2] AT&T was about to clarify that role. In April 1924, DuBois's old colleague, Harry Thayer, had set the wheels in motion. Thayer was more practical than the visionary DuBois; he would never have written, as DuBois did in 1913, "I have been *dreaming* about the future status of the telephone."[3]

Thayer was best suited to whipping an organization into shape to suit the vision of another. His closest business relationship was with Theodore Vail, the Bell System visionary. Thayer's attention to detail complemented Vail's gift for seeing the big picture. It was as if each man could see himself completed in the presence of the other. According to Vail, "sometimes old Thayer comes in to my office and we just sit and look at each other."[4]

In 1924, Thayer was about to retire as president of AT&T, and he

113

Figure 19. The first women employees to "punch in" at the new Kearny works, which began production in late 1924

wrote to his heir apparent, Walter Gifford, with his thoughts about Western Electric. "It was the intention in 1882 that the future of Western Electric Company should be bound up in the future of the Bell System," wrote Thayer. "Subsequent history has shown that any variation from that line has been disastrous to Western Electric Company as well as Bell System." Thayer cited as an example the leadership of his Western predecessor, Enos Barton, who, "in gratification of his personal ambitions, gave the most of his thought to the development of the company as a general electric manufacturing company." Discussion of policy was a healthy thing, but the decision "ultimately rests with the American Telephone and Telegraph Company, [and] it should be assumed that that policy is for the benefit of Western Electric Company."[5] Thayer had made a declaration of Western's dependence.

Gifford did not wait long to act on Thayer's advice. In September he proposed establishing a separate research entity for the Bell System. He had three objectives. One was efficiency and economy: putting all the researchers together better coordinated the scientific work of the Bell System. Second was a spirit of cooperation. Most of the technical work had been done by members of Western Electric's engineering department, and some by AT&T's, resulting in a battle for credit. Third, he saw public relations benefits. To maintain a virtual monopoly without inviting antitrust action, the Bell System needed to show that it was striving for the sorts of improvements that competition created, and to claim credit for "progress of art of telephony."[6] A separate entity would make that easier. On January 1, 1925, AT&T established Bell Telephone Laboratories, Inc., in New York City as a joint venture with Western Electric. Gifford appointed Frank Jewett president of the new company, in charge of 4,000 employees.

Gifford also had plans for Western Electric International, a subsidiary created during World War I to handle the company's foreign business. DuBois "confess[ed] to a great personal interest in and affection for [Western's] foreign business."[7] Sitting in his office was a large globe of the world he had inherited from Harry Thayer; as it passed from president to president, the globe became Western Electric's "unofficial symbol of continuity." Prior to AT&T's divestiture of Western Union, Theodore Vail had commissioned a number of globes for his executives. The globe highlighted the undersea telegraph cable throughout the world, but to Western Electric it also symbolized its overseas operations.[8] In the spring of 1923 DuBois had toured the company's European plants, and in August he had written *The Foreign Business of the Western Electric Company*. DuBois pointed out that Western was the dominant force in the international telephone apparatus business, possessing 47 percent of the market. Western had achieved this market share, not by dominating a few major markets, but by establishing a presence in nearly every country with significant telephone business. There were two exceptions: Germany, where Western had sold its factory on the eve of World War I, and Russia, where Western's affiliate had been seized and nationalized by the Communists after the 1917 revolution.

In early 1925, DuBois had been negotiating with International Telephone and Telegraph (ITT) to coordinate Western Electric's manufacturing with ITT's foreign operations. These negotiations stalled because ITT had committed itself to entering the manufacturing field and had already purchased interests in one of Western's foreign competitors. By June it was clear to DuBois that Western Electric would either have to buy ITT or enter into competition with it in seeking concessions to operate telephone systems abroad.

At that point, DuBois fell ill and spent several months at his farm in Vermont. While DuBois was incapacitated, Gifford continued to pursue the agenda Thayer had recommended. In August, he orchestrated the sale of International Western Electric to ITT. The press release announcing the sale noted that domestic business was making increasing demands upon Western Electric and that, because its primary obligation was to the Bell System, Western had decided to withdraw from the foreign field to devote its resources to business within the United States.[9] DuBois and many others at Western Electric were crushed when they heard the news.

When DuBois returned to work in early November, he explained to Gifford that "my principal efforts are toward restoring and improving W. E. morale."[10] There was no assembly of 40,000 this time. Instead, DuBois explained Gifford's decision to groups of Hawthorne supervisors. It was clear, however, that DuBois was the one who needed a pep talk. "Before I left New York last June," DuBois recalled, "I had expressed my views with respect to these negotiations then beginning. It did not then seem probable they would result in a sale. I hoped they would not."[11] The sale of International had meant the end of DuBois's dream "of a foreign telephone service as great and as universal as the American telephone service."[12] The globe in DuBois's office no longer seemed to symbolize continuity; instead, it was a constant reminder of AT&T's abandonment of the far-flung sweep of Western Electric's operations.

In his November talks, the one area beyond Western's core business where DuBois appeared sanguine was in the future of the supply business, which had contributed some $66 million to Western Electric's sales. He addressed rumors about the status of that department by saying "we have no thought or present intention of selling it."[13] Gifford and the other directors of AT&T proved DuBois wrong. In December, they created the Graybar Electric Company (as a subsidiary of Western Electric) to handle the supply business, while Western would continue to serve the Bell System. In 1928, Western sold Graybar to its employees. By then, DuBois had resigned as president. He cited health reasons, but a conflict in business philosophy with AT&T was probably a contributing factor.

The company DuBois had inherited was one of the world's most advanced industrial researchers, most visible multinational manufacturers, and largest electrical distributors. The name Western Electric was amplified well beyond the reach of the 40,000 employed at Hawthorne: company advertisements appeared in publications with a circulation of nearly 100 million.[14] In June 1924 who would have dared to predict the appearance of a 1950s lament from within Western Electric that all too often employees were introduced "as Mr. Zilch of Westinghouse, or Mr. Hokum of Western Union" because the company's "identity is still relatively obscure"?[15] Yet by the time DuBois retired in 1926, Western Electric was no longer a department store of electricity, or an international power. Western Electric lacked the glamour of Bell Labs and the instant recognition of AT&T. It had become an entirely different enterprise, with more inward-looking principal concerns: productivity and quality.

Ironically, just as Western was abandoning foreign markets and consumer products, it became involved in developments with worldwide ramifications, ranging from the Hawthorne Studies through bringing sound to motion pictures in the 1920s and 1930s, through the development of radar during World War II, to the dissemination of management principles in Japan after the war. Western Electric became more obscure as an organization, but its activities attracted more attention than ever.

WORKPLACE AS LABORATORY

In November 1974, hundreds of people attended a four-day symposium on human relations at the Hawthorne Works auditorium. A joint effort of the Harvard Business School and the Western Electric Company, the symposium showcased some of the brightest lights in industrial psychology, organizational behavior, and management science. Walter Menninger, founder of the Menninger Foundation, spoke about the role of emotion and feeling in the workplace. Stanford's Harold Leavitt and MIT's Edgar Schein spoke about organizational theory. Yale's Victor Vroom spoke about leadership, and Harvard's Jay Lorsch spoke about management's use of behavioral science.[16]

The symposium culminated in a dinner at Oakbrook, which gave the social scientists and Western Electric managers an opportunity to get better acquainted. Yet much of the attention that evening was directed toward three older women. Neither Wanda Beilfuss, Mary Volango, nor Theresa Zajac had completed high school or ever held a supervisory job. All three had spent their careers as assemblers at Hawthorne. In a company as hierarchical as Western Electric, it was unusual for people from the line to receive such attention, except at "long-service anniversary" celebrations and retirement parties. Yet on November 12, 1974, they were seated as guests of honor at the head table.

Robert Jerich helped organize the symposium and later recalled the banquet: "We had world leaders in industrial psychology, and personnel sitting in the audience. When the program concluded, these three ladies were introduced. They were not comfortable being in this kind of setting. As the general manager wished everyone bon voyage, these educators and psychologists made a dash for the dais to have these women autograph their programs. These women just didn't know what to do or say. They couldn't understand why their autograph was so important to these people."[17] Their autographs were important because these three women had been central figures in the Hawthorne Studies, and this banquet celebrated the fiftieth anniversary of the studies' 1924 inception.

The Hawthorne Studies were the most audacious social scientific study ever made in the workplace. During a nine-year period, Western Electric hosted studies of the impact of illumination and other stimuli on productivity and conducted interviews with thousands of employees. The most in-depth aspect of the studies was a five-year observation of the work of six women – including Beilfuss, Volango, and Zajac – in a separate room. The meaning of the studies has been subject of debate ever since, and seemingly no discussion of industrial psychology or industrial sociology is complete without reference to them.

The Hawthorne Studies represented a continuation of the company's interest in the human behavior movement. By 1924, Western Electric was accustomed to dealing with social scientists in general and psychological issues in particular. For Western, the "art of human engineering" began with psychological testing and a relationship with Walter Dill Scott.[18] Scott, a psychology professor at Northwestern University (and the school's future president), introduced professional psychology to business. His first work was in advertising; then he shifted his attention from consumers to employees, establishing a series of psychological tests for the workplace.[19]

Western Electric was one of a handful of companies to request Scott's services. During the 1914–1915 school year, Scott gave a series of six lectures to men in the Hawthorne Club. He was attuned to the sensitivities of his audience; the theme of his series was "Personal Efficiency in Business," and it included a lecture on "Psychology and Modern Business Efficiency."[20] In 1915, Western convinced Scott to develop tests to determine the creative ability of engineers and their potential for growth.[21] Scott's tests at Western suggested a possible link between technical skill and organizational ability. Therefore, not long after Western Electric and the electrical industry had helped turn management into a science, the company found scientific support for their approach to management.[22]

Before the company could apply psychology to other areas, World War I intervened. The birth of psychological testing is often associated with the military's use of it during World War I. Industry, so the story goes, was impressed by the results and began to sponsor its own tests. Actually, it was the other way around. In April 1917, the National

Research Council set up a psychology committee (which included Walter Dill Scott) to establish psychological tests to select and place recruits.[23] Meanwhile, the War Department established a Committee on Education and Special Training (CEST), with Western's Walter Dietz in the Division of Educational Standards and Tests.[24]

After the war ended, Western Electric expanded its use of psychological testing, applying the army "Alpha" test to (male) applicants and transfers in the production branch and the clerical branch, and to applicants engineering and service men in the installation department. The test was also administered to occasional applicants to the merchandise branch, the inspection branch, and the industrial relations branch. A different test, the "clerical test," was given to female clerks and office boys. The company believed that the tests could correlate with "the development and success of the individual in the ordinary course of the day's work."[25]

Western Electric went in for psychological testing in typical fashion – on a large scale. By 1921, the personnel department had grown enough that a separate department was created to handle routine testing, test development, job specifications, and trade tests. In 1922, Western administered psychological tests to nearly 6,000 employees, and in 1923 nearly 8,500. This was an appropriate prelude to the most extensive psychological and sociological examination of a work force ever made.[26]

Ironically, the catalyst for the Hawthorne Studies had little to do with either psychology or management. It was far more mundane than that: an attempt by the electrical industry to encourage the use of its products. Concerned about technological advance that allowed for equivalent amounts of lighting to use less electrical power, electrical manufacturers and utilities tried to compensate for lost business. They conducted a major campaign in the early 1920s to encourage the use of artificial rather than natural lighting. Those companies using adequate lighting, the campaign suggested, would save their workers' sight, prevent accidents, and reap increased productivity and profits.[27] Tests at nine companies demonstrated productivity increases of 15 to 35 percent after more powerful lights were installed.

However, the industry needed results that appeared less like advertising and more like scientific research. To collect more compelling evidence to support their conclusion, the Illumination Engineering Society sought out the National Research Council (NRC). In 1923, the NRC's Division of Engineering and Industrial Research established a Committee on the Relation of Quality and Quantity of Illumination to Efficiency in the Industries. The Committee on Industrial Lighting, as it came to be called, enlisted none other than Thomas Edison as its honorary chairman.[28]

The illumination studies were broadly conceived, including topics ranging from physics to physiology and psychology. The sites for research varied, including scientific laboratories and industrial plants. General Electric, Dennison Manufacturing, and Western Electric appeared especially well suited to this project: each had previously engaged in psychological testing.[29] Western's participation was no surprise in one respect: Frank Jewett, the company's vice president of research, was chairman of the Division of Engineering and Industrial Research, and the company's chief engineer, Edward Craft, was vice chairman. Hawthorne works manager Clarence Stoll offered to host the experiments, keep the records, and bear some expense. With the active involvement of government (the NRC) and academia (MIT), this industry promotion effort bore the imprimatur of disinterested social science.

From November 1924 until April 1925, illumination tests began in three Hawthorne departments: relay assembly, coil winding, and inspection. The researchers found no significant relationship between lighting and output; the output seemed more a function of level of supervision. In the second set of tests, from February to April 1926, the most striking finding was in the relay assembly department, where, although illumination levels were *lower* than those of the 1924–1925 test, output increased. The third set of tests – from September 1926 to April 1927 – pursued that line of inquiry, and again productivity increased as illumination decreased. Not surprisingly, the Committee on Industrial Lighting soon lost interest and never issued a report. Meanwhile, the Hawthorne management *gained* interest.

During the illumination studies, the hosts changed as much as any test variable. Western's research department became part of the separate entity Bell Telephone Laboratories. Further, after having spent the previous forty years as a distributor of electrical lighting equipment, Western Electric spun off its electrical supply business to the Graybar Corporation. The tests, then, appeared to have more to do with Western's past than its future. Instead of diminishing Western's interest, however, the spin-offs appeared to intensify it. Free from the cutting edge of science and the cutthroat competition of the marketplace, there were only so many ways in which a Western manager could make a difference, and productivity was the biggest.

While the electrical manufacturers and power companies sought to collect evidence supporting an answer they accepted in advance (industry needed to use more artificial lighting), Clarence Stoll (now vice president) and the staff at Hawthorne pursued their own agenda: determining the impact of various lighting levels on workers' attitudes, behavior, and productivity.[30] So, after the "failed" illumination tests, the company initiated a new series of studies. Six women – including Wanda Beilfuss, Mary Volango, and Theresa Zajac – assembled telephone relays in a room separate from the rest of the department; and the results led to the title "relay room heard round the world."[31]

Six people in a room was not the usual way at Hawthorne, where participation en masse was the norm. Despite the elimination of research, international, and consumer business, and the departure of a number of managers to the new Kearny plant in New Jersey, Hawthorne's work force returned to 40,000 during the Hawthorne Studies. Photos from the 1920s convey the mass culture that was Hawthorne: the crush at the gate as shifts changed, throngs attending speeches. They played together, too. In 1927, Albright Gymnasium was completed, joining six adjacent baseball diamonds, thirteen tennis courts, and a track. As late as 1931, 94 percent of employees turned out in employee elections. This was the apex of welfare capitalism at Western Electric.

Hawthorne had also added a new wrinkle: the "Hello Charley" phenomenon. In the early 1920s, someone sent a postcard addressed only to "Charley, the Western." Amazingly, it reached its destination, a popular employee named Charlie Drucker. Wags began to call Western Electric "Charley Western." In 1930, Jean O'Rourke was crowned

Figure 20. Hawthorne employees leaving at the end of their workday, 1922

the first "Hello Charley" beauty queen, inaugurating a fifty-year tradition. Her likeness appeared on "Hello Charley" stickers as Western
employees took their mandated two weeks of vacation in July. When
Western employees spotted another car with a sticker, they honked in
solidarity; even on vacation, Hawthorne brought people together. In
such a group culture, having clerks or assemblers doing everything
together was typical of Hawthorne; the fact that there were only six
was not.

The job of relay assembly reflected where Western Electric stood
on the road to assembly-line production. With the exception of the
layout operator, the relay test group had identical jobs, as described
by George Pennock, superintendent of Hawthorne's technical branch:
"Putting together a coil, armature, contact springs, and insulators in a
fixture and securing the parts in position by means of four machine
screws." All told, each assembly took about a minute.[32] Relay assembly
was as repetitive – and measurable – as Hawthorne work ever got.
The number of functions and parts involved indicates that the com-

Figure 21. The crowning of 1957's "Hello Charley" queen was part of a tradition of Western Electric beauty pageants that lasted from 1930 to 1980.

pany had not yet achieved sufficient "job breakdown" to warrant a moving assembly-line process.

For the women, moving to the relay test room was like receiving a promotion. Western Electric extended privileges to the six women the ordinary worker did not receive. Many workers went through an entire career without setting foot in Hawthorne's tower, but the six women were regular visitors. In their separate room, they escaped the noise and dust of the one hundred-person department. The group was also paid based on their own output instead of that of the entire department, so the relationship between their performance and their reward was more direct than it had ever been. The young women (only two were older than twenty when they entered the test room) were not chosen at random but were all experienced workers who performed well above the average. This was to control for any "learning curve" effects.

They also had fun. The women talked and joked with one another while they worked, and after a while began to socialize with each other away from work, with slumber parties and evenings at the theater.[33] "It was very innocent," recalls Mary Volango. It was also interesting,

Figure 22. The relay-room test group, Hawthorne Studies, 1928. Mary Volango is at right.

for both the test subjects and their observers. Don Chipman, who spent six years as an observer in the relay assembly test room, relinquished his supervisor rating to get involved.[34]

From 1927 to 1932, the women's output was measured in response to changing conditions during thirteen periods, which ranged from two weeks to seven months in duration. In addition to pay, other variables explored were rest periods (both in number and in length), length of the workday, and food consumption. When the women were also offered tea, the test room became known as the "T" room.

Productivity rose steadily for the five operators except for periods 10–12. Of particular interest to later observers, however, were two sets of comparisons. In periods 7, 10, and 13, the conditions were identical, but output in period 10 was greater than in period 7, and in period 13 it was higher than in period 10. Similarly, periods 12 and 3 had the same conditions, but output in period 12 was considerably higher. The most common conclusion derived from the results was that rather than tangible factors, such as food, rest, and pay, psychological factors made the difference. This meant the principal issue driving the results was the amount of attention paid to the workers and the fact that their concerns were considered. Hence the expression

"Hawthorne Effect," which refers to social scientific experiments with unexpected outcomes from nonexperimental variables.

Observers came from all over the world to see what was happening in the "T" room. There to explain the results to them, and offering academic advice to Western Electric's management, were a number of academics, most notably Elton Mayo of the Harvard Business School. Mayo's involvement lasted from 1928 to 1933. A product of an Australian and English education, Mayo employed a cross-disciplinary approach to the social sciences at a time when the American approach was becoming more and more specialized. After spending much of his career struggling to obtain funding, Mayo must have felt he had hit the mother lode at Hawthorne, where he received funding from the Rockefeller Foundation and the royal treatment from the Western Electric management. He visited Hawthorne a few times each year, but the first visit made the greatest impression. The company put him up at a Chicago landmark, the Palmer House hotel, where he was extended the same courtesy (or privilege) as Hawthorne works manager C. L. Rice. A bemused Mayo wrote his wife: "Every morning at 8:30 the doorman clears the taxis away from the Wabash St. entrance of the hotel – and a large limousine with a uniformed chauffeur slides noiselessly in. The door is opened and Elton Mayo, formerly of South Australia, gets in and glides off to his alleged industrial researches."[35]

Mayo and his associates tried many approaches, including observing a group of relay assemblers who *were not* physically separated from the larger group. Most significant among the other tests, however, was that of a group of men in the bank wiring room. There, individuals with tremendous ability, potential, and training were among the lowest producers.[36] Whereas the creation of a group among the women relay assemblers appeared to increase productivity, the formation of a group of men in the bank wiring room seemed to limit productivity.[37] Since 1900, Western Electric had succeeded in formalizing the organization of work with detailed organization charts and job descriptions, but the Hawthorne Studies offered evidence of the impact of *informal* groups on output.[38] Many trace the beginnings of industrial sociology to the relay assembly and bank wiring studies.

The aspect of the Hawthorne Studies that involved the greatest number of employees was an interviewing program which ran from 1928 until 1930. The impact of supervision on the women in the relay test room suggested larger possibilities within the company. Channels of communications could be easily blocked in an organization where a group chief, section chief, assistant foreman, foreman, general foreman, assistant superintendent, superintendent, and assistant works manager stood between the works manager and the individual operator. Western Electric's hierarchy became notorious enough to warrant a *New Yorker* "Profile" reference, where someone recited who reported to whom, on and on, and concluded with: "and on the day shift it's worse!"[39] In such a hierarchical and paternalistic organization (works manager Rice liked to be called "Dad"), there is a great risk of individuals abusing their power. So the company instituted a supervisor training program *and* a massive interview program to find out what their employees thought, in true Hawthorne style: from 1928 to 1930, more than *20,000* Hawthorne employees were interviewed.[40]

The lasting impact of the interview program came as much from what the interviewers learned about their craft as from the specific content of the responses. Early on, interviewers came armed with a structured set of questions. What they found was that, regardless of what was asked, the workers would talk about what *they* wanted to say. The interviewers concluded that the unsolicited comments had such value that they changed their approach to *nondirected interviewing* (NDI). That meant that after explaining the program interviewers allowed the subjects to choose topics of discussion.[41] NDI later would become a staple in the counseling field.

The Hawthorne Studies ended in 1933. By then, Elton Mayo had predicted that the impact of the studies would rival that of the industrial revolution. In the immediate aftermath of the studies, Mayo and the other researchers published a blizzard of work about Hawthorne, including more than a dozen books and dozens of articles.[42] They succeeded in fulfilling Mayo's prophecy: a historian of the studies notes that they have "acquired the status of a creation myth in such subdisciplines as industrial sociology, the social psychology of work, industrial psychiatry, and the anthropology of work."[43]

Indeed, the Hawthorne Studies became the most hotly debated social science experiment ever conducted at a business enterprise. It put the field of industrial psychology in the public eye as never before and launched organizational psychology and industrial sociology. This may be because the studies remain unmatched in sheer scale and scope. One scholar of organizational behavior, after acknowledging the impact of the Hawthorne Studies on various fields of study, said: "if the studies hadn't been done we would have had to invent them."[44]

The legacy of the Hawthorne Studies is mixed. Inside the company, a consensus is evident, but measurable impact is not. Outside the company, they made a tremendous impact, but there is little consensus as to what they mean. The range of interpretations is impressive. As Edward Lawler put it: "one of the charms of the Western Electric studies is that they seem to provide data to support almost any conclusion about employee behavior." Some see the studies as a refinement of Taylorism, because they reinforce the idea of an administrative or managerial elite presiding over the work force. Chester Barnard, president of New Jersey Bell, rejoiced: "At last we have something that really is a basis for scientific management."[45] Yet some see the studies as a rebuke of Taylorism, in that the significant outcomes were not always directly associated with tangible incentives such as pay. Some go further, interpreting the results as a nail in the coffin of the idea of "rational economic man."[46] There is not even a consensus as to whether the studies yielded answers or merely questions.[47] The Hawthorne Studies, then, have become something of a Rorschach test of human relations. As Jay Lorsch put it, "When a behavioral scientist tells you about Hawthorne you learn more about that behavioral scientist than you do about the Hawthorne Studies."[48]

The reaction to the studies inside the company was quite different. The company found more consensus about the *meaning* of the studies: they showed that merely letting employees know that supervisors were paying attention to them could increase productivity (and that was their definition of the "Hawthorne Effect"). The *impact* of the Hawthorne Studies inside the company, however, is more difficult to gauge than outside. Despite all the information the company gathered and the money it spent (more than $1 million) on the studies, a report with specific recommendations was never issued to management. The information remained in descriptive form and was not focused on any one management problem.[49]

The most obvious tangible result inside the company was the establishment of American industry's first major counseling program. The beginnings of the counseling program offered a nice bit of symmetry to Western Electric's relationship with psychology. Twenty years after helping to bring psychological testing to the military, Walter Dietz headed the counseling program at Western Electric.[50] Established in 1936, the program employed the new approach of nondirective interviewing.

A counseling program represented a natural direction for a company committed to welfare capitalism, and whose employees were not yet members of national unions. One of Western's counselors commented: "one would have to be extremely naive . . . to claim . . . that counseling does not drain off grievances that might otherwise find expression in other channels [such as unions]."[51] The counseling program grew from 5 counselors handling 600 people at Hawthorne in 1936 to a peak of 55 counselors handling 21,000 people in 1948.[52]

Unions came and the counseling went. By the early 1950s, Hawthorne was represented by the International Brotherhood of Electrical Workers (IBEW). Shop stewards replaced counselors as the recipients of complaints. In 1956, the counseling program was eliminated. In the meantime, some former Western Electric counselors set up a similar program at Sears, which remained nonunion and replaced Western Electric as the leading human relations outpost in corporate America.[53]

THE BELL SYSTEM SHOCK ABSORBER

In 1919, Baltimore's Board of Trade wrote a letter to Western Electric president Charles DuBois: "The Industrial Bureau of the Board of Trade of Baltimore, after some investigation, desires to call to your attention the facilities of the City of Baltimore as a manufacturing center, and a desirable location for your Eastern plant. . . . Baltimore's industrial growth is receiving support of the leading banks and business men of the city, and a branch factory of your company will be most welcome here."[54] Thus began a nine-year courtship. Baltimore was the northernmost southern city (just below the Mason-Dixon Line), but in an attempt to appeal to dubious northerners, it billed itself as the southernmost northern city. By the summer of 1928, Baltimore was a finalist for Western's next major manufacturing facility: a cable and wire plant. After three months of intense negotiations, a combination of proximity to excellent rail and water transport, a large labor pool, a high percentage of home ownership, and a convincing local sales pitch led Western to announce its intention to come to Baltimore.

In the fall of 1928, after committing to build in Baltimore, the company hosted Baltimore civic and industrial leaders at Hawthorne to see how a Western Electric plant operated. This was a big deal. The mayor of Baltimore, one of Maryland's U.S. senators, and the managing editor of the *Baltimore Sun* were part of the entourage.[55] Western chose to build on the site of Riverview Park, an amusement park that had been dubbed "The Coney Island of the South."[56] In early 1929, Western Electric razed the old amusement park, making way for the Point Breeze plant, which became known as "The Playground That Went to Work."[57]

Both the company and the city had big plans for Point Breeze. In October 1928, the Baltimore Association of Commerce honored Western president Edgar Bloom at its annual banquet. Bloom offered his vision of Western Electric's future in Baltimore: "When finally completed to ultimate capacity our Point Breeze plant will provide employment for about 30,000 people." Including families and "accessory population" (those catering to the needs of Western employees and family), Bloom predicted: "our Point Breeze plant at ultimate capacity will sustain a total population of 150,000 people (compared to Baltimore's population of about 830,000)."[58]

This did not happen. Although the plant floor space reached five times that of Baltimore's Fifth Regiment Armory (site of the 1912 Democratic national convention) Point Breeze never employed 10,000 workers, much less 30,000.[59] The one prediction by Bloom that came true was "I should expect we will reach our ultimate capacity within the fifteen year period."[60] Indeed, fifteen years later, in 1943, Point Breeze reached its peak employment level of about 9,000. In the meantime, Western Electric and Baltimore were victims of bad timing. The plant was planned and built during the prosperity of the 1920s, but began operation on the eve of the Great Depression.

By 1934, the *Western Electric News* (the company organ since 1912) had ended its run, and the *Hawthorne Microphone* had temporarily ceased publication. There would have been little good news to report. The depression had driven many businesses into bankruptcy and many individuals out of work. American unemployment levels reached 25 percent. The depression's shrinkage of the American economy was deeply felt at Western Electric, where sales fell from a high of $411 million in 1929 to less than $70 million in 1933. The 1930s was the only decade in the twentieth century when the number of telephones in the United States decreased, falling from 16 to 13 per 100 population (compared to the late 1970s, when the number surpassed 75 per 100 population). Telephones were still a luxury enjoyed by a minority rather than a necessity available to most.

The 1936 presidential election provided an indication of the nature of telephone demand at the time. The *Literary Digest* conducted a telephone poll asking respondents which presidential candidate, the Democrat Roosevelt or the Republican Landon, they preferred. The poll's respondents chose the Republican challenger; President Roosevelt, whose criticisms of "economic royalists" were not designed to curry favor with the telephone-using upper-middle class, won in the greatest landslide in history.[61] In a time of great economic distress, spending on anything but the necessities usually falls, and the telephone had not yet attained the status of necessity in America – hence a Bell System crisis.

Economic crises test the priorities of a business enterprise. How will the burden be distributed among its stakeholders? In March 1936, at hearings before the Federal Communications Commission, AT&T President Walter Gifford was asked: "And I take it that you feel that your responsibility and your loyalty is divided as nearly equal as it may be to [employees, investors, and patrons]?" Gifford answered, "Yes, sir," but his actions spoke louder than his words. Gifford sustained payment of AT&T's dividend at $9.00 per share throughout the depression, although net income fell below $8.00 per share by 1932 and below $7.00 by 1934. Dividend payments actually grew from $116 million in 1929 to $168 million in 1935 because the number of outstanding shares had increased. Gifford's policy was widely praised as helping to maintain the purchasing power of the hundreds of thousands of AT&T shareholders.[62]

In the 1970s, when AT&T vice president Alvin von Auw wrote the policy statement for the Bell System, "there were colleagues of mine that wanted to emphasize the virtues of the continuity of employment that the Bell System offered."[63] Von Auw, who had joined Western Electric toward the end of the depression, argued that those who had worked at his old company "would not accept such a statement."[64] They had good reason: from 1929 to 1933, employment levels at AT&T and the operating companies fell by about 32 percent (from 359,000 to 245,000); Bell Labs also lost about the same 32 percent (from 5,628 to 3,717); while Western Electric lost more than *75 percent* (from 87,000 to 21,000).

The depression sustained a long tradition: during economic downturns, AT&T had to keep a service going, whereas Western could postpone building more equipment. Western's employees, then, were more vulnerable to layoff. The panic of 1907 was a good example: from 1906 to 1908, employment levels at AT&T and the operating companies fell by about 6 percent (from 105,000 to 99,000), while at Western Electric the decrease was more than half (from 23,000 to 10,000). Little wonder that Western Electric came to be known as the Bell System "shock absorber."[65]

When hard times came to Western, who got to stay and who had to go? Ultimately, the two pillars of welfare capitalism became a guide: position in the hierarchy and seniority. When managers' jobs were eliminated, they were offered the first shot at lower-level jobs. Even with such an option available, the managers felt little security. Joseph Juran, who had become a division chief in Hawthorne's inspection group at age twenty-five in 1929, observed people with twenty-five years or more experience laid off. So he got a law degree at night –

Figure 23. Guard by Hawthorne gate no. 1, 1931

just in case: the number of lawyers in Washington, D.C., was beginning to increase. Juran kept his job and never had to practice law.[66]

One approach the company used to keep as many people employed as it could was to reduce the workweek. The reduction of hours hit the operators first. By the summer of 1931, those who had kept their jobs worked a 40-hour week rather than the usual 48. All those at the level of assistant foreman or above stayed at 48 hours, but some of the lower-level supervisors were reduced to 40 hours. The reduction in hours not only reduced pay but damaged social prestige for supervisors. For many, being a supervisor at "the Western" was a badge of honor which they proudly wore. When word got out about their reduced hours, some friends or neighbors would say things like: "Oh, I thought you were a supervisor, but I see your hours were cut like the operators."[67] The loss of prestige and pay was difficult for managers to take, but they stood a better chance of remaining employed than the people on the line.

Consequently, workers at the bottom of the hierarchy, particularly those with less than ten years with the company, were at greatest risk. After a while, even those with excellent work performance were let go. Many supervisors complained about the loss of so many capable young people, but the seniority system held sway.[68] The layoff victims included the six relay assemblers involved in the Hawthorne Studies. They had been given more attention than any assembly workers in the history of Western Electric, or any company. They had been interviewed by curious visitors from Germany, Japan, and all over the world. They had been given unprecedented latitude in determining their own working conditions, incentives, and perks. They had been treated like a valuable resource. Nevertheless, they too lost their jobs and were replaced by women with more seniority.

The company made allowances for those with families to support. The six women would have been let go sooner if they had been married. Operating under the philosophy that married women had another income to fall back on, the company used marital status as the most common exception to the seniority rule.[69] By the same logic, single men were at greater risk than married men. Beyond these policies, managers had some latitude regarding whom to let go. They might suggest, for instance, that a favored employee stay home on the day the ax would fall. Such methods helped little, however, when employment at Hawthorne fell from a high of 43,000 in 1930 to about 6,000 in 1933.

The impact of layoffs on individual departments could be quite dramatic. Ray Russ had supervised a cable forming group at Kearny, but the only way to stay on the payroll was by giving that up and taking a demotion. In the depths of the depression, Russ became the only cable former in a group previously composed of 20–25.[70]

The survival of Joseph Juran and Ray Russ were exceptions; Cuthbert Cuthbertson's experience was more the norm. He joined the company in 1930 as a planning engineer at Kearny and had an excellent relationship with his boss. As the depression deepened, he survived layoffs that claimed five-year men, but kept his job until June of 1932 (his boss, who had once been assistant superintendent, was later demoted to engineer). Cuthbertson might have kept his job longer, but he was single. The next four years were a struggle. A college-trained engineer, Cuthbertson got a series of short-term jobs, as a bakery delivery man, as a rodman on the irrigation survey, and as a surveyor for the Works Progress Administration (WPA). During one winter, he worked with his parents and brother feeding sheep for a combined income of $46 a month.[71] Like many other layoff victims, Cuthbertson's main goal was to rejoin Western Electric, so when an upturn came in the late 1930s, the company had little trouble convincing him, the six relay assemblers, and many others to return.

During the depression, the company created its own "make-work" program. At Hawthorne, Kearny, and the new Point Breeze plant in Baltimore, employees began to make furniture, jigsaw puzzles, and other items. The company even issued a separate catalog for such items. Robert Yaverick was one such worker. He had started as a cable former at the West Side Shops (a nearby temporary location while the Kearny works were being completed) in 1924. He had risen two levels when the depression hit. He was demoted to section chief, then to cable former, before moving into the wood shop. There he built wooden frames for switchboards, but also tile-top tables, mahogany folding card tables, and other products for sale in the employee store, both to employees and the general public.[72] The program failed to keep many people employed for long; like so many other businesses during the depression, Western Electric simply had to wait for the return of demand for their main line of products. In the meantime, the company did the best it could with ancillary lines.

One of the most popular diversions during the depression was

Figure 24. Bookends were just one of many products made by Western Electric craftsmen and distributed throughout company stores as part of the company's depression-era "make-work" program.

motion pictures, and Western's most significant ancillary product line was the introduction of sound to film. As often happens, technological advance in one area had led to breakthroughs in another. In this case, a revolution in the telecommunications industry led to a revolution in the entertainment industry.

In 1922, Western Electric's research administrator, Edward B. Craft, decided to direct the company's developments in amplifiers, loudspeakers, microphones, and electronic recording in a new direction: toward sound motion pictures. Efforts toward that end had been made since the dawn of motion pictures in the 1890s, including the introduction of the Kinetophone by Thomas Edison's laboratory in 1913. The Kinetophone's poor synchronization and sound quality proved more a distraction than an enhancement to films. Edison's failure made Hollywood moguls wary of expending much time or effort on sound, offering an opportunity to other innovators outside of the motion picture industry.

By 1923, a number of companies were working on sound developments, but Craft was undaunted by the competition. He wrote to

Figure 25. Western Electric sound equipment arrives at a Tokyo movie theater, 1929.

Frank Jewett, vice president in charge of research, "it seems obvious that we are in the best position of anyone to develop and manufacture the best apparatus and systems for use in the field." Craft turned out to be right. Western Electric developed an integrated system for recording, reproducing, and filling a theater with synchronized sound. By 1924, Western Electric was ready to sell its system to Hollywood.

Western attracted the attention of a second-tier motion picture studio called Warner Brothers and the Vitaphone Corporation to experiment in the production and exhibition of sound motion pictures. Four months later, the new system, called Vitaphone, debuted with the opening of *Don Juan*, starring John Barrymore, at the Warner's Theater in New York City. Preceding the film were a series of short sound films rather than the usual live vaudeville acts. As for the main feature, an electrical sound system – carrying the recorded strains of the New York Philharmonic – replaced accompaniment by live musicians. The

137

system was a hit, even if the film wasn't: Quinn Martin wrote, in the *New York World*, "You may have the 'Don Juan.' Leave me the Vitaphone."

Western Electric formed a subsidiary the following January to handle the company's nontelephone interests. Electrical Research Products, Inc. (ERPI) developed and distributed studio recording equipment and sound systems to the major Hollywood studios. Recognition for Western Electric's contributions to the film industry soon followed. In 1931, ERPI won an award from the Academy of Motion Picture Arts and Sciences for technical achievement. ERPI's system of noiseless recording was cited as the "outstanding scientific achievement of the past year."

ERPI also made movie theater sound equipment, which was leased rather than sold – just as the Bell System had leased out the telephone equipment Western produced. ERPI equipped 879 movie theaters in 1928, and 2,391 in 1929. By 1932, only 2 percent of open theaters in America were not wired for sound: silent film was dead, and sound was in Hollywood to stay. Western Electric proved better at wiring the nation's theaters than it was at maintaining that customer base, however, and ERPI abandoned the motion picture theater business in 1937. The company continued to produce sound equipment for movie studios until 1956, when as part of a Bell System antitrust settlement, Western Electric abandoned most nontelephone enterprise. The company left a legacy in the motion picture industry, one reminder of which is the credit at the end of many films from Hollywood's Golden Age: "Sound by Western Electric."

COMMUNICATIONS ARSENAL

On January 1, 1940, Clarence Stoll became the first engineer to head Western Electric. For years, Western had been presided over by Harry Thayer, Charles DuBois, and Edgar Bloom, who had fashioned careers from office work. By contrast, Stoll spent his early years on the manufacturing floor, then rose through the ranks. After studying electrical engineering at Pennsylvania State University, he joined Western's training program for engineers at the Clinton Street shops in 1903 (where his class of ten was nearly twice the size of Stoll's high school graduating class). He then had a series of assignments at the Clinton Street shops, and in New York, before he settled in at Hawthorne and quickly rose through the ranks. He replaced H. F. Albright in the tower offices as works manager in 1923, then became vice president in 1926. Stoll's promotion to president meant that an engineer would run a company dedicated to the engineering principles of scientific management.

When Stoll took over much of the rest of corporate America had not yet fully recovered from the impact of the depression. That soon changed, as one crisis replaced another. Stoll, who had been superintendent of the company's Antwerp factory in 1914 when Germany invaded Belgium, must have felt a sense of déjà vu when the German blitzkrieg rolled through the Low Countries in the spring of 1940. In May, President Roosevelt declared a limited national emergency, catalyzing America's war preparedness efforts. Western Electric opened a Washington office two months later, helping transform the company into a "Communications Arsenal." This ushered in an era of more than thirty years where the company's top two customers were the Bell System and the federal government.

For the first time since 1925, Western Electric had a significant independent customer. Since the spin-offs of Graybar and international in the 1920s, about 95 percent of Western's sales had been to the Bell System. By December 7, 1941, when Japan bombed Pearl Harbor, approximately one-third of Western Electric's business was with American military agencies. At the same time, commercial business took a back seat. For example, the process of replacing manual switchboards with dial telephone crossbar switchboards – which would mean less need for operator interruptions – was curtailed. In 1941 Western manufactured about 300,000 lines of crossbar equipment. That declined to 87,000 in 1942 and to only 470 the next year.

Products which a few years earlier had provided merely marginal income now commanded Western Electric production. Four hundred sets of aviation radiotelephone equipment, which prior to the war would have saturated the entire market, by the middle of the war

Figure 26. Western Electric's greatest contribution to America's war effort – radar – was kept secret until May 1943. Then Western Electric ads likened the ability of radar to "pierce the black of night" to "electrical cats."

would not satisfy weekly demand. Public address systems for stadiums and auditoriums were modified and applied to the construction of battle announcing systems. The frequency of ship-to-shore radio sets production was expanded to provide the navy's oceangoing craft with a wider frequency band. Western Electric hearing aids were used in constructing under-the-helmet headsets for frontline communications. Bone conduction receivers, a component of Western Electric hearing aids, became the principal component of special throat microphones used by the navy. Indeed, by 1944 Western Electric was supplying every two weeks communications equipment equivalent to what it had supplied during the entire four years of World War I.[73]

Western's greatest volume of defense work was on "secret equipment of many types which cannot be revealed."[74] The most important secret project was for radar, or "radio distance finding."[75] Radar offered both offensive and defensive capabilities. It made weapons more accurate, and therefore efficient, requiring far fewer shots to register the same number of hits. It also allowed defenses to detect airplanes at any time of day or night and in any type of weather.

Next to the government, Western Electric/Bell Laboratories played perhaps the greatest role in the development of radar. In terms of value, Western manufactured nearly $1.2 billion of radar, more than three times that of the next most prolific producer (General Electric). During the war Western Electric supplied 42 percent of the ground radar, 27 percent of shipboard radar, and 28 percent of airborne search and bombing radar – in value between one-third and 40 percent of the total radar – manufactured in the United States. By the last quarter of 1944, 40 percent of Western Electric personnel was involved in radar manufacture, and by 1945 radar represented more than half of Western's sales to the government.[76]

Radar was a complex item whose construction was more analogous to that of central office switchboards than to telephones and other mass-produced products. Like switchboards, radar equipment had to be modified for each purpose and installation requirement and was, therefore, not readily standardized. Therefore, Western's manufacturing, which had increasingly moved to assembly-line-type processes during the interwar period, reverted toward job-shop assembly. Hawthorne's telephone shop, which had operated on an assembly-line basis, producing millions of phone components each year, was converted to a job shop producing twelve types of radar, with the total production running less than 1,700 sets in 1943.

Radar orders tested the limits of manufacturing at Western Electric. The company established sixteen shops in nine cities to handle the excess work derived from its radar contracts. A shoe factory in Haverhill, Massachusetts, was transformed into a coil-winding facility. A zipper factory in Bayonne, New Jersey, was converted to radar manufacturing. A laundry in Jersey City and a garage in New York, an ordinance plant in Eau Claire, Wisconsin, and an airplane hangar in Baltimore were all conscripted into Western's radar manufacturing program.

Radar at the very least was necessary – if not sufficient – to determine the outcome of the war. In July 1946, President Truman awarded the Medal of Merit to Western Electric president Clarence Stoll. "Under his direction and outstanding leadership," the citation read, "his company produced more than thirty percent of all electronics and communications equipment and more than fifty percent of all Radar manufactured in this country during the war."[77]

Although the end of the war terminated most of Western's defense contracts, the company did not, as it had at the end of World War I, quickly abandon its defense connections. Those connections would soon be put to use to build a defense for the United States in the Cold War, which would also defend the Bell System itself.

THE CHANGING FACE OF WESTERN ELECTRIC

The 1943 Annual Report of the Baltimore Urban League noted: "in the Spring of 1942 Western Electric provided Maryland with its first example of a concern successfully using Negroes and white workers side by side and without segregation as to toilets, cafeteria, dressing rooms or other facilities." Western's Point Breeze plant had become the largest racially integrated defense plant south of the Mason-Dixon Line. The Urban League also reported that Western Electric management claimed: "little or no conflict has resulted."[78] In May 1942, the Office of War Information issued a similar report. The reports were premature. Integration at Point Breeze was about to cause white employees to demand segregated facilities, the company to deny the request, the white employees to strike, and the government to take over the plant.

On the eve of World War II, few would have predicted Western Electric's involvement in one of the early skirmishes in the civil rights movement. The African American presence in the company amounted to a handful of workers at distributing centers and some caricatured figures in *Western Electric News* cartoons. Not one African American worked in any of the company's three major plants – even in Chicago, the "Promised Land" of the great migration of African Americans from the South.

By 1920, many major Chicago manufacturers, including meat packers, steel plants, International Harvester, Montgomery Ward, and Sears, employed blacks. Western Electric, one of the largest employers in the Chicago area, did not. Some of the other employers had less than noble reasons for hiring African Americans, either using them principally for dangerous or dirty work, or hiring them as strikebreak-

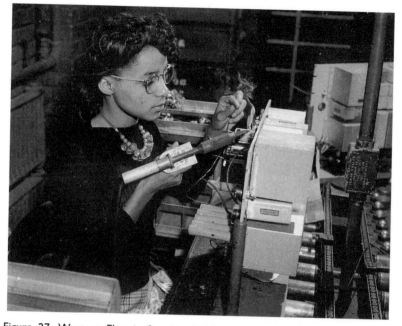

Figure 27. Western Electric first hired African Americans at its plants during World War II. Here is Kearny wirewoman (and future screen actress) Ruby Dee.

ers. The conditions for such employment did not exist at Western Electric: the work was less dangerous than that in many other industries, and the electrical industry had been slow to unionize. This may explain why Western Electric also hired no blacks at the company's two newer plants.

The Kearny, New Jersey, plant was built in the mid-1920s close to New York City to meet the demand for telephone equipment which the company's New York shops once fulfilled. Kearny provided the company with an opportunity to save on shipping costs from the Midwest to the East Coast. Kearny was built as a replica of Hawthorne, and like Hawthorne it produced both switchboard and cable equipment. Supervisors were shipped from Hawthorne to ensure that Kearny's procedures followed the Hawthorne model, including its racial policies. As the new plant's work force grew past the 10,000 level, about 90 percent of the workers, none of whom were black, were recruited from the local area.

As late as 1940, race seemed to be the last issue that would pose a problem at Western Electric in general and at the Point Breeze works in particular. The city of Baltimore enforced segregation of the races, and Western Electric only hired whites at its manufacturing facilities. World War II changed all that. Race became one of the most volatile issues on the homefront. The idea of blacks fighting fascism overseas while denied democratic rights at home stirred considerable resentment. Even before America entered the war, A. Philip Randolph, head of the Brotherhood of Sleeping Car Porters, threatened an equal rights march on Washington. On June 25, 1941, President Roosevelt responded with Executive Order 8802, calling for the integration of government contractors.

Becoming a major defense contractor not only transformed Western Electric's work but also its workplace. After Roosevelt's executive order, Western began to hire blacks in 1941, but did so very slowly. As of March 1942, out of 50,000 employees at the three plants, 103 were black. By the end of 1943, the number had increased to nearly 7,000. Nowhere was the change more noticeable than in Baltimore.

The Point Breeze case provides a classic example of an employer wedged between government policy and local custom. On October 6, 1941, Point Breeze hired Andrew Ridges as a janitor. Ridges was the first African American hired at the plant, but the first segregated facilities preceded his arrival. The company already had posted a "colored" sign on a rest room to be used by visiting chauffeurs and truck drivers. By December, the company added one toilet in the wire building and one in the cable building for blacks. Western Electric was following the Baltimore Plumbing Code, which called for segregation of washrooms and drinking fountains by race and gender. This was Jim Crow in action.

After America's entry into the war, things began to change quickly in Baltimore. The Urban League and a local congressman successfully lobbied the Health Department to eliminate "race" from the plumbing code in February 1942. This reflected a growing activism among Baltimore's African American community. The local NAACP was in the process of growing from 100 members in 1935 to more than 17,000 in 1946.[79] The Baltimore *Afro-American* ran a series called

"Nazi of the Week," suggesting that those who denied blacks their rights were supporting Hitler's policies.[80] In the spring, the War Manpower Commission chose Baltimore as the first "critical labor supply area," and the city was selected as a test of the government's voluntary manpower program (which established a target of 10 percent of the Negro population to be employed in the war industry).[81] In May 1942, amid this environment of escalating concerns about race, Point Breeze first hired black men for production work.

In the summer of 1942, Western Electric removed signs designating race and partitions that separated black and white sections from the bathrooms. Only one other defense employer in Baltimore, Eastern Aircraft, had integrated. Whites and blacks migrating from the South, according to a government report, "brought their racial prejudices with them."[82] Baltimore, and Point Breeze, were no exception. By October, when blacks had reached 10 percent of the work force, whites began to complain about integration.

In August 1943, a spark hit the tinderbox. The company moved a black woman into an inspection department, and twenty-two white women demanded her removal. When management did not comply, the women went on strike and were supported by the Point Breeze Employees Association (PBEA), the Point Breeze employer-sponsored labor union. After meetings between the PBEA and management, the focus became separate facilities. The company denied the request for separate facilities, but the women returned to work without a change in conditions.

Then the PBEA submitted a petition with about 1,500 names seeking racially segregated toilet facilities. The company rejected the petition, and the PBEA called a strike vote. In October, 1,802 voted for, 1,144 against. In the meantime, more than 500 African American workers organized efforts to defeat the strike vote. Eugene Barnes, who presided, pointed out that the PBEA collected fifty cents per month from *all* employees (black and white) but was using the money to fight against the blacks.[83] After their efforts to defeat the strike vote failed, the black group, who called themselves the Non-Partisan Committee of Western Electric Employees, enlisted the assistance of Alexander J. Allen, the Urban League's industrial secretary. The group telegraphed the War Labor Board and the president: "If other means fail we urge President Roosevelt to take over the plant for the duration of the strike threat." That was just the beginning of some hardball played by both sides.

In an open letter to the Baltimore City Council, the PBEA suggested: "If conditions are permitted to continue, the trouble at the plant is going to become more violent and will spread all over the city. . . ." This was a particularly sensitive time to suggest such a possible outcome. Just a few months earlier, the Detroit race riot had killed thirty-four and injured six hundred.[84] PBEA attorney Charles Dorn testified before the War Labor Board: "Nothing short of segregation is going to prevent a strike and possible rioting." Dorn claimed that this was not a threat, but "simply a prediction based on my own personal knowledge of the situation at the Western Electric plant."[85] At the same time, the Non-Partisan Committee recommended that the White House and the Selective Service immediately induct all the male strikers into the military.[86]

After a series of discussions with the War Labor Board, which concluded after the board refused to order separate facilities, on December 13 the PBEA called a strike. Most of the whites stayed out, and production levels fell 10 to 20 percent.[87] President Roosevelt then issued Executive Order 9408, authorizing government takeover of the plant, which the army did on December 19. This was largely symbolic: there were no troops involved, and although Brigadier General Archie A. Farmer "possessed" the plant, Western Electric's management ran it. The order also directed the secretary of war to recommend modification or cancellation of any draft deferments of the striking men.[88]

On March 23, 1944, after three months without riot or major incident, the government returned the plant to the control of management. The following day, the *Baltimore Sun* and the *Afro-American* printed the compromise reached by the government, Western Electric management, and the PBEA. Western agreed to build additional lockers and toilets, which would be assigned "in a manner directed toward the harmonious relationship of those involved."[89] That was a euphemism for "segregated." In the shop, this meant those assigned to a particular group of lockers used one set of facilities, and those assigned to the other lockers used different facilities: one group of lockers was assigned to blacks, the other to whites. Although partitions had been removed from the bathrooms, separate doors (black and white) led to the *same* rest room. Blacks and whites tended to use the washbasins and toilets on their accustomed side. Maybelle Rodgers, who had been secretary of the Nonpartisan Committee, recalls walking down an aisle with a white friend toward the bathroom, then her friend saying, "I'll see you in a few minutes," as they entered separate doors. Inside, they rejoined at adjacent basins.[90]

So, after abandoning its old racial policies and taking a tentative step toward full integration, the company bowed to local custom. The segregation of Western Electric in the 1940s changed the terms of the company's version of welfare capitalism. Previously, most of the activities of the Hawthorne Club and other employee organizations had been open to *all* employees, and the others (such as sports and some classes) were segregated by gender. The addition of race to the mix changed that – particularly in Baltimore. There were black and white dances, black and white baseball teams, and black and white annual picnics – all funded by the company. This situation did not change until the 1960s. By then, Western Electric's top management had committed itself to a leadership position in civil rights and equal opportunity.

5

DEFENSE AND SOCIAL
CONTRACTS: 1950–1972

I N A P R I L 1 9 4 9 , A T & T ' s P R E S I D E N T , L E R O Y
Wilson, presided over a crowded, standing-room-only shareholders meeting at New York City headquarters. AT&T had more
shareholders than any company in the world, and the annual
meeting gave them an opportunity to voice concerns about Wilson's
stewardship of their investment. Some activists pushed for female rep-
resentation on the board of directors. Others voiced concerns about
the company's pension policy. The main concerns, however, were
about a suit the Justice Department had filed against AT&T in January.

Filed under the Sherman Antitrust Act, the suit claimed that the
rates operating companies were charging telephone users – based on
Western Electric's costs – were excessive. The suit grew out of the
FCC's investigation of AT&T in the 1930s. Holmes Baldridge, the
lead attorney in that investigation, had moved to the Justice Department. There he convinced attorney general Tom Clark to attempt to
pry Western Electric loose from the Bell System and divide it into
three parts, as a means of fostering competition.[1]

At the time of the suit, Western Electric was confronting the enormous challenge of postwar reconversion. During the war, while Western focused on defense matters, civilian orders had accumulated until
about two million people were waiting for telephones. Once the company was freed of war commitments, it turned its attention to addressing this enormous pent-up demand for telephones. During the first
full year of peace, Western Electric delivered roughly two-and-one-

half times its 1941 civilian output. By 1947, 91 percent of its business was with the Bell System. Not until 1956 could Western announce that the backlog of telecommunications equipment orders caused by World War II had been met. So intent was the Bell System on satisfying commercial demand that it established internal policies limiting defense work to less than 15 percent of revenue – until the Justice Department filed the antitrust suit.

In the summer of 1949, Western Electric was excluded from crucial decision making about its future, just as it had been in the mid-1920s. Relations between Western Electric and AT&T were quite stable (as they had been since the 1920s). The difference was that in 1949 there was an additional stratum – the government – above AT&T and Western's own hierarchy. AT&T resolved the suit without the spin-off of Western after, among other things, agreeing to have Western manage Sandia Laboratories, which handled America's nuclear weapons arsenal. Ironically, after decades of struggle to focus Western Electric's attention on the telephone business, culminating in Walter Gifford's pruning of Western's ancillary businesses in the 1920s, in 1949 one tactic AT&T employed to keep Western Electric was to order the manufacturer to perform work outside of the Bell System's core business.

The 1949 negotiations reflected how AT&T and the government viewed Western and defined its "core competence." Prior to World War II, Western had been viewed as a maker of things, priding itself on manufacturing high-quality products at low cost. Since spinning off Western's consumer products in the 1920s, AT&T had – at least in peacetime – identified Western as "Makers of Bell Telephones." Beginning in the 1940s, Western was also viewed as a manager of projects, including Sandia. The "Makers of Bell Telephones" became "Managers of the Nation's Nuclear Stockpile."

The next twenty years appeared to offer Americans simultaneously realization of their fondest hopes and of their gravest fears. Any fears of a postwar return to a depression were soon put to rest by the greatest period of prosperity any nation had ever experienced. At the same time, Americans paid a stiff price for their good fortune: an extended arms race with the Soviet Union punctuated by the periodic

Figure 28. The world's largest centrifuge, at Sandia Corporation's environmental test area. Western Electric's management of Sandia helped fend off an antitrust suit.

threat of another world war. As a result of AT&T's negotiations, Western Electric became actively engaged both in helping Americans realize their hopes, by meeting the consumer demands of "the Affluent Society," and in assuaging their fears of Soviet attack.

The antitrust suit's 1956 settlement, which allowed Western to remain with the Bell System, called for Western's only sideline to be defense work. That meant that, in addition to the management of Sandia, Western handled a variety of federal projects, from guided missiles to military communications to radar. By the end of the 1950s, about 18,000 Western Electric employees were engaged in defense work. Although this was not the first time the company had done work for the government, it was the first time it had done sustained government contracting during peacetime.

Involvement in defense work had important ramifications for Western Electric. One consequence, a successful outcome of the antitrust suit, was an explicit goal from the start. Another consequence, the company's involvement in issues of equal opportunity, was utterly unforeseen in 1949.

Two of the most notable themes running through American history have been the attempt to realize the ideas of the Constitution in daily life and the promise of economic opportunity. These two themes converged when the civil rights movement came to corporate America in the 1960s, and Western Electric was one of the focal points. The federal government had the opportunity to impose its civil rights policies on defense contractors such as Western Electric – and exercised it. At Western, the response to government policy took on a life of its own. Led by champions of equal opportunity such as president H. I. Romnes, the company transformed itself from a laggard to a leader in civil rights. Few companies came so far so quickly.

THE BELL SYSTEM'S MANAGERS

In May 1967, the *Mainichi Daily News* reported: "The man responsible for improving management and control in the Japanese telecommunications industry during the Occupation days is back in Japan – and being welcomed heartily by his 'former students.'" The man was Charles Protzman, and his former students had become the heads of Fujitsu, Sumitomo Electric Industries, and Matsushita Electrical Industries, among others. Protzman had retired from the Western Electric company in 1963 after a forty-year career, but his most noted achievement came during an eighteen-month stint when he was on loan to America's occupation forces in Japan. The U.S. government's invitation to Protzman and other Western Electric managers to come to Japan showed the extent of the government's acknowledgment of Western's management skill.

During World War II, Western Electric had acted as both project manager and personnel manager for the government. When Bell Labs brought its technical expertise to the defense program, Western acted as prime contractor, subcontracting research and development to the Labs.[2] Western Electric's hierarchical setup, which many have compared to that of the military, meshed well with the government's wartime needs. Also during World War II, Western Electric's Walter Dietz, who had assisted the government with personnel issues during World War I, helped head a program called Training Within Industry (TWI). The TWI program prepared individuals to learn how to perform jobs different from the ones they had held before the war or to enter the work force for the first time. TWI was later applied throughout the world.

After the war, Western had another opportunity to spread its gospel of management. Following Japan's September 1945 surrender, General Douglas MacArthur headed an occupation force whose immediate tasks were to disarm the Japanese army and to make sure that the Japanese people were fed and clothed. MacArthur realized that in order to avoid rumors that might cause riots or other disruptions, the Americans must help rebuild Japan's communication system. This was no small task. Not only had Japan's communication system been devastated, but the war had destroyed more than 75 percent of its manufacturing capacity for communications products.

So the occupation force's Civil Communications Section called on the Bell System for help. Western Electric sent a crew of managers to solve problems involving communications equipment, wire, and cable. For the first couple of years of occupation, Western Electric's advisors addressed particular manufacturing problems. For instance, beginning in October 1946, the advisors met weekly with representatives of the Nippon Electric Company (NEC) – Western's progeny – regarding vacuum-tube and repeater-tube production and quality. Repeater-tube rejections at NEC were running at 60 percent.[3]

Charles Protzman arrived in 1948. Until then, his career at Western Electric had been quite ordinary. He joined the company in 1922 as an installer, then moved to Hawthorne in 1926 as an engineer. He rose to department head before moving to Point Breeze in 1930 at the same level, but, like so many others, he was demoted during the depression. He had risen to assistant superintendent by the time he went to Japan. There Protzman soon noticed that something was needed besides discussions about quality.

Protzman toured numerous factories that manufactured communications products. He wrote: "This convinced me that the Japanese lacked both practical engineering concepts as related to manufacture and also fundamental management concepts and practices for effective control of the business. . . . The management weaknesses were evident in loose supervision, lack of knowledge of costs, absence of control techniques, failure to recognize the interrelationships of various company functions and, in many instances, one man domination."

What Protzman noticed was the result of a policy in occupied Japan that was very different from the one in occupied Germany. After the war, the Allies reinstated many of the leaders and managers of Germany's wartime industry because they believed nobody else could do the job. In contrast, MacArthur chose to purge Japan's industrial leaders, which resulted in a shortage of management expertise in Japanese industry. Regardless of the cause, the consequences of such management inexperience were serious: "the weaknesses of management were causing a tide of regression which, allowed to go unchecked, might well culminate in the collapse of the industry. Were this to occur, it would have most serious repercussions on the welfare of the national communications systems."[4]

In the meantime, the stakes in Japan had risen. In May 1948, the Russians had cut off Berlin from the rest of the world, resulting in the Berlin Airlift, one of the most dramatic flashpoints of the Cold War. It was no longer sufficient for MacArthur's force to diffuse Japanese resentment against America, make sure the nation's immediate needs were taken care of, and then leave. Rather, Japan had to become a pillar of capitalist strength in the Far East. The sense of urgency about that goal intensified when China went communist in May 1949.

In August 1949, Protzman proposed a management training course for the communications manufacturing industry. If Japan were to anchor resistance to communism in the Far East, it would need to run its own businesses effectively – especially those in communications. Protzman's proposal stated: "A stable national economy demands the existence of firm industrial enterprises; but more than this, it is imperative that the communications networks be supported by an industry which is made up of stable, reliable, progressive equipment suppliers."

Protzman had spent his career in an organization wedded to the principles of scientific management. In Japan, he argued that such principles, "which are the basis of enterprise in a modern society, are largely unknown." In suggesting a management training course, he also suggested an emphasis on developing "practical knowledge of the two most fundamental controls of management – Quality Control and Cost Control." Not coincidentally, those were the two areas in which Western Electric managers had the most latitude and experience.

Protzman concluded that the need for managerial expertise was so widespread that rather than deal with companies individually he would conduct seminars that representatives of many companies could attend. Protzman and his colleague Homer Sarasohn presented their course twice: once in Tokyo beginning in September 1949 and once in Osaka beginning in November. The course lasted for eight weeks at each location, four afternoons a week. The subjects covered included organization design and construction, policy, and cost control. In addition, more than 60 pages of the 400-page course guide were devoted to issues of quality.

The seminars were offered as the occupation was winding down; indeed, Protzman returned to America, and to his Western Electric career, in May 1950. While Protzman and his colleagues at first despaired over their inability to offer the course more than twice, their departure did not end "CCS," as the course came to be known. In March 1950, Protzman received a letter from members of the Osaka seminar. They informed him of their plans to continue offering their version of his course: "The seed which the CCS has planted in the industrial city of Japan is thus growing, and the seed shall not stop growing until they be flourished in glorious trees."

If the subsequent success of the companies of attendees (Matsushita, Sanyo, Sharp, Sumitomo, Fujitsu, Hitachi, NEC, Toshiba, or their predecessor companies) is any indication, that is what happened. The Japanese Management Association sponsored two executives to sustain the course. By the end of 1952, about 1,300 Japanese executives had attended. Bunzabmon Inoue, one of the two executives who carried on for the departed Americans, believed that the lasting impact of CCS on Japan was the introduction of scientific management. One of the signers of the March 1950 letter, and later chairman of Sumitomo

Rubber Industries, Inoue referred to the CCS course as "the light that illuminated everything."

Subsequently, there has been debate about the role Americans played in Japan's postwar economic "miracle." For example, American-quality gurus Joseph Juran (who had begun a consulting practice after leaving Western Electric in 1941) and W. Edwards Deming brought their ideas to Japan after Protzman left. Afterward, they disagreed about the source of Japan's subsequent success. Deming attributed it to American expertise; Juran credited Japanese openness to new approaches. In any event, CCS helped the Bell System to reinforce its position as the government's manager of choice. Western Electric's role as manager in CCS ended just as the company was beginning a project much closer to home: the management of Sandia Laboratories.

THE BEST DEFENSE IS DEFENSE

One of the aspects of the twentieth-century American experience which has distinguished it from that of other world powers has been its avoidance of foreign invasion. Europe, East Asia, and the Middle East have been battlegrounds for much of the century, but not the United States. In that respect, Americans may have been mentally less prepared for the dangers of the atomic age than those more accustomed to living at risk. So, in 1948 and 1949, when the Soviet Union imposed a blockade on Berlin then tested its first atomic bomb, and China fell to the communists, Americans felt a new sense of vulnerability. During the 1950s, the Bell System and Western Electric were entrusted with the primary corporate responsibility for easing those concerns.

The Bell System's first major contribution to Cold War defense was Western Electric's management of Sandia Laboratories. Located in Albuquerque, New Mexico, and administered since 1945 by the University of California, Sandia was responsible for development of America's nuclear arsenal. By 1948, its staff had grown from fewer than 400 to more than 1,700. Sandia had a management problem, struggling with its shift from research to the manufacture of nuclear weapon components. In December 1948 the regents of the University of California announced that they would abandon the contract to manage Sandia.[5]

Even before the university announced its intention, Roger Warner, associate director of the military researchers working at Sandia, approached Oliver Buckley, president of Bell Telephone Laboratories, suggesting that the laboratories might manage Sandia. Buckley rejected the possibility, pointing out that operation of Sandia would place his firm well over the internal policy limits on government contracting at 15 percent of the firm's revenues.[6]

Buckley's rejection of Warner's invitation shifted the government's sales pitch to the highest levels. On May 13, 1949, President Truman wrote to AT&T president Leroy Wilson and Dr. Buckley, informing them that the Atomic Energy Commission (AEC) would seek a contract with Bell Laboratories to manage Sandia and urging them to accept the contract.[7] This was only a few months after the Justice Department had instituted antitrust proceedings against the Bell System. Wilson now found in Truman's letter a way of defending Western Electric's role in the Bell System. His response to the president made no commitments other than seriously to consider the AEC's proposal.

A series of meetings ensued. Wilson and Buckley convinced AEC officials to follow the wartime precedent of contracting through Western Electric, in other words, to have Western and Bell Telephone Laboratories jointly administer Sandia. Bell Laboratories would be best suited to handling the research, while Western Electric could best address the manufacturing problems.

Wilson raised another concern. If the Justice Department antitrust suit succeeded, Western and the Laboratories would be unable to fulfill their contractual obligations to the AEC. The suit would destroy the very relationship between Western Electric and the rest of the Bell System that might bring the Sandia situation under control. As Wilson not so subtly put it, the antitrust suit "made us question with you whether it would in fact be desirable in the national interest for us to undertake this project."[8]

Thus, Wilson conditioned his acceptance of the contract on the AEC's and president's assurances about the antitrust action. On August 15, AEC head David Lilienthal met with President Truman, who, Lilienthal told Wilson, appreciated Wilson's concerns and indicated that neither AT&T nor the AEC need worry about Justice Department action. This is what Herbert Bergson, head of the Justice Department's Antitrust Division, had told the AEC's general counsel in June.[9] Subsequent events confirmed those explicit and implicit promises. The antitrust matter was shelved until the Eisenhower administration took office in January 1953.

Meanwhile, Western Electric's involvement with defense projects grew, from the Nike guided missile program beginning in 1950 to discussions of one of the biggest military engineering jobs in history: the Distant Early Warning Line (DEW Line), a 3,000-mile system of radar outposts across the Arctic to detect approaching bombers. Various studies sponsored by the Department of Defense from 1950 to 1952 concluded that America's continental air-defense system was not capable of preventing a devastating nuclear attack. The existing defense system provided only one hour's warning that bombers were on the way, although it would take four to six hours to prepare to defend against such an attack. Only an early-warning radar fence could provide the additional time necessary to prepare adequately.

In November 1952, AT&T's new president, Cleo Craig, turned down the Defense Department's request that Western Electric construct the "northern radar fence" and associated communications facilities during the next two years. Craig complained that the Bell System was already overburdened with meeting the expanding demands of public communications services and heavy defense obligations. Craig also feared that the Bell System might have to abandon at least some of its defense commitments if the antitrust action were not delayed. Craig's fears abated during the subsequent year as the Bell System garnered some powerful advocates in the executive branch.

In 1953, the incoming Eisenhower administration brought a lower level of interest in pursuing antitrust than its predecessors. Attorney General Herbert Brownell publicly advocated a review of pending antitrust actions, suggesting that many of them ought to be dismissed.

The new administration provided Western Electric and the Bell System with important allies in the Defense Department. Deputy Secretary of Defense Roger Kyes advised Bell Laboratories president Mervin Kelly that AT&T and Western should give "full time to defense activities and not be concerned about preparation for the suit."[10]

In July, Kyes's boss, Secretary of Defense Charles Wilson, wrote Brownell a letter expressing "serious concern" about further antitrust prosecution against the Bell System. The case, Wilson asserted, threatened the continuation of important national defense work that the Bell System was performing. Were the Justice Department to sever Western Electric from the Bell System, they would effectively "disintegrate the coordinated organization" that was "fundamental to the successful carrying forward of these crucial defense projects." Should the Justice Department succeed, it would virtually destroy Western's "usefulness for the future."[11]

This advocacy gave the Bell System the assurances it needed to go ahead with the DEW Line. Awarded the contract in December 1954, Western Electric used the development work of Bell Telephone Laboratories and the Massachusetts Institute of Technology, and enlisted the assistance of 2,700 U.S. and Canadian suppliers and contractors.

The biggest threat to the project did not come from the Soviets but from the forbidding Arctic weather. To protect themselves against -40 degree temperatures compounded by stiff winds, Western Electric men wore thirty pounds of clothing and carried twenty-pound sleeping bags whenever going out for a stroll. The logistical challenges were enormous, involving bulldozers, enormous quantities of steel and cement, hundreds of miles of cable, not to mention provisions for the workmen. Supplies had to be shipped during the few weeks in late summer when the Arctic Ocean was sufficiently free of ice to navigate safely.

The Arctic segment of the job was completed on schedule in July 1957. In the spring of 1959, Western Electric completed the communications and electronics phases of the 700-mile westward segment of the DEW Line through the Aleutian Islands, and in November 1961 completed the 1,200-mile eastern segment to Iceland. The *New*

Figure 29. Western Electric was prime contractor for the Distant Early Warning (DEW) Line. This radar station was in Greenland.

York Times called the DEW Line "one of the modern wonders of the world."

In the meantime, the value that the government put on Western's contribution to the national defense program had been confirmed by the outcome of the 1949 antitrust suit. A 1956 consent decree culminating the 1949 antitrust case called for the Bell System to divest all of its nontelephone activities – except those involving national defense. At the same time, the Justice Department abandoned its original goal in the case: removing Western Electric from the Bell System.

Western Electric also had to relinquish its interest in Northern Electric of Canada, the last vestige of its international operations. Since its 1895 incorporation, Northern Electric had acted as a subsidiary of Western Electric and had expanded well beyond telephone equipment, selling radio and broadcasting sound equipment, electric sound equipment, and other lines of electrical equipment. So the government's decree not only shrank the Bell System, it created a potential new competitor.

Military considerations both hindered Western Electric's telecommunications development and advanced it. The company diverted to military contracts economic resources that otherwise might have been applied to telecommunications development in the 1950s. At the same time, military needs for microelectronic products pushed technology ahead at a rate faster than would otherwise have been economically viable.

CHANGING PROCESSES

Before he took a job at corporate headquarters in the late 1930s, one of Joseph Juran's most memorable moments at Hawthorne came when he solved a serious manufacturing problem. Hawthorne was regularly scrapping about 15 percent of the production of a circuit breaker it manufactured in enormous quantities. Juran found that the addition of two inches to each piece could transform a problem-laden soldering process into one nearly without defect. As Juran recalled: "We analyzed the manufacturing process to find the sources of our problems and then fixed them by improving the production process. We not only improved the quality of the circuit breakers, we also lowered the cost of producing them."[12]

Juran saw dramatic possibilities in this episode and excitedly told his boss: "I know that problems like this exist throughout the plant. Why don't we search them out and fix them?" His boss agreed that it was a good idea, but insisted that wasn't their job: "We're the inspection department, and our job is to look at these things after they're made and find the bad ones. Making them right in the first place is the job of the production department. They don't want us telling them how to do their job, just as we don't want them telling us how to do ours." So an opportunity was lost because, as Juran put it, "production was the job of one unit, quality of another unit, and no one was in charge of process improvement."[13]

Juran always sought practical applications of statistical methods and at times was better able to do so after hours than on the job. Al Capone, whose gang was headquartered a half-block away on Twenty-second Street, owned a couple of gambling establishments across Cicero Avenue from Hawthorne. Many Western Electric veterans recall the danger having such a neighbor involved, especially when gunmen from a rival gang would drive down Twenty-second Street, past Hawthorne's telephone apparatus buildings, with guns blazing.[14] For Juran, however, Capone's gambling house called "The Shop" represented an opportunity to turn his statistical talents to good use. Juran observed that one of Capone's employees was "a robot as far as operating the roulette wheel," and so repetitive in his motions "that data collection and analysis could be applied." Juran won $100, "and that was several weeks' pay."[15]

Statistical quality control was one of the most likely areas to yield process improvement, and at the time during which Juran worked in inspection the Bell System already had some of the world's leading theorists. In 1924, Western Electric's Walter Shewhart launched the modern scientific study of process control through the invention of the first statistical control chart. Control charts display observations on processes over time to see whether changes in output are random or reflect changes in process. Applying statistical techniques to quality assurance, control charts go beyond the deficiencies of individual items to offer evidence regarding the stability of an entire process.[16]

Shewhart's work received worldwide attention but did not change the way things operated at Western Electric. Shewhart was a skilled theoretician, but he could not successfully convey quality ideas to a manufacturing work force. Therefore, at the onset of World War II, you could walk through the Hawthorne plant – seedbed of a quality revolution – without seeing any control charts. Process improvement was still no one's job.

The 1947 invention of the transistor at Bell Labs led to a dramatic change in manufacturing processes. The transistor signaled the end of the electromechanical era (symbolized by vacuum tubes and bulky electrical equipment) and the beginning of the electronic era (symbol-

Figure 30. Walter Shewhart's control chart revolutionized statistical quality control.

ized by solid-state devices and the miniaturization of components). For Western Electric, the initial demand for small lightweight devices was for guided missiles such as the Nike system, which was capable of carrying nuclear weapons; but Western also applied solid-state technology to civilian projects such as switching systems.

The first Western Electric plant to mass-produce the transistor was the one at Allentown, Pennsylvania. There, in the early 1950s, quality control was a major problem. What Western needed was a translator of Shewhart's quality-control theory into practice – and it found one in Bonnie Small. Small was familiar with statistical control charts, having used them in her photography business before the war. Her World War II experiences at Hawthorne convinced her that Shewhart's abstract ideas alone were of little help in a factory. At Allentown, she decided to translate these ideas into practical methods: sell the idea of improving process, with the control chart as tool. By the time she left Allentown, there were 5,000 control charts posted in the plant, and performance had dramatically improved.

Small then shifted from quality advocate in one location to advocate

Figure 31. No one event transformed Western Electric postwar manufacturing more than the 1947 invention of the transistor by William Shockley, Walter Brattain, and John Bardeen at Bell Labs.

for the company. In 1955, she was appointed chair of the writing committee for a book that would translate statistical quality-control principles into layperson's terms. She assembled a committee of quality professionals from throughout the company to write a quality guide for factory use. The resulting handbook represented a confluence of Western Electric's long-standing traditions of quality control and education and training. Much of the material for the book was based on company training courses given to managers, engineers, and shop-floor people from 1949 to 1956. The *Western Electric Statistical Quality Control Handbook* appeared in 1958, and has been the shop-floor bible of quality control throughout the world ever since.

Western Electric's increased attention to process in the 1950s also led to organizational change, most notably the establishment of the Engineering Research Center (ERC) in Princeton, New Jersey. The ERC handled issues of automation, such as how to automate assembly

Figure 32. Bonnie Small brought statistical quality control to the shop floor.

of some miniature components. The ERC applied mathematical models to production planning and control, and scientific principles to manufacturing problems.[17] Indeed, in 1962, Bonnie Small took her statistical expertise from Allentown to the ERC. The most visible mission of the ERC was to determine the "best way" to perform processes that were quite repetitive and involved substantial amounts of production. This goal was congruent with an organization that had embraced scientific management. Frederick Winslow Taylor, the father of scientific management, had emphasized the search for the "one best way" to perform manufacturing tasks. So the ERC would seek the best approach to, say, soldering a printed wiring board, then disseminate the information to various works locations.[18] This was the sort of thing Joseph Juran had tried – and failed – to institutionalize at Hawthorne. The ERC was the ultimate in scientific management: not only

Figure 33. The Engineering Research Center was established in 1958 to focus on "how" (processes) while Bell Labs focused on "what" (products).

the separation of tasks between planners and producers but the physical separation of planners into their own facility.

ORGANIZING LABOR

Wayne Weeks started work at Hawthorne in 1956 on the fourth floor of building 24, at the corner of Cermak and Twenty-second. "The room was huge," he recalled, "with hundreds and hundreds of people as far as you could see."[19] The room did not have air conditioning, so they relied on window monitors for climate control: "They had big windows that folded out and you used a pole to open them. At a given time, the head window monitor would stand up at the front of the room, blow a whistle, [and] the window monitors would open the windows. Then, at a specified time, he'd blow the whistle again and they'd close them."[20]

Four of the five Western Electric presidents in the 1940s and 1950s – Clarence Stoll, Stanley Bracken, Frederick Kappel, and H. I. Romnes – came from the engineering ranks. At the time, however, it seemed a long way from the equipment engineering rooms to the executive suites. You would never guess the exalted position of the engineer by observing the phalanxes of engineers sitting at identical desks.[21] This was the impersonal, en masse environment of Western Electric engineering when Tim Shea became the vice president of engineering in 1957 and set out to create a more professional environment.

Tim Shea had a varied background. By the time he was twenty-one he had earned bachelor and master of science degrees from MIT and a bachelor of science degree from Harvard. He joined Western as an engineer at Hawthorne in 1920, then went to Bell Telephone Laboratories when it became a separate entity. From 1929 until World War II, he was involved in acoustical, optical, and electrical work on sound motion pictures, including a stint as vice president of engineering for Western Electric subsidiary Electrical Research Products, Inc. Shea's wartime efforts in antisubmarine electronics earned him the Medal for Merit. During the next ten years, he served as president of the Teletype Corporation, vice president of Sandia Corporation, and held executive positions in personnel at AT&T and Western Electric. Shea's career was testimony to the variety of technical challenges besides telephony available to engineers in the Bell System.

Shea was passionate about the creative process and helped champion a number of reforms to support it. He believed that Western emphasized management ability and performance to the detriment of able technical professionals. Management was rewarded with perks but the professional engineer was not. He persuaded Western to develop a "parallel ladder of promotion" for engineers, which introduced various levels of engineer from junior to senior. This meant that those who were not on the track to the executive ranks could be recognized and promoted *as engineers.*

Under Shea's influence, physical and professional changes were made. The rows of desks were broken up by cubicles, offering more individualism and privacy, and increased attention was paid to lighting, ventilation, and noise. In June 1957, in conjunction with six colleges, Western Electric initiated a graduate engineering training program with centers in Chicago, New York, and Winston-Salem,

Figure 34. Tim Shea helped to professionalize the role of engineering at Western Electric in the 1950s.

North Carolina. The program offered formal training and postgraduate study to 2,500 company engineers each year. Even before assuming his new position, Shea had fostered the creation in 1957 of a new quarterly magazine, *The Engineer*, which published technical articles, acknowledged the accomplishments of individual engineers, and promoted professional development.[22]

Previously, a union called the Council of Western Electric Professional Employees (CWEPE) had organized a number of Western Electric engineers. As long as they were treated en masse, engineers were more likely to be receptive to union organizers. Yet by the time votes were taken at Western's various locations, Shea's reforms were in place. In nearly every case, 60 percent voted against, 40 percent for unionization. By 1963, when Shea retired, the high tide of efforts to unionize engineers had passed.[23]

National unions had greater success with Western Electric's blue-collar workers. After the end of World War II, the most contentious labor relations in the company had been at the Kearny works. During a period of nationwide labor unrest – between V-J Day and March 1946, when more than four million workers went on strike – the

Western Electric Employees' Association (a company union) at Kearny demanded a 30 percent wage increase. The resulting sixty-five-day strike beginning in January 1946 brought the first violent labor confrontation to the telephone industry. The *New York Times* reported the most dramatic moment, when, "using fists and clubs to compensate for their comparative lack of members, 42 pickets succeeded . . . in denying entrance to 1,000 non-striking executives, supervisors, and maintenance employees who made a mass dash to get into the huge plant." Nobody was seriously hurt. The strike ultimately failed to secure the requested wage increase.[24]

For Western, the Kearny strike's contentious nature was the exception, not the rule. At Hawthorne, for instance, by 1955 the hourly, salaried, and craft employees were represented by the International Brotherhood of Electrical Workers (IBEW). For many years, the president of IBEW Local 1859 was Leo Becker. Becker's "long service anniversary" showed how Western's labor relations status quo melded into, rather than conflicted with, the company's hierarchy and system of welfare capitalism.

Nominally, Becker's job was capacitor-inspector, but heading one of the biggest union locals in the country was a full-time job. So Becker would routinely arrive at the Inspection Department at about 7:45 in the morning, catch up with his friends, and then head off to conduct union business. Becker's manager, Charles M. "Chick" Gayley, recalls that "a long-standing special 'understanding' permitted the Local 1859 president some unusual flexibility: he 'punched in' on the clock but rarely, if ever, 'punched out.' " Becker once needled Gayley about not having received a merit increase. Gayley responded, "The next time you inspect something, maybe we can talk about it."[25]

Gayley may not have been prepared to raise Becker's salary, but he did want to acknowledge a "long-service" anniversary. Traditionally, on major service anniversaries, such as twenty-five years with the company, employees were invited to come up to the sixth floor of building 27 (just below the tower) to "Mahogany Row" to meet with their department's fifth-level manager and receive congratulations, a certificate, and other tokens of appreciation. For many employees, this was their first meeting with an individual of such high rank in the organi-

Figure 35. Long-service anniversaries (such as this one from 1931) were important rituals at Western Electric.

zation, and was also their first visit to the sixth floor. For most employees, the "long-service" ceremony was special and not to be missed.

For Leo Becker, it was different. He was a regular visitor to Mahogany Row when he was not testifying at congressional hearings or attending national union meetings. Usually the manager was the one straining to fit long-service celebrations into his schedule, but in Becker's case the roles were reversed. It took months before Gayley could get on Becker's calendar. Finally, instead of coming to Gayley's office on Mahogany Row, Becker took Gayley to lunch at the Old Prague restaurant on Cermak Road, where Becker often went after conducting union business.[26]

Such labor–management accommodation appeared to be at risk in 1963 when the Teamsters arrived in Baltimore to organize the Point Breeze plant. This was the beginning of the Teamsters' campaign to organize the communications industry. The week of the Point Breeze vote, Teamster head Jimmy Hoffa spoke at Point Breeze.[27] In the days leading up to the vote, Baltimore county police stayed at the home of Robert Bach, head of the Communication Equipment Workers, Inc., which had represented the plant since 1949.[28] Bach had reported receiving an anonymous phone call offering bribes if he would step down and threatening violence if he did not.[29]

As part of an all-out effort to defeat the Teamsters, Western's management negotiated with a group it was still learning about: black leadership. During the months leading up to the union vote, black employees at Point Breeze suggested that they might help to defeat the Teamsters if the company would take a more enlightened approach to promoting blacks. Four representatives of Western Electric management came down to Baltimore and met with leaders of various groups, including one meeting with black leaders arranged by AT&T's Raymond Scruggs, who had previously worked for the Urban League.[30] On October 16, 1963, the Teamsters lost by more than 1,000 votes (out of about 4,300), and a major threat to the status quo at Western evaporated.[31] The impact of meetings with black leaders was not the determining factor in the October vote but was more indicative of the direction in which the company was heading. Western Electric's education about equal opportunity was under way.

PLANS FOR PROGRESS

In 1961, Western Electric's president, H. I. Romnes, warned his company and the rest of corporate America: "increasingly, we are finding it necessary to take account of complex social, economic, even political factors, which do not figure in the contents of the Engineer's Handbook."[32] These were prescient words from a man trained as an engineer. Romnes recognized that, although engineers sometimes see themselves as agents for change, they rarely apply that sensibility beyond their craft. Romnes was a humanist, however, and regarded the larger community as part of the businessman's responsibility.

Romnes found his issue in equal opportunity. In late 1961, years before the civil rights movement attracted the attention of most major corporations, Romnes insisted: "Equal opportunity is a fine phrase. Making it come true is an arduous, sometimes painful process. But there are many good reasons why management needs now to demonstrate not merely good faith but practical initiative in support of this basic American tenet. The good opinion of the world is only one of them."[33] Romnes intended to catapult Western Electric into a leadership role on civil rights, and explained why: "In the final analysis there is one reason above all others for giving our best management attention to making equal opportunity come true – and that is because it is right."[34]

As important as Romnes's message was his venue: the annual meeting of the Chamber of Commerce and Associated Industries of Arkansas in Little Rock. Seated beside Romnes on the dais was Governor Orville Faubus, one of the twentieth century's prominent symbols of segregation. Faubus had confronted the federal government over federally mandated integration of schools in 1957, which led to President Eisenhower's dispatch of the National Guard to Little Rock. At Little Rock in 1961, Romnes's speech took the high road, but not necessarily the safe one.

The president of Western Electric usually focused on guaranteeing the Bell System a continued flow of high-quality, low-cost products. Resumés of those heading Bell System companies tended not to feature achievements of social change. Although Romnes had spent his entire career in the Bell System – he had worked at AT&T, Bell Labs, and two operating companies – businessmen, educators, and journalists recognized him as a different breed. In 1972, when the *Saturday Review* named Romnes its "Businessman of the Year," the Little Rock speech was the example of leadership the article most emphasized.[35]

Romnes was far from a quixotic visionary. His company addressed the issue of equal opportunity because the government wanted it to. Defense contracts comprised about 25 percent of Western Electric's business. In May 1961, Western had been one of fifty defense contractors invited to Washington to discuss President Kennedy's Executive Order 10925 regarding equal opportunity in government contracting. Every president since Franklin Roosevelt had signed an executive order on equal opportunity and government contracting. Kennedy's version was noteworthy for its language, which has since become so familiar: "The contractor will take *affirmative action* to ensure that applicants are employed, and that employees are treated during employment, without regard to their race, creed, color, or national origin."[36] Romnes was not a catalyst; instead, he transformed Western's involvement from mere compliance to leadership.

Western Electric and the Bell System felt particularly vulnerable to government action. Like other defense contractors, they faced loss of government business if they did not comply with the executive order. Unlike other defense contractors, the Bell System might have its telephone rates challenged by the Federal Communications Commission or its monopoly challenged by the Justice Department. So Western Electric was particularly eager to demonstrate that it was a good corporate citizen, and especially wanted to do so after the government issued an amendment to the executive order requiring that the commercial businesses of defense contractors comply with the order's civil rights directives.

On July 12, 1961, with Vice President Lyndon Johnson hovering over his shoulder, H. I. Romnes became one of the first major defense contractors to sign a Plan for Progress, a company-specific blueprint for equal opportunity. The plan involved "dissemination of policy," recruiting, promotion, and training.[37] There were no numerical goals. Western Electric, which so often followed the policies of AT&T, was ahead of its parent on this issue. Its example was crucial because other Bell System companies might use Western's plan as a model to follow.[38]

The results of Western Electric's equal opportunity push came very slowly. Two years after Romnes signed the company's first Plan for Progress, the percentage of black employees at Western had increased from just over 3.5 percent to just under 4 percent. Meanwhile, the number of black supervisors had increased from one to eleven – still less than one-tenth of 1 percent of the total. More than 70 percent of Western's black employees continued to be unskilled workers, although unskilled workers comprised less than 30 percent of the com-

Figure 36. In July 1961, President John F. Kennedy met with industrial leaders who signed "Plans for Progress," dedicated to equal opportunity. H. I. Romnes, Western Electric president, is fourth from the right.

pany's total work force.[39] Western Electric had a sense of urgency about improving its equal opportunity performance.

One manifestation of that urgency was the special assignment given Norman Rubin in January 1963. Instead of remaining in his office in Western's public relations department at 195 Broadway, Rubin's mission was to go out in the field and learn about the leading groups in the rising tide of America's civil rights movement. Rubin was thrilled to have the chance for what he later called "a great liberal education."[40] Prior to coming to Western Electric, he had been a newspaperman, then worked as a congressional staffer. This assignment fulfilled both the journalist's desire for the big scoop and the political activist's desire to act on a matter of conscience.

Rubin interviewed Martin Luther King Jr. of the Southern Christian Leadership Conference, Roy Wilkins of the National Association for the Advancement of Colored People, James Farmer of the Congress on Racial Equality, Whitney Young of the National Urban League, and Julian Bond of the Student Nonviolent Coordinating Committee. During his three-month assignment, he spoke with most of the prominent black leadership of America, with the exception of Malcolm X, who sent one of his lieutenants. Rubin told his interview subjects that he was from Western Electric and that the company wanted to learn what their goals were. The civil rights leaders were surprised – and impressed – that a major corporation was paying such attention. Neither Rubin nor the man who sent him, Alvin von Auw, was aware of any other company taking such an initiative.[41]

Rubin reported back to his superiors that, yes, Western Electric could work with these leaders and their organizations. His findings became a subject of discussion at the highest levels of the Bell System. At a Bell System vice presidents' meeting on July 30, 1963, and at a presidents' meeting two days later, the world's largest corporate entity wrestled with the most daunting social issue of the century. Attendees were reminded that "it is a measure of the explosive pace of the civil rights movement that what was considered long-range six months ago is one of our major preoccupations now."[42]

The meetings addressed issues of hiring, qualifications, and "prerequisites" for employment. At the time, the South had become known for separate requirements (including tests) for blacks and whites for voting, hiring, bar exams, and various other important aspects of citizenship. Western Electric had not been immune from such practices. For instance, blacks hired at Western's Point Breeze plant during World War II had been required to show evidence of at least twelve years of education; whites had not. This had led to awkward situations, such as Maybelle Rodgers (an African American woman who not only had completed high school but had taken college courses at night) having to report to a white woman with a third-grade education, and being called on to do much of her supervisor's writing.[43] Little wonder that in 1961 a reporter for the *Wall Street Journal* had written to Romnes, asking: "Do you see an economic advantage in hiring Negroes, especially for some low-pay 'white-collar' positions?

Figure 37. Western Electric president Paul Gorman (right) with National Urban League president Whitney Young (center) at a 1964 equal opportunity conference

Many firms I have talked with . . . believe they can hire a better-educated Negro than white worker for some clerical jobs."[44]

H. I. Romnes concluded: "our experience indicates the value of establishing working relationships with Negro leaders – including organizations once considered 'radical.' . . . The interests of the business require that we have a sophisticated knowledge of people who can effect our future in many ways – just as we do with politicians."

Consequently, Western hosted two conferences devoted to equal opportunity, where the company's managers had the opportunity to meet civil rights leaders. In January 1964, after Romnes became AT&T's president, Western's new president, Paul Gorman, addressed an equal employment conference just outside of Chicago. Wilkins, Farmer, Young, James Forman, and Dr. Kenneth Clark attended. Gorman explained what the expression "affirmative action" meant to Western Electric: "to seek out in the communities where we operate non-white candidates who have the capacity to learn and do a Western

Electric job, and to seek out in our own ranks as well non-white employees who can take on larger responsibilities." Now, in front of Western Electric managers, president Gorman singled out the civil rights leaders: "one day it will be noted that what you have said and done in these last few historic months will have done as much or more to shape the future of our country as the words and deeds of anybody in our time."[45]

GEOGRAPHIC DIVERSITY

During the first two years after signing the Plans for Progress, Western Electric was uncertain about how to proceed where local custom was likely to conflict with federal law and company policy. One of the conclusions at the July 1963 vice presidents' meeting had been to pursue equal opportunity in the South more aggressively: "Not so long ago, we soft-pedaled equal employment practices for fear of repercussions on and from our friends in the South. Today the situation is reversed. Unfavorable notice based on a handful of employees in a small location can be seriously damaging to the national stature of our Company and the Bell System with effects not limited to employment practices."[46] Not long afterward, Western had a chance to implement equal opportunity policy at a new telephone manufacturing plant in Shreveport, Louisiana.

Plant location was not a major concern for Western Electric before World War II because the company had only three major plants (in Illinois, New Jersey, and Maryland). By 1950, the company had additional plants in Pennsylvania, Massachusetts, Indiana, and North Carolina (Allentown, to manufacture new electronic equipment; Merrimack Valley, to supplement production of electronic devices; Indianapolis, to manufacture consumer telephone equipment; Burlington and Winston-Salem, to handle defense work). In the 1950s, Western Electric developed a routine for researching prospective locations. First, the company let it be known that it was going to build a new plant *somewhere*, so representatives from various states could make their sales pitches. At the same time, the company sent a representative from plant design and construction to investigate various locations. This was done very discreetly: nobody ever knew that Western Electric was interested in the particular property. If the local real-estate market caught wind of Western's plans, prices would be sure to rise. Western's representative would fly over the prospective site in a helicopter to see if it fit the company's requirements. What were the surrounding residential areas like? Did roads offer adequate access? Was there a railroad siding for the shipment of heavy materials? Meanwhile, the company assessed the local labor market, the tax situation, the local community, and educational opportunities. Finally, if the site was desirable, Western made an offer through an intermediary.[47]

By the 1960s, Western Electric added another variable to the formula. The company could see political advantages to geographic dispersal. Each new state meant two senators who could promote Western's goals in Congress. As Western's public relations director, Alvin von Auw, put it: "Western Electric's plants were fairly strategically located with respect to influential senators."[48] Its political strategies and civil rights policy combined to lead Western Electric to negotiate simultaneously with representatives of civil rights groups and politicians representing segregationist constituencies in 1964. Louisiana Senator Russell Long was head of the Senate Finance Committee and majority whip. Although Long came from a family of racial moderates, he represented a segregationist state.

Western's plant was to be the largest in Shreveport's history and would become one of the largest employers in the state. Western Electric knew that Russell Long wanted jobs for the area. Gorman told Long that for each new Western job, another ten would appear in other industries as a result. Yet Western made it clear that it would not open a plant in Shreveport unless it could follow the company's policy of equal opportunity. That meant completely integrated facilities – the first in the city of Shreveport. Aside from his personal feelings on the issue, Long knew that the appearance of softness on segregation had ended many a political career in the South. After six months of negotiation, however, he chose economics over segregation.

After keeping "one of the biggest . . . secrets in the industrial history of [the Shreveport] area," in January 1965 Western announced that it would open a new plant in Shreveport.[49]

So Western opened an integrated plant, but to enable Long to save face – and to avoid resentment among local whites – the equal opportunity aspect of the plant was not mentioned in opening ceremonies or in Western Electric's publications. The company had been through this before. When it had integrated the Point Breeze annual picnic in 1962, the *Pointer* made no reference to the change. Therefore Western's integration of Shreveport was at first only highlighted in the monthly Plans for Progress reports which the plant submitted to New York.

Carrying out Western's equal opportunity policies in Shreveport was Floyd Boswell, the works manager. Boswell had general guidelines from headquarters on how to proceed, but the details were up to him. Boswell was well aware there might be personal risks involved. The mayor of Shreveport, for instance, tried to reassure him, "in case there is a burning cross on your front lawn, give me a call, and I'll take care of it in ten minutes." Boswell never had to make the call.[50]

In January 1967, Paul Gorman gave a status report to the Shreveport Chamber of Commerce. The title of his speech ("Why W.E. Is Happy with Its Choice") suggests how pleased he was with how things had gone.[51] Gorman reminded his audience that "Western Electric was one of the original corporate signers of President Kennedy's Plans for Progress, whereby employers pledged themselves to follow a nondiscriminatory hiring policy. We have followed this policy in Shreveport, and I am happy to say there has not been a single incident in our plant."[52]

Meanwhile, Senator Long got more than the Western Electric jobs for his state. He had been raised in Shreveport but had never been able to carry his home parish. So, every time Long came to Shreveport, he visited the Western Electric plant, reminding his constituents what he had done for them. Meanwhile, every time Boswell made a public appearance, he credited Long for bringing Western Electric to town. In Long's last election, he carried 80 percent of the parish. The next day Boswell received a letter from Long's office manager: "[Long] got 80 percent, and knows *why* he got 80 percent."[53]

THE COLOSSUS OF CICERO

In 1965 – the same year Western opened its Shreveport plant – the civil rights movement shifted its focus from segregation and voting rights in the South to housing and jobs in the North. Martin Luther King Jr. settled on Chicago as the next target for the movement and set up shop in a dilapidated apartment in Lawndale, about two miles from the Hawthorne works. After spending months negotiating with Chicago's political establishment, including Mayor Richard Daley, in the summer of 1966 King led a number of marches into all-white Chicago neighborhoods before announcing plans to march in Cicero.

Cicero had a reputation that exceeded any of Chicago's white enclaves. Although thousands of blacks worked in Cicero during the day, including at the Hawthorne works, no black families lived there at night.[54] In 1951, when a black family moved in, a riot ensued, chasing them out. For the civil rights movement in the North, this was the belly of the beast. Speaking to Mike Wallace, King said: "Cicero in the North symbolizes the same kind of hard-core resistance to change as Selma in the South. And I think it will in fact eventually be the Selma of the North in the sense that we've got to have a confrontation in that community."[55]

Cook County Sheriff (and future Illinois governor) Richard Ogilvie warned movement leaders against such a "suicidal act," then asked Illinois Governor Otto Kerner for National Guard troops.[56] Kerner agreed, and the Guard used the Hawthorne plant as a staging area. Through gate 1 off Twenty-fourth and Cicero came armored personnel carriers, tanks, and other vehicles. At the September march, which King could not attend, there were more troops than marchers. Compared to previous marches, the Cicero march was quite peaceful.[57]

King sensed little progress was being made in housing rights for African Americans, however, and spoke of having another march in

Cicero: "just as we confronted the colossus of Selma in the South, we're going to confront the colossus of Cicero in the North."[58] Fate intervened, however, and King was assassinated in April 1968. Later that year, a group of African Americans came to Cicero. They were there not to march, however, but to sell.

On the El riding downtown in early 1968, Hawthorne's manager of industrial relations, George Johnsen, told two of his staff: "What we really need to do is to find a way to bring the small black business people, the entrepreneurs, together with the purchasing people from the major corporations in Chicago."[59] Johnsen was a member of the Chicago Economic Development Corporation (CEDC), where he had become familiar with the challenges faced by black entrepreneurs. "What we need to do is have a meeting. . . . We could probably hold it at Albright Gym in Cicero." Bob Jerich responded: "George, it's a ridiculous idea. It's never going to work. Do you think you could bring a group of black business leaders into Cicero?" Echoing Richard Ogilvie's warning to civil rights leaders, Jerich declared, "That's suicidal."

Johnsen was savvy enough to realize that in a hierarchical organization such as Western Electric, he needed to enlist top management's support first. Then he worked with the Chicago Urban League and the CEDC to hold a day-long conference hosted by Western at Albright Gym. "Suppliers Opportunity Day" was the first conference of its kind in Chicago. It attracted representatives from fifty leading Chicago companies and 170 suppliers representing 125 black businesses. At the end of the day, one of the black businessmen from Chicago's South Side commented, "It would have taken me years to make the contacts I made today in a few hours."[60]

The inaugural meeting was such a success that it was moved outside to the International Amphitheater the following year to accommodate 570 buyers from 150 companies, 510 minority business owners, and 150 guests. Within a few years, Johnsen's idea had been transformed into the Chicago Purchasing Council, and the annual meeting moved downtown. This was the forerunner of the National Minority Supplier Development Council.[61]

Meanwhile, the company's attention to equal opportunity was

changing the environment inside the walls of Hawthorne and Western Electric's other northern plants. Such change could not come so quickly without some crucial institutional changes being made within the company. The first was the establishment of an "open enrollment" program for supervisors. Previously, Western Electric management had operated like a private club. You could not apply for membership. Instead, if you had a sponsor, you were invited to join. This approach dictated promotional strategy at the highest levels of the company. The advantage of this approach was that it discouraged self-promotion, which might interfere with satisfactory job performance. The disadvantage was that it tended to perpetuate the status quo: sponsors often looked for reflections of themselves (white males).

Western realized that certain groups were being systematically excluded from management because of this approach, so in 1962 it began to periodically allow individuals to nominate themselves. This change reflected top management's impatience with middle management's lack of commitment to equal opportunity goals. Open enrollment was called a "primitive form of affirmative action."[62] Indeed, the number of minority supervisors grew rapidly after the change.

Achieving supervisor status was a goal, but it was also the beginning of greater challenges. Those blacks who aspired to supervisory jobs realized that they would face considerable requirements beyond their job descriptions. At Hawthorne, a black engineer named Bill Alexander organized a support group. The group – four or five at first – met at Alexander's home or onsite to discuss what it took to succeed and how best to bring about change. They decided that any gains they made had to come within the context of the company's success. The group grew rapidly during the late 1960s and needed more space. They finally became sufficiently established and well known that works manager Wyllys Rheingrover circumvented the line of command and met with them.[63]

Val Jordan, who attended Alexander's meetings, recalled: "When they first started promoting those supervisors I always had my pencil out to see what percentage of the new promotees were blacks and Hispanics. And I remember at one time getting to the point where we were always exceeding my level of expectancy because the figure I had written down was 13 percent and we were getting 20 percent, 21, 22. So I just stopped following that figure."[64]

From the summer of 1963 to the end of 1969, the number of minority employees at Western Electric increased from about 6,800 to more than 28,000. The minority percentage of Western's work force tripled in that period, from 4.6 to 13.9 percent.[65] In 1963, Western had only about a dozen minority supervisors, but by 1969 there were more than two hundred.[66] This was a stunning change for a company with a long history of not hiring minorities.

Western Electric's success in achieving equal opportunity goals for minorities was not matched by equal opportunity advances for women. A 1980 reference book of Western Electric executives – present and past – listed only one woman out of nearly five hundred names in the index: Juanita Kreps, an outside director. The path to Western Electric's executive suites usually included a six-month program of management training known as "charm school." By the end of the 1970s, no woman had ever been invited to charm school.

In 1972, an engineer at Kearny named Cleo Kyriazi sued the company, alleging discrimination in promotion and access to training. She was joined by about 2,000 women in a class action, which they won in 1979.[67] Eighteen years after signing its first Plan for Progress, Western Electric agreed as part of the suit's settlement to initiate plans to promote equal opportunity for women.[68]

As Western Electric instituted programs and policies in the 1960s and 1970s to address equal opportunity, the original catalyst for change – Western's defense contracting – was dissipating. In 1972, the United States negotiated the Strategic Arms Limitation Treaty (SALT) with the Soviets, which signaled a decline in American defense spending. One result was the cancellation of Western Electric's Safeguard contract for the Anti-Ballistic Missile (ABM) System. The end of ABM brought a sharp decline in Western Electric's government contracting, which represented less than 2 percent of the company's business by 1977.

In the case of Western's new president, Don Procknow, the decline in defense work gave him the chance to follow Romnes's advice: "keep our military work in perspective. We are, after all, telephone makers."[69] For the first time since the late 1940s, Western Electric had the opportunity to focus its efforts on serving the Bell System's telephone customers. The decline of defense contracting on the one hand allowed Western to focus more on the telephone business, but it also left the Bell System more vulnerable to antitrust action. The coming years would also bring increased competition and the greatest level of upheaval for Western Electric's workers since the Great Depression.

A SHOCK TO THE SYSTEM:
1972–1984

FROM THE MID-1920S TO THE EARLY 1970S, Western Electric manufacturing was a self-sufficient operation. When Bill Marx started at Kearny in the 1960s, "we were building virtually everything we needed ourselves . . . buying raw material and converting it into [finished products]." Western's flagship plants of Hawthorne and Kearny had tool and die shops, metal shops, wood shops, paint shops. They even made their own nuts, bolts, screws, and washers. So when Marx was assigned to investigate the subcontracting of nuts and bolts, he was struck by how foreign the idea seemed to Western Electric's company culture. Years later, the slogan of Lucent Technologies became "We make the things that make communications work." Marx laughingly noted that in the period prior to the 1970s, "we made *all* the things."[1]

As a captive supplier, Western Electric needed to market almost nothing it made and manufactured virtually everything it needed. Consequently, the real heart of the action was at the factory – whether it was a shop, a plant, or a works – and the position of works manager was one of tremendous responsibility and power. Works managers were entrusted with the productivity and welfare of as many as 40,000 employees. A military-like hierarchy permeated the entire Western Electric organization, but the works manager was the highest-ranking individual to have close proximity to the people in the ranks.[2] Works managers presided over what Sanford Jacoby called "modern manors," with all the trappings of despots, from limousines to special suites.[3]

Some were benevolent despots, but others were not. The extent of contact between some works managers and their employees was a brief meeting at the plant's main gate at about 8:30 in the morning. The works manager would shake the hand of the employee, introduce himself, and pronounce, "You're late."[4] More often, works managers were remote figures occupying tower suites at Hawthorne and Kearny, or, in the case of Point Breeze, working in an office in downtown Baltimore, miles from the plant.

In November 1971, Wyllys Rheingrover became the Hawthorne works manager. Rheingrover knew how distant managers could be. Just before World War II, he had worked as an accounting clerk at Twenty-sixth Street, a few blocks from Hawthorne. He later recalled: "I can honestly say that in the year and a half I spent over there, I *never once* saw my department chief, my assistant manager, or my manager. Not once. I didn't even know what my managers looked like." It wasn't until a closing party, at which the accountants celebrate once the books are closed for the year, that Rheingrover met his managers. He told them: "You don't know me from a load of hay. I've been here a year and a half and none of you have ever come to our section. That's no way to treat people, to give them any incentive. Maybe I'm only a two-bit clerk, but that's what I think." The next day, Rheingrover was back at his desk and heard a voice behind him say, "Here's the guy who wanted to see us." When Rheingrover turned around, there was his manager, assistant manager, department chief, and section chief.

Rheingrover never saw most of them again. He did, however, promise himself: "If there ever comes a time when I have some executive responsibility, when I can help direct the work of others, they're going to know *who* I am, and what I'm thinking about, and how we can work together. And I'm going to find out the same things about them."[5]

That's what he did. It was rare enough for an accountant to become works manager, but what distinguished Rheingrover is what he did when he got the job. In essence, he practiced "management by walking around" before the style associated with Hewlett and Packard became well known. He became one of Hawthorne's most beloved works managers.

Rheingrover also sustained a tradition of paternalism that had begun with Enos Barton. When Rheingrover spoke of Hawthorne as "a
family here of 16,000 people" he must have reminded some oldtimers
of previous benevolent works managers.[6] C. L. Rice, for example, was
works manager from 1926 to 1939. Hawthorne was the largest single
manufacturing unit in the state of Illinois, and the patriarch of this
industrial family was known as "Dad" Rice.

Although Wyllys Rheingrover carried on a company tradition of
paternalism, he also posed a threat to another Western institution: its
hierarchy. He did so with a series of "skip-level" meetings, in which
he met with people who were neither directly above nor directly below
him in the organization chart. One of the first such meetings was with
Bill Alexander's group of black supervisors.[7] Val Jordan recalled another: "A group of us would meet once a week early in the morning
before work. We would pray and discuss the Bible. Rheingrover heard
about it, came in one day unannounced, and prayed with us. That
made a tremendous impact. . . . When word got around that he was
praying with us, the next time we didn't have enough seats."[8] Rheingrover institutionalized morning skip-level meetings as "Waffles with
Willie," a mix of all levels of supervision, engineers, accountants, shop
people.[9] He left a lasting impression, although he held that position
for only five years.

In 1976, Rheingrover took on the job of corporate director of personnel. The move to personnel prevented him from conducting some
unfinished business at Hawthorne. The man who initiated skip-level
meetings at Hawthorne kept his office in the tower, where his secretary
had a secretary. It was Rheingrover's successor, Virgil Schad, who
finally moved out of the tower and dismissed his secretary's secretary.
In the mid-1980s, Schad also presided over the closing of Hawthorne
– an event that had been rumored from the day of Rheingrover's
arrival. The work force had expanded from 16,000 in 1968 to 25,000
in 1970, then had contracted to 16,000 again when he took over in
November 1971. Rumors were flying that Hawthorne would be closed
down and become a giant warehouse.[10] Rheingrover was so successful
at quashing such rumors that people began to sing a song, "There

Will Always Be a Hawthorne."[11] And people associated Rheingrover with that promise.

One of his staff believed there would always be a Hawthorne "until business took me to the plant in Dallas. And I saw their modern plant. And I visited the Atlanta plant. And it was a modern plant. And I could see the trailers backing up to the back door with the materials, putting it on the rollers, and that stuff would roll on down the line and they'd start working on it right there. And they would finish it. Then it would roll on down and they would inspect it. And it would roll down and they would load it up and deliver it. Whereas at Hawthorne we'd have to put it on an elevator, take it upstairs, take it downstairs, wheel it across the courtyard. . . . So I began to see that Hawthorne's days might be numbered."[12]

Although Rheingrover was viewed as an agent of change, there was nothing he could have done to save the plant had he stayed. The sort of change he promoted paled in comparison to the technological, political, and competitive forces Western Electric faced during its final years. The new world was one of solid-state components, miniaturization, clean rooms, and automation. The new plants, more suited to microelectronics, needed fewer people than the ones based on electromechanical processes.

Both transmission and switching manufacturing had been transformed from general component manufacturing to specialized manufacturing requiring relatively large capital investments with significantly lower labor costs.[13] The days of a fourth-level supervisor having 3,000 people were over.[14] During the 1970s, Western Electric followed the same path as much of corporate America, transforming itself from a manager of labor to a manager of material.[15]

At Western Electric in the 1970s and 1980s, not only did the nature of manufacturing change, but also its relative importance. Previously, manufacturing had been the heart of the business. The number two man in the company was the vice president of manufacturing, and the works managers were masters of all they surveyed. A company with only two main customers did not need particular marketing or sales expertise. The final years of Western Electric as a separate company brought with them a new competitive environment. The resultant rise of marketing and sales would challenge the power of works managers.

Between the promotion of C. L. Rice to Hawthorne works manager in the mid-1920s and the arrival of Wyllys Rheingrover in 1971, the distinctive aspects of Western Electric – its position in the Bell System, its hierarchy, the rewards accruing to service and loyalty, and the dominant role of the works managers – remained relatively constant. From the early 1970s to the mid-1980s, all those defining features would change. In many ways, the Western Electric of 1971 when Wyllys Rheingrover took over at Hawthorne bore more resemblance to the Western Electric he first saw in 1937 than to the Western Electric that disappeared in 1984.

A CHANGE OF PLANS

In early 1971, Western Electric president Harvey Mehlhouse informed employees that the company had survived "a most demanding year in which our people and our productive capacity were put to a severe test." Western Electric was in an expansion mode, part of a frantic attempt to meet the production needs of a rapidly expanding Bell System. In the mid-1960s, the operating companies had cut back on construction in an effort to improve their earnings. Their subsequent attempts to keep up with customer demands required a crash program of construction beginning in 1968. John O'Neill, then general manager of the Columbus works, recalls a "crisis" in the company: "[W]e couldn't supply enough equipment particularly in the major cities, especially in New York. And the demand far exceeded what we could produce."[16] The Columbus works grew from around 6,000 employees to over 13,000 in about eighteen months.[17]

In April 1970, Western was building new facilities at a faster rate than ever before, with factories under construction at Dallas, Denver, and Atlanta, and having announced the purchase of land for a new plant in San Ramon, California. A month later the company added plans for a new crossbar plant in Vancouver, Washington. By the end of the year, after announcing plans for another plant in Naperville, Illinois, Western had scheduled six plant openings over the next six years.

By the end of 1970 a softening economy reduced demand for telephones and PBX units, and Western Electric's work force had declined to about 206,000 from a high of about 215,000 in July. Nevertheless, in early 1971, Mehlhouse predicted that Western Electric construction would continue, adding some larger plants and a few smaller special-purpose plants over the remainder of the 1970s.[18]

The new plants were increasingly specialized rather than general-purpose. In the fifties, Western had developed specialized shops for the production of wire and cable, but these had been components of larger factories at Kearny and Hawthorne. Now Western Electric began focusing on product specialization in its plants. The Denver plant would produce PBX equipment; the Dallas plant would produce state-of-the-art switching equipment; the Atlanta plant would provide automatic wire and cable production.[19]

Electronic chips handled increasingly complex circuit functions, part of a tremendous change in Western's manufacturing process catalyzed by the 1947 invention of the transistor by William Shockley's group at Bell Labs. Components that in the fifties and even early sixties could be hand-assembled by skilled workers using microscopes no longer relied upon a skilled work force for assembly. Automated construction of complex circuit boards made increasingly complex electronic devices cost-effective. Chemical processes and computer controls replaced soldering irons and wire. Lasers, high-vacuum machines, and automatic component insertion equipment replaced skilled mechanical labor. Clean rooms and laboratory-like settings replaced traditional factory assembly lines.

The new electronic production required a new type of worker, prompting Western Electric to establish a program for retraining its work force. Some of the training was ad hoc: Wayne Weeks recalled that he would get a new piece of automatic equipment and then train an operator to run it. Most of the training was more formal. Four

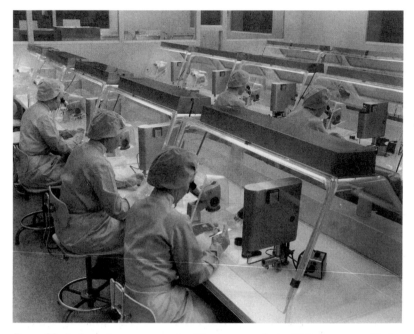

Figure 38. A clean-room scene at the Allentown works in 1969 contrasts with the work scene fifty years earlier (opposite).

thousand of Merrimack Valley's seven-thousand-member work force underwent job retraining between 1972 and 1974 to prepare them for new skills needed in the manufacture of the new products.[20]

The new technology also had implications for Western's expansion plans. In 1972, Larry Seifert, an engineering assistant manager, was assigned to the headquarters long-range planning group. Western's failure to predict the rapid growth of the business in the late sixties had led to establishment of the group.[21] Each division sent someone to represent its interests, and Seifert was the "transmission guy." Seifert particularly remembered a discussion he had with Kurt Rahlfs, who represented the electronic components division of the company. Rahlfs told him, "something's wrong with our planning because we're extending the future based on what we know today." The ever-growing importance of microelectronics, according to Rahlfs, might change the equation regarding Western Electric's manufacturing needs. "I keep looking at the semiconductor learning curve where you

double the number of transistors on the chip every 18 months." Rahlfs was referring to "Moore's Law," a 1965 statement about technical rates of change made by Intel cofounder Gordon Moore. "If that's the case. . . . we shouldn't need these [plants]."[22]

The planning team did a rudimentary analysis and determined that rather than opening a factory a year, as they were then doing, Western would have to *close* a factory a year. This was a stunning revelation. Seifert and Rahlfs brought their findings to Morris Tanenbaum, vice president of engineering. Tanenbaum agreed with their analysis, and Western abruptly changed course.

Western dropped plans to expand the San Ramon pilot plant into a factory and for expansion of the Vancouver plant. The San Ramon plant was a temporary facility, so its closing was not a monumental event. Vancouver, however, was different. In the early 1970s, the city of Vancouver had a big celebration to mark the opening of Western's new plant. Senator Henry Jackson shared the spotlight at the ceremony. It wasn't long before 1,000 people were working there. Western Electric president Don Procknow had the unpleasant task of informing Jackson, who had already basked in the glory of a thousand new jobs for his constituents.[23] Procknow later announced plans to phase out plants in Buffalo, New York, and Greensboro, North Carolina.[24] "We closed a factory, on an average about every year . . . over the next ten years," Seifert recalled. "And it had to do solely with semiconductors."[25]

The reversal of policy had a profound impact on the size of Western Electric's work force. The number of Western employees fell from a high of more than 215,000 in 1970 to less than 153,000 by 1975. The 1970s was only the second decade of the twentieth century when Western's labor force declined. During the 1930s Western Electric's annual revenues had declined by over 48 percent while its labor force was reduced by nearly 62 percent. The 1970s were different. From 1970 through the antitrust settlement in 1982, Western's revenues *increased* by nearly 115 percent while its labor force declined by just over 29 percent. Layoffs had always been a part of Western Electric culture, but in the 1970s the company's labor needs had been transformed more by new technology than by the cyclical needs of the business. For the first time, the company made no promise to bring the workers back when conditions improved. The old social contract changed.

In the new manufacturing environment, the value of paternalism, the role of loyalty, and the rewards for length of service were supplanted by more merit-based incentives. This was particularly striking in the realm of layoffs. During the first half of the twentieth century, the predominating determinant in who survived layoffs was length of service. By the time of the great layoffs of 1974–1975, that was no longer the case. Personnel procedures had been gradually overhauled beginning in the 1950s, and by the 1970s such decisions (for nonunion workers) were based on merit.

This phenomenon became relevant to corporate equal-opportunity goals. In the late 1960s, Western had made tremendous strides in hiring and promoting black workers. Yet massive layoffs put all those gains in jeopardy – if those layoffs were made based on seniority. It would be the classic case of "last hired, first fired." Therefore, one argument used in favor of merit as opposed to seniority was to preserve the equal-opportunity gains of the late 1960s. For Western Electric, equal-opportunity policies served as a catalyst toward a merit-based system – one that would come to be necessary in an increasingly competitive environment.

A STILLBORN TECHNOLOGY

During the 1970s the new technology produced a bumper crop of new products. A good example was the Merrimack Valley transmission equipment plant, where 60 percent of the plant's product line in 1974 had been introduced since 1972 – a rate of change equal to that which took place between 1961 and 1971. Merrimack Valley introduced eleven new transmission products between 1961 and 1971. An equivalent number were introduced in 1972 and 1973, and nearly as many – ten new product lines – were introduced in 1974.

Sometimes during a period of great change a promising technology is never employed because it is upstaged by a subsequent, superior approach. Transmission equipment manufacture at Western Electric in the 1970s provides a good example. As of the end of World War II, Western provided AT&T Long Lines with three different transmission systems: copper line, coaxial cable, and microwave radio. Copper-wire systems had been used since before the turn of the century, when they had replaced steel wire. Western introduced coaxial cable in the 1930s, and microwave transmission became commercially viable by 1948.

Once Western began installing microwave transmission systems for AT&T Long Lines in 1948, copper wire played a proportionately smaller role in new Bell system transmission. By the late 1960s, just

Figure 39. Millimeter waveguide manufacture

about all of the long-distance transmission mileage was either micro-wave or coaxial cable.

In 1969 Western Electric's Engineering Research Center formed a team to develop manufacturing methods for a new technology of transmission called "millimeter waveguide." Like its predecessor tech-nology, microwave radio, millimeter waveguide grew out of World War II radio development, but promised better performance. The frequencies used in microwave transmission limited the number of telephone conversations that could be carried. Higher-frequency trans-mission, capable of carrying increased transmissions, could not be sent through the atmosphere because of disruptive weather conditions. Millimeter waveguide eliminated this problem by guiding the trans-mission along a continuous copper-coated tube buried underground. Long-distance transmission could further take advantage of digital transmission to multiply telephone conversations further.

Digital transmission, developed in the 1960s for use in existing media, became the centerpiece of millimeter waveguide. Digitized in-formation packets would be modulated at frequencies between 40 and 102 gigahertz and the signals guided down copper-lined polyethylene tubes at nearly the speed of light. Set within the tube at specified distances would be a helix waveguide around which copper wire and fiberglass would be tightly wound. The helix waveguide would filter out signal distortions. One 2¼-inch tube could carry up to 250,000 signals.

A pilot plant was created at Forsgate, New Jersey, and by 1972 Western was prepared to manufacture millimeter waveguide.[26] But this transmission system of the future never went into regular production. The reason: Bell Laboratories was preparing to move optical fiber transmission from research to the development-for-production stage. Fiber optic systems promised more reliability, greater transmission capacity, and less expense to build and maintain.[27] Microwave transmission could handle AT&T's transmission growth over the next five years or so. By then, fiber optics, the new technology coming out of Bell Labs, would be ready for the market.[28]

Western Electric's experience of "skipping" the technology of millimeter waveguide confirmed Kurt Rahlf's application of Moore's Law to corporate long-range planning. In an environment of increasingly rapid technological change, such as that of telecommunications in the 1970s, a company had to be prepared to reject projects promising only marginal value or to do what Western did with millimeter waveguide: pull the plug on a successful but superseded technology.

A COMPETITIVE ENVIRONMENT

On November 20, 1974, the Justice Department again filed an antitrust suit against AT&T and Western Electric. Like the 1949 antitrust suit, the later suit sought to divest Western Electric from AT&T, forcing AT&T's purchasing to take place in a competitive environment.[29] Therefore, one way in which AT&T sought to ward off antitrust action was by creating a semblance of competition for Western Electric. In 1975, AT&T chairman John deButts told the National Association of Railroad and Utilities Commissioners that "there are a great deal of organizations besides our own whose talents could effectively be brought to bear on the growth and improvement of the

nationwide telephone network."[30] Toward that end, AT&T formed
the Bell System Purchased Products Division (BSPPD) to establish
standards for non-Western manufactured equipment. Presumably the
operating companies would be pressured to buy at least some of their
equipment from alternative sources.

After AT&T set up its Purchased Products Division, it required
Western to assist in seeking out alternative suppliers. "We had to
provide competition to AT&T and that a was a very sore point at
Western Electric," Procknow recalled. "We had to go out deliberately
and set up other sources of supply."[31]

Thus began the most awkward period in Western Electric history.
Bound by a consent decree that forbade it from entering competitive
markets, and under attack from the Justice Department for not encouraging competition to supply the Bell System, Western appeared
to be caught between a rock and a hard place. Western's tightrope
walk is best demonstrated by its establishment of an account management system, and with it the beginnings of a marketing structure.

The idea came from outside the company. In 1974, McKinsey &
Company testified before the FCC on Western's behalf. Their report
was essentially an update of an in-depth study they had done in 1969
of Western's effectiveness: they concluded that Western was effectively
run. Nevertheless, after his testimony, McKinsey's Fred Gluck told
John O'Neill: "You know things have changed dramatically since [our
earlier] study. You guys need to get better. . . . You've got to act like a
competitive company. . . . you've got to be prepared [for] competition
in electronics and telecommunications." His advice: "You, Western
Electric Company, have to take care of your own destiny. You have to
build a competitive sales force. You can't let AT&T decide everything."[32]

O'Neill needed little convincing. He recalled the period of rapid
Bell System expansion in 1969 and 1970 as the time when he first
sensed that potential competitors might be catching up. Unable to
supply the Bell System demand for wire spring relays, Western purchased millions of relays from OKI, NEC, Fujitsu, and Hitachi.
"[T]hey wanted desperately to break into our market," O'Neill, then
general manager of the Columbus Works, recalls. "So they shipped us

Figure 40. Don Procknow was the last president of Western Electric.

millions of relays . . . and their prices were competitive with ours. . . . There were a few people in the United States that made small quantities of these things, [and did so at] three times our cost. But we began to see that the Japanese were close."[33]

Gluck gave the same advice to Procknow and the executive staff. Procknow already knew something was needed: after becoming Western president in 1972, he had visited each of the operating companies. Not all the visits had been friendly.[34] One operating company president had told Procknow he had received a great product at a good price with excellent and enthusiastic service. Unfortunately, he added, the supplier was not Western Electric.[35] Other companies were increasingly capable of doing what Western Electric did.

Account management involved a different form of going about Western's business. Previously, Western had not performed the sort of customer-by-customer sales, profitability, and analysis of competitors that the new environment required.[36] Account management also introduced product-line profit analysis to Western Electric and life-cycle costing – the analysis of the cost of a product sold to a customer over its useful life. Western had to keep up certain appearances: Western's lawyers, concerned with the development of a sales force while the company remained technically a monopoly, forbade the use of the terms selling and marketing.[37]

Meanwhile, the focus of Western Electric competition expanded from inside to outside the company. For years, Western had encouraged competition between plants – competition that intensified when plant closings were becoming commonplace. Now the rules of the game were changing. Unlike the monthly "M-1" reports, which quantified interplant rivalry with measures of plant productivity, account management increasingly measured how well the customer was being served. Simply making a product efficiently was no longer enough.

The new competitive environment also changed the locus of power in the company. Bill Marx recalled: "There was a sense that the guys that used to be at the seat of power were the guys that ran the factory ... and that ... power [was] moving to the people closer to the customer."[38] By the mid-1980s, "the product manager was king."[39]

DIGITAL SWITCHING

Western Electric's shift to account management and competitive marketing was intertwined with technological competition. As the 1970s began, Western was essentially the sole supplier of switching systems to the Bell System. The development of the 5 ESS (electronic digital switching system) reflects the changing environment and the Bell System's competitive ambivalence in the 1970s.

Western Electric began manufacturing analog electronic switching systems (ESS) in 1963, installing the #1 ESS switching system at New Jersey Bell's office in Succasunna in 1965. ESS promised greater flexibility, advanced features, and reduced costs. Western rapidly expanded analog ESS from 10 percent of its local switching production in 1967 to 88 percent ten years later. In 1972, solid-state electronics provided the impetus for modularized switching systems, reducing the amount of time required for installation of both mechanical and electronic switches to one-third of what it had previously been.[40] The growth of circuit board technology further reduced ESS size while increasing capacity.

In the mid-1970s digital transmission remained limited primarily to the short-distance range between local switches and AT&T's toll switching systems. The power required for the customer loop continued to be seen as a problem for local digital transmission. Although long-distance analog transmission remained more cost-effective than digital, the future of telecommunications would clearly be digital.

In 1976 Western introduced the first digital switch, the #4 ESS toll-switching system. The state of Western's digital switching reflected the tensions within AT&T. Western Electric had spent nearly five years and some $400 million in developing the new switch. Meanwhile, AT&T held off on the decision to implement development of a local digital switch, preferring to rely on incrementally improved analog electronic switching systems that Western had been installing since 1965. Not until the mid-1970s did Bell Labs begin developing a local digital switch that could be utilized by the operating companies. AT&T did not announce official plans to develop a local digital switch until 1977.[41]

By then, under pressure from Bell operating companies and hopeful that increased outside purchases would stave off antitrust action, AT&T provided information and assistance to Northern Telecom in the development of their DMS-10 digital switch. The DMS-10 did not compete directly with Western's analog electronic switches. It was a niche product designed for exchanges too small to use the smallest Western Electric ESS system. Shortly after the DMS-10 was introduced, Bell System Purchased Products standardized it for Bell System use in local markets. A year later, Northern Telecom began to market the DMS-100, which *did* compete with Western's analog electronic switches.

The year 1978 brought more competition: Northern Telecom introduced a larger 100,000 line DMS-100, and Stromberg-Carlson brought its 20,000 line DCO local switch to the market. ITT's North – formerly North Electric – introduced its DSS switch, capable of either local or transit switching. By 1981, when Western finally intro-

Figure 41. The #5 ESS, the switching system that brought Western Electric into the digital age

duced its #5 ESS system for local switching, Siemens, L. M. Ericsson, Nippon Electric, Fujitsu, Hitachi, Thomson CFS, Philips, and TRW Vidar also had local switches on the market. GTE's supplier, Automatic Electric, which followed Western's strategy of introducing its long-distance digital switch first (in 1978), brought a local switch to the market about the same time as Western.[42]

Ironically, the delay in introducing Western's #5 ESS local digital switch may have benefited more than it hurt Western Electric. By the time Western installed the first #5 ESS switch in 1982, it had refined its software development skills crucial to utilizing the power of the digital switch. Technology had moved so fast that even minor delays in digital switching development would have eliminated a first-generation local digital switch from the market. In addition, Western's account management system bore fruit as Western adapted its switch to meet the market needs of the operating companies.

Western Electric began the decade with little competition in the switching market, where it had long been the sole supplier to the Bell System. It ended the decade with burgeoning competition in that market. But it entered the 1980s better prepared for the increased competition that the Justice Department's antitrust activity would thrust upon it.

THE END OF WESTERN ELECTRIC

In September 1981, John O'Neill was in the final stages of a huge project. A vice president of sales, he was about to testify before Judge Harold Greene as part of AT&T's defense against the Justice Department's antitrust case. The case had not gone well for the Bell System: for instance, the Supreme Court had refused to hear AT&T and Western's appeal that antitrust laws do not apply to regulated industries. So, after the Justice Department rested its case in July, some began to wonder if the Bell System would prevail.

O'Neill had worked for about a year preparing three hundred pages of testimony regarding customer relations, from sales to installation to repair. About a week before he was scheduled to testify, O'Neill learned that Judge Greene was getting tired and did not want to read that much. Could O'Neill reduce it to a hundred pages? "So I went back," O'Neill recalled, "and worked the whole weekend taking this magnificent testimony and cramming it into 100 pages rather than 300."[43]

The day before his scheduled appearance before the judge, O'Neill's lawyer said: "The issue has shifted from vertical integration to horizontal integration. So tomorrow I'd like to ask you for your direct testimony about horizontal integration, not vertical." Vertical integration – the addition of any stage in the creation of products, from the collection of raw materials to sales and service – represented Western Electric's link to the Bell System. Horizontal integration – the collection of businesses performing similar functions – described the role of the operating companies. So O'Neill sat down with his lawyer and they agreed on several questions likely to be asked about horizontal integration. Then O'Neill worked past midnight writing the answers. It seemed ridiculous to him: "So I go on the stand after a year of preparation, not to say a word about what I did for a year, but what I wrote at 1:00 in the morning. I didn't even give a damn about horizontal integration."[44]

O'Neill's testimony did not turn out to be the nightmare his preparation for it had been. He had, however, learned something significant about the case. Although the Justice Department had originally sought to separate Western from the Bell System, "Western Electric being part of the Bell System may not be the issue now." Instead, it appeared to be the operating companies.

In November, at a Bell advanced management meeting, AT&T chairman Charles Brown was asked what the Bell System would do once they lost Bell Laboratories and Western Electric. Brown thought for a minute and then responded that his job as chairman of AT&T was to represent the stockholder. Telecommunication's future lay, he said, with research at Bell Labs and with manufacturing at Western Electric. Therefore, his duty might be to divest the operating companies and keep Western Electric. As they had not been privy to John O'Neill's experience in Washington earlier that fall, most of the people in the audience did not take Brown's comments seriously.[45]

Two months later, on January 8, 1982, AT&T and the Justice Department announced a settlement. AT&T agreed to let the regional operating companies go, and they became known as the "Baby Bells." AT&T kept Western Electric and Bell Labs, in line with Brown's November comment. Western Electric president Don Procknow was not involved in the decision; once again, Western's future had been determined by others. On December 31, 1983, the Bell System as Theodore Vail had envisioned it would cease to exist.

Western Electric had two years to prepare for life with AT&T but not in the Bell System. Western had numerous plans to make in terms of establishing an "arms'-length" relationship with the operating companies, but the most pressing issue in 1982 was excess capacity and what to do about it. Bill Marx was part of a team that performed a company-wide capacity study. The conclusion: Close Hawthorne. Close Kearny. Close Point Breeze. Close Indianapolis.

The 1982 committee, like its 1972 predecessor, was not just a group of outside consultants offering disinterested advice. Many of them had begun their careers at one of these four plants, including Bill Marx. He recalled his role on the committee: "here's a guy who started in Kearny bringing forth the decision to close the place."[46]

On January 27, 1983, Western announced the phase-out of the Kearny works and the reduction of capacity at Hawthorne and Baltimore. Six months later, citing overcapacity, it announced plans to close the Hawthorne works. Within months, plans for closing Baltimore and Indianapolis were revealed. Their analysis had shown that "if you added up the number of square feet we had in total and the number of square feet we needed . . . the difference between [the two numbers] was roughly the size of these places we were closing."[47] This was the culmination of the advice Larry Seifert and Kurt Rahlfs had offered as representatives of the company's long-range planning committee in 1972.

When they presented their findings to Procknow, his response was, "You mean 'downsize,' don't you?" They didn't. Procknow knew that the company had too much capacity for the new technology. He knew that to replace relays with semiconductors would require clean rooms the old plants did not have. He knew that a multistory building hindered work flow.[48] And he had presided over numerous plant closings since 1972. Nevertheless, he was taken aback by the idea of completely retiring the factories that had been the workhorses of Western Electric for most of the century.

Naturally, Marx heard from his old coworkers: "They didn't know I had anything to do with it, they just knew I was one of them and [had become] a big guy in Western Electric, [so they were] looking for jobs. . . . I couldn't really help much because the only jobs were going to be in Oklahoma or someplace but not where they'd want to move because their whole life was living in Jersey City or Bayonne or Union or wherever."[49]

The plant closings were another step in the declining power of the works managers. Marx's old plant, Kearny, was a good example. Works manager Ron Butterfield had led a number of programs to "rejuvenate Kearny," including a pep-rally-style parade to kindle enthusiasm. Butterfield was not, however, involved in the decision to close the plant. As Marx put it: "All the while we're doing the [capacity study], he's still beating the drum, [saying] we gotta do better. . . . He was saving the place at the time we were deciding to get rid of it."[50]

In January 1984, at the same time as the end of the Bell System and announcements of the closing of the venerable old plants, came the demise of Western Electric. "Western Electric . . . has ceased to operate as we knew it," pronounced Victor Pelson, AT&T's executive vice president for sector planning and administration. AT&T announced that Western Electric and its former subsidiaries would be restructured along lines of business (LOBs) into network systems, technology systems, and international groups. Technology systems would comprise three lines of business: computer systems, component and electronic systems, and federal systems. Network systems would manufacture switchboards and transmission equipment. PBX and consumer products went into AT&T Information Systems, a fully separated subsidiary briefly mandated by the FCC.[51]

Various Western functions scattered. Some of its purchasing, for instance, went to the operating companies.[52] Some of its engineering and design staff, along with comparable units from Bell Laboratories, were transferred to the new AT&T Information Systems. Many former Western Electric functions would be a prominent part of a new AT&T Technologies, Pelson noted, "but AT&T Technologies certainly is not the same company with a new name."[53]

Indeed it was not. After spending more than a hundred years as captive supplier to the Bell System, and enjoying a virtual monopoly for most of the twentieth century, Western Electric found itself in a changed world. The controlled environment that Enos Barton sought to create in 1882 – and for which he was willing to risk his dream of Western becoming the "department store of electrical apparatus" – began to give way with the rise of competition in the mid-1970s, then disappeared with the breakup of the Bell System. Although many who remained in AT&T Technologies considered themselves standard-bearers of the Western tradition, the disappearance of Western Electric's name in 1984 was altogether appropriate.

7

AFTER THE WESTERN:
1984–1995

THE NEW AT&T "WILL BE A POWERHOUSE OF money, research talent and manufacturing muscle," declared *Time* magazine in discussing the changes transforming the telephone system on January 1, 1984. AT&T's television advertisements stressed its new unregulated activities: providing information systems for business, teleconferencing, and data processing. The former Western Electric, absorbed into the parent company, would manufacture "telephone equipment for sale to consumers and all kinds of exotic electronic whizmos like powerful memory chips for computers."[1]

The key immediate issues after divestiture for AT&T manufacturing, however, were relationships with the seven regional Bell operating companies (RBOCs, also known as the "Baby Bells"). The seven RBOCs remained monopolies providing local service, but sought more. They pushed for growth opportunities either by entering the competitive long-distance market or by manufacturing telecommunications equipment, even though the Modified Final Judgment barred the RBOCs from these areas. Entering the long-distance market placed the Baby Bells in competition with Communications Services. Manufacturing meant they would compete with AT&T Network Systems, which comprised the lion's share of the old Western Electric.

Robert T. Blau, of Bell South, noted in *Communications Week* that the RBOCs had diminished their reliance on AT&T equipment because AT&T was competing with them for large customer local private-line networks. Why should the RBOCs buy from Network Systems if the profits might help finance AT&T's efforts to limit their expansion? Few analysts thought that the Baby Bells would actually construct their own factories. Rather, they expected them to establish exclusive contracts with one of the established manufacturers. As the Baby Bell companies began to view AT&T as a competitor, or at least as an opponent to their expansion programs, Network Systems found it increasingly difficult to sell its equipment. It would be unlikely that the RBOCs would turn to Network Systems for an exclusive contract should they be granted the right to manufacture.

Thus, Network Systems had to overcome the opposition engendered by AT&T's competition with the RBOCs. Bill Marx was vice president of Network Systems sales during the immediate postdivestiture period. "I spent a disproportionate amount of time," Marx recalls, "but not disproportionate to the need from my point of view, building some personal relationships with some of those people in the RBOCs so that there was someplace to talk. . . . [S]ometimes they just wanted to vent. [S]ometimes you'd go for a meeting and you'd want to talk about some proposal you were trying to make or a piece of business you were chasing. But they just wanted to tell you about how you know they were getting harassed by AT&T in the regulatory [process]."[2]

Consequently, AT&T manufacturing entities faced stiffer competition than Western had. The RBOCs actively shopped for equipment. Robert Blanz, president of Mountain Bell Telephone Company, reported that "Divestiture had brought us millions of dollars in cost savings by opening up competition among vendors." AT&T Technologies vice chairman Donald Procknow noted, "the world does change when every bid you make is competitive."

There was no getting away from the problem divestiture had created – namely, that AT&T Network Systems was trying to sell equipment to seven companies which loomed as AT&T's potential competitors. That conflict of interest would not be resolved until 1995. In the meantime, Network Systems would revisit two issues from Western Electric's past: managing for quality and global manufacturing.

A LESSON RELEARNED

In 1986, a group of AT&T manufacturing officials visited Japan. Japanese manufacturers had developed a reputation for superior quality, and the purpose of the visit was to bring home some lessons that AT&T could apply in America. Each member of the group visited five factories, where they saw examples of "Total Quality Management" (TQM), where quality was not just the responsibility of the inspection group. The Japanese clearly did not believe that you could "inspect quality" into the product; they were more concerned with overall processes.[3]

AT&T's interest in the Japanese approach was symptomatic of America's general obsession with the Japanese postwar economic resurgence, and its specific interest in Japanese quality methods. Pundits, management experts, and business school professors emphasized the irony of the situation: American businessmen, who had once taught the Japanese and the rest of the world how to run manufacturing businesses and how to make a quality product, were now swallowing their pride and asking how it was best done.

The AT&T visit was particularly ironic. The group visited a number of companies, including Fujitsu and Ricoh, but their host was NEC.[4] NEC had been the creation of a Western Electric joint venture in 1899. When NEC's Tokyo plant was destroyed by earthquake in 1923, Western Electric officials oversaw the construction of a replacement plant that was a replica of Hawthorne, including the tower. Representatives of NEC and other Japanese companies had attended the Hawthorne Evening School and later had visited to learn about the Hawthorne Studies. After World War II, the Bell System sent managers to assist in the resurrection of Japan's telecommunications industry and to teach management methods. Finally, management consultants W. Edwards Deming and Joseph Juran (a Western Electric alumnus) arrived in Japan in the 1950s bearing their gospel of quality. So, by 1986, what was once Western Electric had shifted from exporter to importer of ideas, and the Japanese had become a "reexporter." In a sense, in 1986 AT&T was asking the Japanese to act as the company's institutional memory.

AT&T became increasingly interested in quality issues. In 1988, the company began a corporate-wide reevaluation of quality, adopting the "Baldridge criteria." Between 1981 and his death in 1987, U.S. Secretary of Commerce Malcolm Baldrige had urged American companies to look beyond short-term competition and focus on excellence. After his death, Congress established the U.S. National Quality Award in his honor.

A 1989 restructuring of Network Systems led to an increased emphasis on quality. Five business units – switching systems, transmission systems, media products, operations systems, cellular systems – became the core of AT&T manufacturing. John O'Neill recalls the transformation from the single-enterprise policy to individual business units as the basis for an expansion in the understanding of quality at Network Systems. "[W]hen we broke into business units and we had the president of the business unit [address quality-related issues], then I think we made a step forward." Previously, quality had been the focus of the shop floor and inspection. After the shift to business units in 1989, O'Neill recalls: "we found out that 80% of the quality breakdown or defects weren't caused by the people on the floor. They were caused by an engineer or a designer, or somebody else that's doing the paper work, by some people that didn't specify – didn't work with the purchasing people, didn't work with a supplier to make sure they met this [specification]."[5]

That realization led to a shift from inspecting to designing quality into products. The new notion of quality forced manufacturing to look at quality in terms of value added for the customer and the cost that the market would bear for that value. In 1992 the Network Systems Transmission Business Unit won the Baldrige Quality Award for manufacturing. It had been a finalist the previous year. Also in 1992, AT&T Power Systems, another business unit derived from Western Electric, won the Shingo Prize for excellence in American manufacturing. Two years later, Power Systems became the first U.S. manufacturer to win Japan's Deming Prize, which salutes companies for successful dedication to the concepts of Total Quality Management (TQM).

Network Systems accrued important benefits from its attention to quality. As the focus shifted from product quality to process quality, Network Systems cut in half the time it took to bring a product to the market. It reduced its inventory by 40 percent and product returns by about 50 percent. The improvements in quality had come from a shift in the understanding of quality processes rather than a focus on products. "Using Baldrige guidelines, we've learned a lot about what our customers want and expect from us," asserted transmissions quality manager Lou Monteforte.[6] That was important, as Network Systems relied for its business more and more on new customers – particularly overseas.

GOING GLOBAL (AGAIN)

In 1977, Western Electric agreed to install a microwave communications network in Saudi Arabia, and in 1979 it contracted to provide the government of Taiwan with an electronic switching system. The U.S. government had asked Western Electric to perform these tasks, which represented Western's first direct selling to the international market since 1925. Two agreements did not, however, a global giant make: at the time of divestiture, AT&T had fewer than a hundred employees outside the United States.

The return to international business in 1978 would aid Western in the transition to manufacturing for market demand that it would eventually face at home. Western's return overseas also led to a diversification of its product line. Multiplex equipment designed for the Bell System had to be modified to meet international standards. Therefore, the company formed Western Electric International to adapt Bell System equipment and standards to meet the needs of international markets. Western Electric International also reflected the diversity of business operations. No longer could Western manufacture for a single business culture. Every country required different operating mechanisms, different equipment standards, and different business practices.

It was not, however, an immediate success. Robert Allen recalled: "We had come from a position which was pretty much a Western

Electric established product business in some parts of the world, and still operating with [the attitude that] we'll do it the way we do it in the United States . . . as opposed to adapting to the needs of the countries in which we were trying to sell the product." For instance, AT&T shipped products to Europe that could only use American-style 110 volt electrical outlets. In Europe, 220 volts were quite common, so AT&T had to buy adapters and ship them to make the devices usable there. Allen also recalled that there was "very little understanding about the political environment in each of those countries."[7]

One way to achieve such crucial understandings was through establishing joint ventures with foreign corporations, and in 1984 Network Systems began to do so. A joint venture with Phillips in the Netherlands eventually led to Network Systems International. In 1988, AT&T and Sumitomo Electric Industries, Ltd. announced the formation of a joint venture to manufacture optical fiber cable, the future mainstay of AT&T transmission systems. The arrangement would introduce AT&T into markets in Asia where Sumitomo had a significant presence. This amounted to a return to Western's international roots: the announcement failed to mention that Sumitomo had begun in 1920 as a joint venture between Western Electric and Nippon Electric.[8]

Network Systems' globalization efforts accelerated after August 1991, when Rich McGinn, then president of AT&T Computer Systems, accepted a position as senior vice president for strategy, sales, and customer operations at Network Systems. This freed Bill Marx to focus on global manufacturing as a corporate executive vice president, and Network Systems rapidly expanded into the Asian market. By 1992, AT&T Cable Network Systems had joint ventures with two Japanese firms and a Chinese firm.

The end of the Cold War brought opportunities for Network Systems in the Eastern Bloc countries. Indeed in 1990, before the crumbling of the Soviet Union, the company reached an agreement to provide switching and transmission equipment to Armenia, which became the first Soviet Republic to establish international phone service.

Previously, all of the Soviet Union's international calls were routed through Moscow, where central authorities determined which calls had priority, and where limited capacity created overload problems. In 1992, Network Systems International began installation of digital switching systems in Kazakhstan, and in 1993 it formed a joint venture to update Ukraine's telecommunications network.

By 1993, AT&T had more than 50,000 employees abroad. In a few short years, Network Systems had reestablished much of the international presence that Western Electric had abandoned in 1925.

A FRESH START

In 1978, Robert E. La Blanc, a Salomon Brothers general partner, argued that Western Electric should be an independent company. In *Business Week* he predicted that "If you take Western Electric out of the Bell System, you're going to turn a whale into a shark that would eat competition alive."[9] Nearly two decades later, his theory would be put to the test. On September 20, 1995, AT&T Chairman Robert Allen announced that AT&T would spin off its manufacturing divisions and NCR, the computer manufacturer it had acquired in 1991. The new company, Lucent Technologies, would be made up of the manufacturing components of AT&T and the old Western Electric in addition to Bell Laboratories; NCR would be sent off on its own.

The idea of restructuring had been around awhile. After divestiture, relations between AT&T and the "Baby Bells" had never been great, although, Allen noted, "we'd done a number of things over the years to try and heal the rift."[10] Therefore, twice in the early 1990s, Allen called for "strategic reviews" to discuss "whether some structural change would make a difference."[11] Both times, after some general discussion including the Network Systems leadership, Allen shelved the idea.

The third time around, in 1995, the political environment acted as catalyst. The Telecommunications Act of 1996 was in the formative stages when the spin-off decision was made. Allen's expectation – which

Figure 42. Robert E. Allen, architect of trivestiture

was later borne out – was that the act would allow AT&T to compete in the local phone market against the Baby Bells. That would have put AT&T's Network Systems in the awkward position of attempting to maintain its position as the principal equipment supplier for the Baby Bells at the same time that Baby Bells were competitors of AT&T. Yet another compelling reason for the timing had to do with the transformation of Network Systems: "There was a long, hard transition from the old captive supplier to a competitive marketplace," Allen recalled, "but they were not ready to go off on their own much before [1995]."[12]

"Trivestiture" brings an ironic end to this story. When it held a virtual monopoly of American telephone service, AT&T struggled mightily to integrate Western Electric into the Bell System, then vigorously defended against Justice Department suits in the 1940s and 1970s aimed at separating Western Electric from the Bell System. No longer a monopoly in the 1990s, AT&T voluntarily spun off its long-time manufacturing unit.

The new company Lucent Technologies employs many onetime Western Electric employees, manufactures in several former Western Electric plants, and retains some remnants of the old Western Electric culture. Shades of the old Western Electric? Not Western Electric at its high tide, which represented a type of industrial operation distinctive to the mid-twentieth century. Western Electric was characterized by plants of thousands of workers. At times, the company had two plants (Hawthorne and Kearny) with more than 20,000 each. The era of the large, multistory, densely populated plant of the electromechanical era has given way to the smaller, specialized, highly automated plant of the solid-state era. Western Electric represented a combination of powerful welfare capitalism and weak unions. It embodied the quintessential paternalistic and hierarchical organization, one that promoted from within and rewarded seniority. The era of employees placing their future in the hands of their company has given way to a more entrepreneurial type of corporate career. A combination of technological and social change makes it unlikely that we shall see the likes of the post-1925 Western Electric again.

It is striking, however, how Lucent represents a reconstruction of elements from the pre-1925 Western Electric. Lucent houses Bell Labs, just as Western Electric housed most Bell System research prior to the establishment of Bell Laboratories as a separate entity. Lucent has extensive overseas manufacturing operations, just as Western Electric did before it spun them off. Lucent has marketing and sales functions, just as Western Electric once did but abandoned when its only major customers became the Bell System and the federal government.

Yet the Lucent whole is quite different from the sum of the Western Electric parts. Most significantly, Lucent has the autonomy that Western Electric craved but gradually compromised during the process of vertical integration which culminated in 1925. This means that Lucent is free from a parent's dictates regarding the scope of its product line, when and how to expand, the nature of its relationship with the government, and the leadership of the company. For a company with a 127-year history, this is as close to a fresh start as it gets.

CONCLUSION

N 1907, AT&T'S PRESIDENT, THEODORE Vail, wrote: "the Western Electric Company stands in a very different position from that of an ordinary manufacturing company having the ordinary relations between the company and the consumers or purchasers of its product." Indeed, Western Electric was anything but ordinary. Its story is the tale of a manufacturing company with two masters: AT&T as parent and the government overseeing AT&T. The most distinctive aspect of Western Electric's history, then, was its predicament: as captive supplier to a regulated monopoly, it was circumscribed as perhaps no other. Again and again, outside decision makers limited the company's possibilities. Relations with parent and government shaped Western's approach to some of the key business issues of the century: innovation, globalization, and equal opportunity. They also combined to make the Western story almost entirely American.

In many ways, however, Western Electric's story diverges from those of other major American manufacturers. One of the great themes of twentieth-century U.S. business history is the increasingly international nature of American firms. Yet the continual influence of AT&T and the government made the Western story a distinctly domestic one. On the eve of World War I, no American company had manufacturing facilities in more countries than Western Electric. AT&T's 1925 spin-off of Western's overseas operations and the 1956 agreement with the government to spin off Northern Electric drove Western to another extreme. During the years 1925–1975, when erstwhile competitors General Electric and Westinghouse went abroad, Western operated almost exclusively in the United States. At the same time, Western's progeny, including NEC and Northern Electric, began to test the American market.

Western also did not practice image building as did other American firms. In the early twentieth century, America became the world's leader in marketing and gave birth to the profession of public relations. In so doing, American firms institutionalized a distinctive aspect of the American character: self-promotion. Western's predicament with respect to AT&T reinforced restraint rather than encouraging self-promotion. As a captive supplier, Western Electric had little use for marketing pizzazz or projecting an exciting image to the outside world. It offered the electrical equivalent of steak, not sizzle. America's other large American electrical manufacturers, General Electric and Westinghouse, became ubiquitous through their appliances and ad campaigns. "You can be sure if it's Westinghouse" and GE's "We bring good things to life" became part of American culture. Western was simply "Makers of Bell Telephones." Western's role even paled within the Bell System, where Bell Labs scientists made headlines – and won Nobel Prizes – with the transistor, the laser, and other inventions. Western Electric's role was the less glamourous one of bringing transistors into mass production, or applying lasers to manufacturing processes.

The world's foremost private scientific research laboratory offered Western Electric a constant source of innovation. Creativity became a continual source of tension for Western, as technical innovation acted like a centrifugal force pulling the company in various directions against the gravitational pull of the Bell System's core mission. Consequently, Western Electric's paths taken but not sustained – from introducing sound to motion pictures to developing typewriters to manufacturing calculating machines to distributing appliances – are among the most noteworthy in American corporate history.

Western Electric's style of leadership also fit its predicament: its presidents kept their charisma in check. Western was imbued with a low-profile approach dating to the company's early days. Cofounder Enos Barton frowned on displays of individual ego, preferring the greater glory of the company. Barton's successors followed his example, and finally the company came to reflect that approach.

Western's position as subordinate to a regulated monopoly combined with a very hierarchical organizational structure to prevent the company from making quick, dramatic changes. The history of Western Electric includes some of what David Halberstam calls the "hard drama" of headline-making events, such as the completion of a transcontinental connection in 1915, the successful application of sound to motion pictures in 1927, and the erection of the Distant Early Warning (DEW) Line in the 1950s. All those events made headlines, yet such headline making hardly adds up to this company's history, which is predominantly a "soft drama" of more gradual or behind-the-scenes change.

The Western Electric story offers prime examples of the difficulty of quickly implementing a strategy or policy. Vertical integration is often described as a single event, whereas the vertical integration of Western Electric into the Bell System was a process lasting decades. Other forms of innovation did not immediately change the landscape at Western. For instance, Walter Shewhart invented the statistical control chart there, sparking a revolution in quality control. During the next two decades, however, Western barely used it. One of the presumed advantages of Western's great size was the ability to perform assembly-line production, but not until the 1960s was this method successfully introduced into the company's largest plant on a large scale.

One exception where change occurred quickly was in the area of civil rights. But even Western's civil rights experience grew out of its predicament. As a defense contractor, its business was subject to executive order by activist presidents. The government took the initiative in promoting equal opportunity, and some defense contractors responded by going only as far as they were required to. Western Electric's leadership, in contrast, seized the opportunity to take bold action in one of the few areas where its actions were not circumscribed and acted ahead of its parent. In so doing, the company transformed itself from laggard to leader in civil rights.

Although most of its history evolved in an unusual relation to parent company and government, the Western Electric experience offers ample material that can be applied to more conventional situations. One of the key subjects is the area of institutional change. Western had mixed results when it tried to alter the way things were done, either with respect to social issues or processes and efficiency. When faced with resistance by the company culture, should a company that wants change simply build a new plant or seek another new environment? Western sometimes pioneered in an area such as human relations or quality control, then seemed to forget the lessons it learned by so doing. This was most striking in the case of its relationship with NEC, which changed from an importer to an exporter of ideas. One of the hallmarks of Western's monopolistic situation, then, seemed to be an abundance of ideas and innovation, but slow implementation or change.

Therefore, many were surprised when two years after its initial public offering, the value of Lucent Technologies stock skyrocketed to the ranks among America's top ten public companies in market capitalization (ahead not only of International Business Machines Corp., but also ahead of Lucent's former parent, AT&T). While the market embraced Lucent, we have no comparable measure for Western Electric, whose stock was never publicly traded. The *Wall Street Journal* hinted at a rapid transformation: "Lucent evolved out of AT&T's Western Electric manufacturing arm, a stodgy monolith that dominated 'circuit-switched' technology."[1] How did a "stodgy" subsidiary become the darling of Wall Street?

Did Lucent's performance really represent a turnaround, or was Western Electric imbued with the sort of efficiency and discipline we do not usually associate with a monopoly? As early as 1939, N. R. Danielian of the Federal Communications Commission (FCC) raised the issue in *AT&T: The Story of Industrial Conquest*: "Western Electric's efficiency," he concluded, "remains an unexplored problem."[2] Western Electric's performance was subsequently explored by two corporate consulting firms. In the 1960s, Western hired McKinsey & Co. to do an assessment, and McKinsey concluded that Western was efficiently run. A few years later, the FCC hired Touche-Ross to assess Western's efficiency, and received a similar conclusion. Both studies focused on process rather than product, and did little comparative analysis.

A detailed analysis of Western Electric's efficiency – including comparison to companies such as Siemens, Ericsson, NEC, and Northern Telecom – is beyond the scope of this corporate biography, but promises to be a fascinating project for others. Until that project is complete, we will conclude by revising the usual order of things. Traditionally, the past is believed to foreshadow the future. For now, we will rely on Western Electric's future (Lucent) informing its past: perhaps this particular monopoly had achieved a pattern of efficiency that would represent, according to Danielian, "a gratuitous favor not contemplated nor expected in the theory of competitive private enterprise."[3]

APPENDIX A

CHIEF EXECUTIVES

Gray & Barton
Anson Stager, president — 1869–1872

Western Electric
Anson Stager, president — 1872–1885
William A. S. Smoot, president — 1885–1886
Enos M. Barton, president — 1886–1908
Harry B. Thayer, president — 1908–1919
Charles G. DuBois, president — 1919–1926
Edgar S. Bloom, president — 1926–1939
Clarence G. Stoll, president — 1940–1947
Stanley Bracken, president — 1947–1954
Frederick R. Kappel, president — 1954–1956
Arthur B. Goetze, president — 1956–1959
Haakon I. Romnes, president — 1959–1963
Paul A. Gorman, president — 1964–1969
Harvey Mehlhouse, president/chairman — 1969–1971
Don Procknow, chairman — 1971–1983

AT&T Network Systems
Wayne Weeks, president — 1984–1989
William Marx, president — 1989–1994
Rich McGinn, president — 1994–1995
Dan Stanzione, president — 1995–1996

APPENDIX B

COMPANY SALES AND EMPLOYEES

Year	Sales ($000)	Employees (approx.)
1872	100	50
1873		
1874		
1875		100
1876		
1877	273	
1878		
1879		
1880	877	400
1881		
1882	1,044	
1883	1,756	
1884	1,535	
1885	1,312	500
1886	1,526	
1887	2,306	
1888	2,639	
1889	2,833	
1890	4,097	1,400
1891	4,082	
1892	4,598	
1893	5,153	
1894	4,822	

Year	Sales ($000)	Employees
1895	6,523	2,500
1896	8,005	
1897	8,775	
1898	10,516	
1899	17,850	
1900	24,472	8,486
1901	23,877	9,379
1902	28,627	10,744
1903	30,257	9,293
1904	32,454	9,550
1905	44,146	16,439
1906	69,245	22,609
1907	52,724	12,305
1908	32,314	9,640
1909	45,575	14,559
1910	68,375	19,192
1911	66,212	16,774
1912	71,727	17,857
1913	77,533	19,856
1914	66,408	15,650
1915	63,852	17,135
1916	106,987	26,878
1917	150,340	30,737
1918	145,226	26,126
1919	135,722	27,584
1920	206,112	39,650
1921	189,765	45,243
1922	210,941	51,162
1923	255,177	63,808
1924	298,281	49,157
1925	297,729	39,460
1926	263,105	45,110
1927	253,724	40,749

Year	Sales ($000)	Employees
1928	287,931	57,522
1929	410,950	87,322
1930	361,478	67,763
1931	228,956	47,812
1932	117,850	23,368
1933	69,511	20,613
1934	91,807	22,876
1935	105,417	23,314
1936	146,421	36,172
1937	203,467	45,131
1938	175,163	31,395
1939	186,860	33,699
1940	241,618	43,746
1941	385,418	63,720
1942	553,282	76,779
1943	685,906	89,016
1944	886,344	94,025
1945	832,309	80,029
1946	598,585	114,525
1947	980,982	132,927
1948	1,116,163	103,770
1949	840,980	72,086
1950	737,252	73,458
1951	950,291	90,161
1952	1,270,247	104,887
1953	1,460,487	106,024
1954	1,486,302	98,141
1955	1,822,617	120,054
1956	2,319,417	138,520
1957	2,447,755	141,123
1958	2,142,929	122,101
1959	2,278,742	134,867
1960	2,597,415	143,352
1961	2,563,139	145,781

Year	Sales ($000)	Employees
1962	2,718,940	151,174
1963	2,783,254	147,210
1964	3,056,695	157,626
1965	3,289,584	168,846
1966	3,534,780	168,369
1967	3,629,383	169,699
1968	3,944,576	176,970
1969	4,776,289	203,608
1970	5,856,160	215,380
1971	6,045,216	207,015
1972	6,551,183	205,665
1973	7,037,290	206,608
1974	7,381,728	189,972
1975	6,590,798	152,677
1976	6,930,942	151,052
1977	8,165,911	161,909
1978	9,521,835	161,537
1979	10,964,100	175,292
1980	12,032,100	174,372
1981	13,008,000	162,063
1982	12,579,900	153,000
1983	11,154,700	N/A

NOTES

INTRODUCTION

1 John Brooks, *Telephone: The First Hundred Years* (New York: Harper & Row, 1976), pp. 137–139.

2 Theodore Vail, *Views on Public Questions* (privately printed, 1917), p. 11.

3 *AT&T Annual Report 1909*, p. 3.

4 H. B. Thayer to U. N. Bethell, Feb. 23, 1916, 125 04 03 09. See Louis Galambos, "Theodore N. Vail and the Role of Innovation in the Modern Bell System," *Business History Review* 62 (Spring 1992): pp. 95–116.

5 *AT&T Annual Report 1909*, p. 4.

6 Brooks, *Telephone*, p. 138; Robert Millikan, *Autobiography* (New York: Prentice-Hall, 1950), quoted in Oliver E. Buckley, "Biographical Memoir of Frank Baldwin Jewett, 1879–1949," *National Academy of Sciences, Biographical Memoirs* 27 (1950): 247–248.

7 Leonard S. Reich, *The Making of American Industrial Research: Science and Business at GE and Bell, 1876–1926* (Cambridge: Cambridge University Press, 1985), p. 160.

8 Hugh G. J. Aitken, *The Continuous Wave: Technology and American Radio, 1900–1932* (Princeton, NJ: Princeton University Press, 1985), pp. 242–246.

9 Brooks, *Telephone*, pp. 125–128.

10 Ibid., p. 168

11 Alvin von Auw, *Heritage and Destiny* (New York: Praeger Publishers, 1983), p. 211.

12 See Samuel Haber, *Efficiency and Uplift: Scientific Management in the Progressive Era* (Chicago: University of Chicago Press, 1967); Daniel Nelson, *Frederick W. Taylor and the Rise of Scientific Management* (Madison: University of Wisconsin Press, 1980).

13 Joseph Juran interview, Sept. 5, 1996;

14 *AT&T 1994 Annual Report*, p. 15.

15 See Richard Gillespie, *Manufacturing Knowledge* (Baltimore: The Johns Hopkins University Press, 1991).

16 Thomas J. Peters and Robert H. Waterman, *In Search of Excellence: Lessons from America's Best-Run Companies* (New York: Harper & Row, 1982), pp. 5–6.

17 Vallmer Jordan interview, Nov. 14, 1996.

18 *Bell System Statistical Manual 1920–1962*, p. 1304.

19 Arthur W. Page, *The Bell Telephone System* (New York: Harper & Brothers Publishers, 1941), p. 140.

20 Brooks, *Telephone*, pp. 253–255.

21 *AT&T 1992 Annual Report*, p. 10; *AT&T 1993 Annual Report*, pp. 10–12.

I. BEFORE THE BELL

1 Paul Israel, *From Machine Shop to Industrial Laboratory* (Baltimore: The Johns Hopkins University Press, 1992), p. 55.

2 Alfred D. Chandler, Jr., *The Visible Hand: The Managerial Revolution in American Business* (Cambridge, MA: Harvard University Press, 1977), p. 197.

3 Joseph Frazier Wall, *Andrew Carnegie* (New York: Oxford University Press, 1970), p. 90.

4 Matthew Josephson, *Edison: A Biography* (New York: McGraw-Hill, 1959), p. 41.

5 Steven Lubar, *Infoculture* (Boston: Houghton Mifflin Company, 1993), p. 94.

6 Israel, *Machine Shop to Industrial Laboratory*, p. 78.

7 *WE*, Jan. 1953, p. 45; *Journal of the Telegraph*, Feb. 15, 1869, p. 1.

8 James D. Reid, *The Telegraph in America* (New York: Derby Brothers, 1879), pp. 187–188

9 Israel, pp. 50–51.

10 *WE*, Jan. 1953, pp. 45–46. In 1869, the *Journal of the Telegraph* noted that "A good deal has been said about the exploit of receiving messages by tongue, and no doubt when first done, it was a curious and very smart operation." The *Journal* admitted not knowing "who first executed this lingual feat," but noted an 1853 story from the *Telegraph Review* that described one such achievement in detail. "Receiving by Tongue," *Journal of the Telegraph* (Mar. 1, 1869): 78.

11 William R. Plum, *The Military Telegraph during the Civil War in the United States*, 2 vols. (Chicago: Jansen, McClurg & Co., 1982), 1:130.

12 Ibid., pp. 131, 234.

13 Ibid., 2:107.

14 Ibid., 2:348; Reid, *Telegraph in America,* p. 483.

15 Lubar, *Infoculture,* p. 94.

16 Israel, *Machine Shop to Industrial Laboratory,* p. 71.

17 Josephson, *Edison,* pp. 62–64

18 *The Telegrapher* Sept. 26, 1864, p. 1; Reid, *Telegraph in America,* p. 541.

19 Israel, *Machine Shop to Industrial Laboratory,* p. 72.

20 Enos Barton address, n.d., 92 01 161 08; William Chauncy Langdon, "This Mortgage Made History," *Nation's Business,* Jan. 1926, p. 45.

21 *Journal of the Telegraph,* June 15, 1870, p.174; George J. Gray Jr., "A Century of Service," p. 12.

22 *WE,* Jan. 1953, p. 47.

23 *Journal of the Telegraph,* Mar. 15, 1870, p. 96.

24 *The Telegrapher,* Jan. 15, 1870, p. 168; *Journal of the Telegraph,* Jan. 15, 1869, p. 43.

25 Three years later, after selling out to Elisha Gray, Shawk went into business with George Hicks, *Journal of the Telegraph,* Nov. 15, 1871, p. 293.

26 *Western Electric News,* Apr. 1912, p. 1.

27 Frank H. Lovette, "Meet Mr. Barton," 1956, pp. 238–239, 92 01 162 02.

28 George J. Gray Jr., ed., "A Century of Service," Mar. 15, 1970, p. 15.

29 Elisha Gray, *Extended Research in Electro-harmonic Telegraphy, 1867–1878* (New York: Russell Brothers Printers, 1878), p. 6.

30 "Dictation by Carroll Churchill," Sept. 26, 1962, Elisha Gray Papers, box 1, folder 11.

31 "All in a Lifetime," p. 3, 92 06 176 05.

32 "Dictations by Carroll Churchill," Sept. 26, 1962, Elisha Gray Papers, box 1, folder 11.

33 Josephson, *Edison,* p. 86.

34 Reid, *Telegraph in America,* p. 564.

35 Israel, *Machine Shop to Industrial Laboratory,* pp. 203–204, n. 38. If it was Pond who arranged the demonstration, Gray was in no hurry to give him credit: "Pond is running around and trying to buy an interest but he dont succeed." Gray to wife, Nov. 6, 1867, 92 02 165 08. Pond did, however, move to Cleveland, where he continued his career as a Western Union telegraph operator. *Journal of the Telegraph,* Dec. 1, 1868, p. 5.

36 Reid, *Telegraph in America,* p. 189.

37 Israel, *Machine Shop to Industrial Laboratory,* pp. 69, 71.

38 Gray, "A Century of Service," p. 15.
39 When Barton was a teenager, his mother had let it be known she believed "that a parent has a right to the earnings of their minor children" (Fanny Barton to "sir," Mar. 1858, 92 10 160 03). Barton had complied, and continued his habit of sending money to her as an adult (even helping her pay for the farm). Fanny Barton Diary, May–Oct. 1868, 92 01 161 09.
40 Frank H. Lovette, "Western Electric's First 75 Years: A Chronology," *Bell Telephone Magazine*, Winter 1945, p. 273.
41 "Meet Mr. Barton," 92 01 162 02.
42 *Journal of the Telegraph*, Apr. 1, 1869.
43 *Journal of the Telegraph*, Jan. 15, 1869, p. 43.
44 Gray, "A Century of Service," p. 16.
45 Ibid., p. 14.
46 When Gray bought in, George Shawk returned to telegraph supply in a shop on Center Street. His first partner there was William Foote, then George Hicks, Shawk's original go-between with Barton (*The Journal of the Telegraph*, Nov. 15, 1870, and Jan. 1, 1871; L. L. Evert to Frank H. Lovette, Feb. 24, 1944, 92 03 166 01). There, Shawk dabbled with inventions, including an annunciator for hotels he had patented in 1873. U. S. Patent Office, patent no. 136,465, dated Mar. 4, 1873, 92 03 166 07.
47 L. L. Evert to Frank H. Lovette, Feb. 24, 1944, 92 03 166 01.
48 "Anson Stager," *WE*, Jan. 1953, p. 44–48.
49 Gray, "A Century of Service," p. 17.
50 Reid, *Telegraph in America* pp. 235–247; Gray, p. 21.
51 *Journal of the Telegraph*, Feb. 1, 1869 p. 1[?].
52 *WE* (Jan. 1953), p. 48.
53 Ibid.
54 L. L. Evert to Frank H. Lovette, Feb. 24, 1944, 92 03 166 01.
55 92 02 164 13.
56 *Journal of the Telegraph*, Aug. 1, 1868, p. 4.
57 Gray and Barton to Wives, Nov. 13, 1869, 92 01 160 03.
58 Barton memoir, *Western Electric News*, Apr. 1912, p. 2.
59 Frank H. Lovette to F. B. Wright, Feb. 28, 1946, 92 03 167 01.
60 *Telegrapher*, Oct. 21, 1871, pp. 65–66.
61 Western Union Executive Committee Minutes, Mar. 1872. Western Union Papers, box 8, vol. B, p. 70.
62 "Shawk and Barton, and Gray and Barton changes in capital accounts from various periods between December 1, 1868 and August 31, 1871," 92 03 167 01; *Journal of the Telegraph*, Apr. 2, 1877, p. 98.
63 Gray, "A Century of Service," pp. 21–22.

64 Executive Committee Minutes, Western Union, Apr. 29, 1874; p. 374; Apr. 28, 1875, p. 491.
65 "Chats with Pioneers: John Young," *Western Electric News*, Nov. 1919, p. 50.
66 Don Graf, *Convenience for Research* (New York: Voorhees Walker Foley & Smith, 1944), pp. 7–8.
67 Lewis pay book.
68 More than sixty years later, Hobart – by then a minister, like his father – and Stanley, who had started his own business, visited Western Electric's Hawthorne works and reenacted some 1870s-style packaging.
69 Gray, "A Century of Service," pp. 21–22.
70 Ibid., p. 12; "Chats with Pioneers, " *Western Electric News*, Nov. 1919, p. 48.
71 Ibid., p. 354.
72 Gray, "A Century of Service," p. 24. Smoot would become Western Electric's second president after Anson Stager's January 1885 retirement.
73 Ibid., p. 25.
74 George B. Prescott, *Electricity and the Electric Telegraph* (New York: D. Appleton & Company, 1877), pp. 792–793; Hounshell, *American System to Mass Production*, p. 161.
75 Elisha Gray, "On the Transmission of Musical Tones Telegraphically," *Journal of the American Electrical Society* 1, no. 1 (1875): 3–4.
76 David A. Hounshell, "Two Paths to the Telephone," *Scientific American*, Jan. 1981, p. 157.
77 Deposition of William Goodridge, p. 80.
78 Deposition, Milo Kellogg, p. 179; William Goodridge, p. 80.
79 *Journal of the Telegraph*, May 15, 1869, p. 134.
80 Deposition, Anson Stager, pp. 184–186.
81 Hounshell, "Two Paths to the Telephone," pp. 157–163.
82 John Brooks, *Telephone:The First Hundred Years* (Harper & Row: New York, 1976), p. 37.
83 George David Smith, *The Anatomy of a Business Strategy* (Baltimore: The Johns Hopkins University Press, 1985), p. 203.
84 Gray to wife, Nov. 21, 1867, 92 02 165 08; Hounshell, "Two Paths to the Telephone," p. 163.
85 Hounshell, p. 163.
86 Lloyd W. Taylor, "The Untold Story of the Telephone," *The American Physics Teacher*, Dec. 1937, p. 251.
87 Reid, *Telegraph in America*, pp. 574–575.
88 Smith, *Anatomy of a Business Strategy*, p. 38; W. Bernard Carlson, "Entrepreneurship in the Early Development of the Telephone; How

Did William Orton and Gardiner Hubbard Conceptualize This New Technology?" paper presented at the Business History Conference, Mar. 11–13, 1994.

89 Frank H. Lovette, "Western Electric's First 75 Years: A Chronology," *Bell Telephone Magazine*, Winter 1945, p. 275; "Telephone Patents— List of Patents owned by the Western Union Co.," box 1217, "Western Union Telegraph Company—Patents Owned By—1871–1881."

90 "History of the American Independent Telephone Manufacturing Industry," working papers for Dewey, Ballantine, Bushby, Palmer & Wood, Nov. 1955, p. 6, 450 05 02 12.

91 Ibid., pp. 5–6; Smith, *Anatomy of a Business Strategy*, p. 97.

92 Lovette, "Western Electric's First 75 Years," p. 275.

93 Gray, "A Century of Service," p. 26.

94 Smith, "Anatomy of a Business Strategy," p. 41.

95 Ibid., p. 112.

96 Ibid., p. 111.

97 Ibid., p. 42.

98 Ibid., pp. 82, 106.

99 Ibid., p. 112.

100 Brooks, *Telephone* p. 65.

101 Smith, *Anatomy of a Business Strategy*, p. 64

102 Ibid., pp. 224–225, n. 9.

103 Vail to Forbes, Dec. 14, 1880, box 1113, folder 25.

104 Smith, *Anatomy of a Business Strategy*, p. 116.

105 Ibid., p. 116.

106 Ibid., p. 117.

107 Ibid., p. 119.

108 Ibid., p. 120.

2. IN BELL'S WORLD, BUT NOT OF IT

1 Theodore Vail, *Views on Public Questions* (privately published, 1917), p. 11.

2 Cochrane to Barton, June 13, 1901, Pres. AT&T Letterbook 3 (July 26, 1900–Aug. 31, 1901).

3 Allen wrote: "The telephone system of the future must give, and it will give a *universal public service*, bounded neither by arbitrary political lines nor by rivers and mountains, but covering in one whole the vast extent of this continent." See "History of Telephone," 1903, p. 7.

4 Barton to Kellogg, July 16, 1881, 92 01 160 06.

5 Barton to Kellogg, Feb. 5, 1880, 92 01 160 06.

6 Ibid.
7 Agreement "Between the undersigned Messrs. Gardiner G. Hubbard and E. T. Gilliland," Oct. 24, 1881, 92 01 160 06. George David Smith, *The Anatomy of a Business Strategy* (Baltimore: The Johns Hopkins University Press, 1985), p. 116.
8 "The Factory of the Bell Telephone Manufacturing Company of Antwerp," *The Electrical World,* May 23, 1885, p. 203.
9 Wilkins, p. 67; "Western Electric Company: Report as to the Business of the Foreign Houses from Their Beginning to November 30, 1896," box 1139, folder 02.
10 Mira Wilkins, *The Emergence of Multinational Enterprise: American Business Abroad from the Colonial Era to 1914* (Cambridge, MA: Harvard University Press, 1970), pp. 212–213.
11 Barton to Vail, Aug. 2, 1882, 92 01 160 06.
12 W. R. Patterson, "Cable and Cable Making—Some Stray Recollections," *Western Electric News,* July 1915, p. 2.
13 Ibid., p. 5.
14 Barton to Vail, Aug. 2, 1882 92 01 160 06.
15 Vail to C. Williams, June 23, 1884, 65 05 01.
16 Gilliland to Vail, Feb. 18, 1885, "Annual Report of the Mechanical Department," 250 06 17.
17 Hudson to Vail, Dec. 23, 1885 (letter no. 345); Hudson to Smoot, Dec. 31, 1885 (letter no. 349).
18 "Notes from Other Associates," *Western Electric News* (June 1916), p. 8.
19 Bowditch to Williams, Apr. 3, 1886, Letterbook 3G, p. 455.
20 Bowditch to Fay, Aug. 31, 1886, Letterfile 44.
21 Williams to Forbes, Aug. 14, 1886, 92 04 170 06.
22 "Notes from Other Associates," *Western Electric News* (June 1916), p. 8.
23 John Breckenridge Jackson, *Memoirs of John Mason Jackson* (Chicago: University of Chicago Press, 1908), p. 462.
24 John Brooks, *Telephone: The First Hundred Years* (Harper & Row: New York, 1976), pp. 90–91.
25 *Telephone Switch Boards. Report of a Conference Held at the Offices of American Telephone and Telegraph Company, December 19, 20 and 21, 1887*, p. 87; "The Genesis of the Telephone Multiple Switchboard," pp. 18–20.
26 Cf. "Chapter III: New Switchboards for Central Office," p. 9, in "Telephone in Illinois, 1877–1900," Typescript, Feb., 1945, AT&T Archives, box 1040; *Telephone Switch Boards. Report of a Conference*

Held at the Offices of the American Telephone and Telegraph Company, December 19, 20 and 21, 1887, pp. 72, 80–83. AT&T Archives, box 1141.

27 *Telephone Switch Boards,* p. 93; "The Genesis of the Telephone Multiple Switchboard," p. 21; Hudson to Barton, Nov. 25, 1887, General Manager's Letter Book (GMLB) 246, pp. 172–173; Hudson to Barton, December 5, 1887, GMLB 246, pp. 436–437.

28 Brooks, pp. 85, 97.

29 Smith, p. 128; 226, n. 22.

30 *Telephone Switchboards. Report of a Meeting of the Switchboard Committee held at the office of the American Telephone & Telegraph Company, No. 18 Courtlandt Street, New York, July 21, 22, 23, 1891.*

31 Ibid.

32 Alan Trachtenberg, *The Incorporation of America* (New York: Hill and Wang, 1982), p. 218.

33 David Nye, *Electrifying America: Social Meanings of a New Technology, 1880–1940* (Cambridge, MA: MIT Press, 1990), pp. 37–38.

34 Trachtenberg, *Incorporation of America,* p. 208.

35 Ibid., p. 215.

36 Barton to Hudson, Nov. 23, 1886, box 1216, folder 13.

37 Trachtenberg, *Incorporation of America,* p. 209.

38 Smoot to The American Bell Telephone Company, July 25, 1885, box 1239, folder 08.

39 J. P. Barrett, *Electricity at the Columbian Exposition* (Chicago: R. R. Donnelly & Sons Company, 1894), p. 13.

40 Ibid., p. 15.

41 Ibid., pp. 468–469.

42 Ibid., p. 315.

43 Ibid., p. 334.

44 Ibid.

45 Ibid., p. 498.

46 Ibid., p. 495.

47 Barton to Welles, July 20, 1896, box 1139, 131 10 02 22.

48 Western Electric Company, *Catalogues,* 1884, 1887.

49 "Marshall Field," *Dictionary of American Biography* (New York, 1958), p. 367.

50 Hudson to Barton, Apr. 16, 1895, "Western Electric Company—Operation—1893–1895," 136 03 01 20.

51 Memo of telephone conversation between Hudson and Barton, Apr. 16, 1895, "Western Electric Company—Operation—1893–1895," 136 03 01 20.

52 "Memorandum by E. W. Rockafellow," May 17, 1944, 92 09 186 01.
53 Ibid.
54 For a discussion of computing devices before the modern computer, see Steven Lubar, *Infoculture* (Boston: Houghton Mifflin Company, 1993), pp. 301–302; Martin Campbell-Kelly, "Punched-Card Machinery," in William Aspray, ed., *Computing Before Computers* (Ames: Iowa State University Press, 1990), pp. 122–147; Emerson W. Pugh, *Building IBM: Shaping an Industry and Its Technology* (Cambridge, MA: MIT Press, 1995), pp. 1–28; and Geoffrey D. Austrian, *Herman Hollerith, Forgotten Giant of Information Processing* (New York: Columbia University Press, 1982).
55 Austrian, *Herman Hollerith*, pp. 39–40, 45–46.
56 Ibid., p. 46.
57 Thayer to Welles, Apr. 7, 1890, 94 04 137 01; Austrian, *Herman Hollerith*, pp. 53–54.
58 Austrian, pp. 82–83, 129.
59 Ibid., pp. 131–32.
60 Ibid., pp. 152–53.
61 "Telephone Development in the United States, 1876 to 1957," American Tel & Tel Co. Chief Statistician's Division, June 1958.
62 C. J. French to E. M. Barton, May 25, 1899, AT&T Archives, GMLB 565, pp. 284–285.

3. SYSTEMS OF MANAGING AND MANAGING OF SYSTEMS

1 Thayer, DuBois, and Patterson to Barton, July 13, 1900, 92 01 160 09.
2 "Proposed Plan of a Definite Organization," Oct. 9, 1900, 11 10 02 08.
3 Thayer, DuBois, and Patterson to Barton, July 13, 1900, 92 01 160 09.
4 Ibid.
5 Charles G. DuBois, "Some Undeveloped Uses of Accounts," Mar. 30, 1909, 92 05 173 05.
6 Ibid.
7 Vail to Barton, July 14, 1908, President's Letterbook 6, 3/11/07–8/05/09, p. 123.
8 Enos Barton to Adelia Barton, Feb. 17, 1908, 92 01 160 09.
9 Vail to Barton, Feb. 13, 1908, President's Letterbook 6, p. 79.
10 "Tributes to the Memory of Enos M. Barton from Some of His Associates in the Western Electric Company," *Western Electric News*, June 1916, p. 5.

11 Sanford Jacoby, *Employing Bureaucracy: Managers, Unions and the Transformation of Work in American Industry, 1900–1945* (New York: Columbia University Press, 1985), p. 41.

12 David Noble, *America by Design* (New York: Oxford University Press, 1977), p. 263.

13 Walter Dietz, *Walter Dietz Speaking* (Summit, NJ: N.P., 1972), pp. 23–27.

14 Noble, *America by Design*, pp. 178–179.

15 David Montgomery, *The Fall of the House of Labor* (Cambridge: Cambridge University Press, 1989), p. 217.

16 George F. Will, "A Faster Mousetrap," review of Robert Kanigel, *The One Best Way*, in the *New York Times*, Book Review Section, June 15, 1997, p. 8.

17 "His First Job," *Bell Labs Record* (1925), 1:61.

18 See, for example, Gilliland to Vail, Dec. 23, 1884; Hayes to R. W. Devonshire, Nov. 23, 1886, Mechanical Department Letterbooks, AT&T Archives 65-04-03; Hayes to Hudson, Mar. 6, 1888, AT&T Archives, 65-05-01.

19 Vail to Smoot, July 14, 1885, GMLB 198, p. 59; July 24, 1885, GMLB 198, p. 235; Hudson to Barton, Sept. 26, 1886, GMLB 200, pp. 117–118; Dec. 6, 1886, GMLB 219, p. 206; June 10, 1887, GMLB 239, p. 145; July 30, 1888, GMLB 273, p. 199; Oct. 12, 1888, GMLB 276, pp. 334–335; Oct. 15, 1888, GMLB 276, pp. 358–359; French to Thayer, Aug. 30, 1893, GMLB 380, pp. 274–275; Sept.14, 1893, GMLB 380, p. 496; May 15, 1895, GMLB 439, p. 299; June 8, 1895; GMLB 452, p. 256; Nov. 22, 1895, GMLB 457, pp. 60–61; Aug. 15, 1896, GMLB 486, p. 390; French to Barton, Feb. 10, 1898, GMLB 524, pp. 294–295; Jan. 7, 1899, GMLB 561, p. 361; May 9, 1899, GMLB 565, p. 41; French to Thayer, May 25, 1899, GMLB 565, p. 283; French to Barton, May 25, 1899, GMLB 565, p. 284–285.

20 Dick Greene, "Henry Fleetwood Albright: Western Electric's Master Builder."

21 Enos M. Barton, "H. F. Albright—An Appreciation," *Western Electric News*, May 1913, p. 25.

22 H. B. Thayer, "Operating Methods and the Handling of Irregular Calls from the Manufacturer's Point of View," typescript of paper read before the Telephone Society of New York, 1905, pp. 7–8, 11. Thayer biographical materials, AT&T Archives 92 11 190 01.

23 Ibid., p. 5. Thayer biographical materials, AT&T Archives 92 11 190 01.

24 Statement of Harry B. Thayer, New York, Jan. 8, 1906, 92 11 190 01; "Pioneer Factory Builder Rose from Office Boy to Executive," unidentified newspaper clipping, 92 04 170 02.

25 Thayer to Welles, Oct. 13, 1904, 94 05 238 01.

26 "General Manufacturing Department—Hawthorne Personnel 1908," Historical Information, Western Electric Company, Inc., 1868–1930, 250 06 16.

27 C. W. Houger, "Before Hawthorne Was Born," *Western Electric News* 19 (March 1930): 42–43.

28 A. J. Steiss to Fish, Oct. 24, 1901, box 1332, folder 14.

29 Thayer to Devonshire, Feb. 3, 1899, box 1332, folder 07. This folder contains numerous complaints about Western's work.

30 Barton to Hudson, Dec. 23, 1899, box 1139 131 10 02 22.

31 "Bell Telephone," Boston News Bureau, Mar. 14, 1899, box 1332, folder 07.

32 "Proceedings of the Bell System Educational Conference—Economics and Business," New York City, June 23, 1926, p. 98.

33 This issue gets lost in the obsession of Americans – and American business historians – with success stories. Most companies do *not* succeed, but often there is an ex post facto excision of fears from corporate stories, the focus being placed on hopes. The attitude of a company about its future – much like that of an individual – is often reflected in its housing arrangements. Those who find themselves in truly doubtful situations, such as Gray and Barton in Cleveland, will rent rather than buy to conserve cash flow and hedge their bets. Even those who buy may not be sanguine about their future. During Hewlett-Packard's first decade, David Packard had the company's factory designed in the shape of a supermarket, so if the new enterprise did not pan out, their building could easily revert to another use. "Packard Foundation Set to Shape New Era," *San Jose Mercury News*, Nov. 2, 1997, p. 28A.

34 By 1902, Chicago had more than 240,000 trade-union members. Montgomery, *Fall of the House of Labor*, p. 269.

35 Enos Barton to Adelia Barton, Mar. 1, 1900, 92 01 160 09.

36 Enos Barton to John Hudson, Apr. 21, 1900, box 1316, "Labor Situation in Chicago, Illinois—1900"; *Volume VIII of the Reports of the Industrial Commission: Chicago Labor Disputes of 1900, with Especial Reference to the Building and Machinery Trades* (Washington, DC: 1901), p. vi.

37 Thayer to Thyrza Barton, Mar.1, 1905, 94 05 238 02.

38 Barton to John Hudson, Dec. 23, 1899, box 1139, 131 10 02 22.

39   Thayer to Barton, May 2, 1900. 92 01 160 09.
40   *Volume VIII of Reports of the Industrial Commission,* p. v.
41   Barton to John Hudson, Apr. 21, 1900, box 1316, "Labor Situation in Chicago, Illinois—1900." Attempts to establish a closed shop at the Clinton Street plant continued in earnest through 1902. Barton to Fish, Dec. 4 and 6, 1902, box 1316, "Labor Union Demand for Closed Shop—1902"; Fish to Barton, Dec. 6, 1902, AT&T President's Letterbooks, Nov. 24, 1902–Jan. 3, 1903, p. 171.
42   Fish to Cochrane, June 5, 1902, AT&T President's Letterbooks, May 12–June 20, 1902, p. 255.
43   "A Quarter Century Once Over," *Western Electric News,* March 1930, p. 3.
44   "The Maid Undismayed," p. 36, and "By-Product—Good Citizens," p. 22, *The Western Electric News,* March 1930.
45   "By-Product—Good Citizens," p. 23.
46   Cohen, *Making a New Deal,* p. 33.
47   "By-Product—Good Citizens," p. 24.
48   Thayer to J. M. Keller, March 17, 1908, 94 06 241 01.
49   American Social History Project, *Who Built America? Volume 2* (New York: Pantheon Books, 1992), p. 167. By 1920, Schenectady had 16,000 workers. Gerald Nye, *Image Worlds: Corporate Identities at General Electric, 1890–1930* (Cambridge, MA: MIT Press, 1985), p. 75.
50   Thayer to Welles, Nov. 4, 1904, 94 05 238 01.
51   Fish to Cochrane, June 5, 1902, AT&T President's Letterbooks, May 12–June 20, 1902, p. 255.
52   Fish to Barton, May 13, 1904. AT&T President's Letterbooks, April 26–June 30, 1904, p. 144.
53   Fish to Barton, Oct. 9, 1906, AT&T President's Letterbooks, July 30–Oct. 23, 1906, p. 152.
54   Thayer to Welles, Nov. 4, 1904, 94 05 238 01.
55   Vail to Barton, Oct. 8, 1907, AT&T President's Letterbooks, Mar. 11, 1907–Aug. 5, 1909, p. 38.
56   F. A. Ketcham, "Five Decades of Selling," *Western Electric News* 8 (Nov. 1919): 37–38.
57   Ibid.; Annual Report for 1919.
58   Western Electric Company, *The President's Report for the Fiscal Year Ending December 31, 1912,* pp. 17–18.
59   *The President's Report, 1912,* p. 13.
60   John Brooks, *Telephone: The First Hundred Years* (New York: Harper & Row, 1976), p. 136.
61   Alexander to Vail, Aug. 23, 1912, 125 03 02 01.

62 Allen to Vail, Sept. 7, 1912, 125 03 02 01.

63 "The Story of July Twenty-fourth," *Western Electric News,* August 1915, p. 3.

64 George W. Hilton, *Eastland: Legacy of the Titanic* (Stanford, CA: Stanford University Press, 1995), p. 137.

65 *Western Electric News,* Aug. 1915, p. 1.

66 Hilton, *Eastland,* p. 134.

67 Ibid., p. 141.

68 Ibid., p. 134.

69 "The Story of July Twenty-fourth," p. 7.

70 Hilton, *Eastland,* p. 141.

71 "Third Annual Report of Employee's Benefit Fund Committee, Western Electric Company and Its Successor, Western Electric Company, Incorporated," *Western Electric News* May 1916, p. 21.

72 Helen Repa, "The Experiences of a Hawthorne Nurse," *Western Electric News,* Aug. 1915, p. 19; Hilton, *Eastland,* p. 133.

73 The club had originally been the Hawthorne Men's Club, but in 1915 accepted women and became the Hawthorne Club.

74 Noble, *America by Design,* p. 157.

75 Addams to Sarah Alice Addams Hamilton, Jan. 5, 1980, Jane Addams Papers, reel 2, frame 1145, New York Public Library.

76 "Seven Stars," *The Western Electric News,* Apr. 1918, p. 2.

77 At the turn of the century, one-fourth of America's labor force was foreign-born, including half of all the unkilled workers. Sanford Jacoby, *Employing Bureaucracy: Managers, Unions and the Transformation of Work in American Industry, 1900–1945* (New York: Columbia University Press, 1985), p. 32.

78 Addams to Barton, Nov. 6, 1896. Addams Papers, reel 3, frame 492.

79 David Loth, *Swope of GE* (New York: Simon and Schuster, 1958), p. 31.

80 Montgomery, *Fall of the House of Labor,* p. 240.

81 "Telephone Pioneers of America Hold Their Third Annual Convention," *Western Electric News,* Dec. 1913, pp. 16–17.

82 Walter S. Allen to Kingsbury, Sept. 26, 1912, 125 03 02 01; Sanford Jacoby, *Modern Manors: Welfare Capitalism since the New Deal* (Princeton, NJ: Princeton University Press, 1997), p. 4.

83 Jacoby, *Modern Manors,* p. 11.

84 Stuart D. Brandes, *American Welfare Capitalism 1880–1940* (Chicago: University of Chicago Press, 1976), p. 28; Lizabeth Cohen, *Making a New Deal: Industrial Workers in Chicago, 1919–1939* (Cambridge: Cambridge University Press, 1990), p. 430.

85 Jacoby, *Modern Manors,* p. 20.

86   "E. W. Rockafellow Goes to National Pole Company," *Western Electric News*, June 1923, p.7.

87   R. A. Pook, "A Story of Hawthorne in Years 1919–1934," *Hawthorne Microphone*, June–July 1985, pp. 5–6.

88   Jacoby, *Modern Manors*.

89   Joseph Juran, "Memoirs," vol. 2, chap. 2, p. 10.

90   "The Young Man's Company," *Western Electric News*, July 1913, p. 20.

91   "To Office Boys—Past, Present, and Future," *Western Electric News*, May 1914, p. 36.

92   "Up from the Ranks," *Western Electric News*, May 1914, pp. 20–21.

93   *Western Electric News*, May 1914, pp. 12–13.

94   "To Office Boys—Past, Present and Future," May 1914, p. 36.

95   *Western Electric News*, May 1914, p. 12.

96   George Hopf to C. G. Stoll, July 31, 1947, 96 01 633 02.

97   Noble, *America by Design*, p. 170.

98   "Employment and Training of Engineering Graduates in Bell System Employment," May 1933, p. 3, 96 01 633 02.

99   J. W. Dietz, "Getting an Education with the Company," *Western Electric News*, June 1915, p. 2.

100   Joseph Juran, "Memoirs," vol. 2, chap. 2, p. 11.

101   Noble, *America by Design*, p. 51.

102   Ibid., p. 169.

103   Ibid.

104   Juran, "Memoirs," vol. 2, chap. 2, p. 11.

105   *Western Electric News*, May 1915, p. 27.

106   College-educated women began at lower rates than college-educated men. See "History of Personnel Practices at Western Electric—Education—1924," 91 03 134 01A.

107   *Western Electric News*, May 1915, p. 27.

108   Trigge was a transitional figure to the "welfare manager," who performed this service full-time in the personnel department. See Nikla Mandell, "A Human Contact Mechanism: Gender and the Development of Labor Relations, 1890–1930," Ph.D. diss., University of California, Davis, 1997.

109   "Service Awards: Mary A. Richardson," *Western Electric News*, Sept. 1919, p. 29.

110   Thayer to Frank W. Clark, Sept. 7, 1917, 94 05 242 01A.

111   Mira Wilkins, *The Emergence of Multinational Enterprise* (Cambridge, MA: Harvard University Press, 1970), pp. 212–213.

112   [Gerard Swope], "A Trip through Europe Just Ahead of the Crest of the War Wave," *Western Electric News*, Sept. 1914, p. 7.

113 Swope, "Autobiography," (Sept. 1944), pp. 30–31. Gerard Swope Papers, MIT, box 3.

114 "Foreign Notes," *Western Electric News*, January 1915, p. 24.

115 "Foreign Notes," *Western Electric News*, October 1914, p. 21; "The Month in Europe," *Western Electric News*, Nov. 1914, p. 7; "Organization Changes," *Western Electric News*, Nov. 1914, p. 7.

116 "Conditions in Europe Shown by Recent Cablegrams," *Western Electric News*, Nov. 1914, p. 9; "The Bombardment of Antwerp and the Flight to Holland," *Western Electric News*, Jan. 1916, p. 28.

117 "At Antwerp Again, We Walk In as the Germans Run Out," *Western Electric News*, March 1919, pp. 1–6.

118 Ibid.

119 Gerard Swope, "An Important Communication to All Western Electric Employees," *Western Electric News*, Oct. 1914, p. 1.

120 See, for example, "Belgian Soldiers in the Antwerp Factory," *Western Electric News*, Sept. 1914, p. 25; C. D. Minor, "Paris in War Time," *Western Electric News*, Oct. 1914, pp. 3–5; "When the Zeppelins Visited Antwerp," *Western Electric News*, Nov. 1914, p. 6; "On the Firing Line Near Liège," *Western Electric News*, Nov. 1914, p. 7; "The Month in Europe," *Western Electric News*, Dec. 1914, p. 7.

121 "G. H. Nash, C.B.E." *Western Electric News*, Jan.–Feb. 1920, p. 23.

122 *The Fortieth Milestone: Being a Record of Forty Years' Achievement of the Western Electric Company, Limited in the advancement of International Communication*, 1923, AT & T Archives, p. 35.

123 Ibid., p. 37

124 Memorandum. J. J. Carty to Theodore N. Vail, June 7, 1917, AT&T Archives, 125 05 02 15.

125 Gerard Swope Papers, Autobiography, MIT Archives, p. 23.

126 Ibid., p. 34.

127 Ibid., p. 54.

128 *Bell Statistical Manual, 1900–45*, p. 1307; "Share Owners, Employees and Manufacturing Facilities, 1892–1952," courtesy of George Wise.

129 Charles G. DuBois, "Our Place in the Sun: An Exposition of the Western Electric–Bell System Relationship," *Western Electric News*, May 1922, p. 2.

130 E[dgar] S. B[loom], H. P. D[avis] and D[avid] S[arnoff], Memorandum G, May 20, 1925, quoted in Archer, *Big Business and Radio* (New York: American Historical Company, 1939), pp. 219–220.

4. HEARD ROUND THE WORLD

1   "President DuBois Dedicates Hawthorne's Public Address System," *Western Electric News*, July 1924, p. 19.

2   Charles G. DuBois, "The Bell System—Its Constituent Companies and Their Relations to Each Other," *Western Electric News*, June 1913, pp. 1–4; Gerard Swope, "The Western Electric Company's Place in the Bell System," *Western Electric News*, Jan. 1914, pp. 7–9; H. B. Thayer, "The Western Electric Company and Its Relation to the Bell System," *Western Electric News*, Sept. 1916, pp. 1–5; Charles G. DuBois, "Our Place in the Sun," *Western Electric News*, May 1922, pp. 2–4;

3   DuBois to Vail, Nov. 11, 1913, 92 05 173 05.

4   John Brooks, *Telephone: The First Hundred Years* (New York: Harper & Row, 1976), p. 148.

5   Thayer to Gifford, April 29, 1924, 125 03 01 20.

6   Walter Gifford, "Bell Telephone Research Laboratories, Inc.," Sept. 19, 1924, 126 07 02 25.

7   "Remarks at Friday Luncheon, November 6, 1925," p. 3, 92 05 173 05.

8   "Bracken Is W. E. President," *Observer*, Oct.1947, 92 10 188 05.

9   Memorandum for the Press, Aug. 14, 1925, AT&T Archives 140 08 02 06.

10   DuBois to Gifford, Nov. 11, 1925, 92 05 173 05.

11   "Remarks at Friday Luncheon," p. 2.

12   Ibid, p. 3.

13   Ibid, p. 5.

14   Western Electric Company, *The President's Report for the Fiscal Year Ending December 31, 1912*, pp. 17–18.

15   Memo, Frank H. Lovette, Oct. 20, 1958, 96 02 664 02.

16   Eugene L. Cass and Frederick G. Zimmer, eds., *Man and Work in Society* (New York: Van Nostrand Reinhold Company, 1975).

17   Robert Jerich interview, Oct. 17, 1997, p. 4.

18   William H. Whyte Jr., *The Organization Man* (Garden City, NJ: Doubleday & Company, 1956), p. 27.

19   Loren Baritz, *The Servants of Power* (New York: John Wiley & Sons, 1965), pp. 26–27.

20   J. W. Dietz, "Getting an Education with the Company," *Western Electric News*, June 1915, p. 3; "Activities of the Hawthorne Men's Club," *Western Electric News*, May 1914, p. 19.

21   Personnel director Walter Dietz gave the test to fifteen engineering graduates, and reported that two of the fifteen scored well above the

others: Stanley Bracken (Nebraska, class of 1912), and Heine Beal (Purdue, class of 1914). Bracken became president of the company in 1947, and Beal served as vice president in the 1940s and 1950s. By then, the percentage of companies using psychological testing had risen from a handful to 75 percent. Baritz, *Servants of Power*, p. 38; Walter Dietz, *Walter Dietz Speaking* (Summit, NJ: privately published, 1972), p. 42; "Chronological Outline of Western Electric Personnel Activities," section &a ("Education"), 91 03 134, folder 1a; Kim McQuaid, "Corporate Liberalism in the American Business Community, 1920–40," *Business History Review* 52 (Autumn 1978): 345–357.

22 Dietz, *Walter Dietz Speaking*, p. 42.
23 David Noble, *America by Design* (New York: Oxford University Press, 1977), p. 207.
24 Ibid, pp. 214–215.
25 A. H. Dyon, "Annual Report—Testing Department, Employment Division, Industrial Relations Branch for Fiscal Year Ending December 29, 1923," p. 7, 91 03 134 02 01b.
26 Baritz, *Servants of Power*, p. 77.
27 Richard Gillespie, *Manufacturing Knowledge* (New York: Cambridge University Press, 1991), p. 38.
28 Ibid., p. 39.
29 Noble, *America by Design*, pp. 318–319; Baritz, *Servants of Power*, p. 74.
30 Gillespie, *Manufacturing Knowledge*, p. 42.
31 Bob Boardman, "The Relay Room Heard Round the World," *Western Electric News*, March–April 1964, pp. 40–43.
32 Elton Mayo, *The Human Problems of an Industrial Civilization*, (New York: Macmillan, 1933), p. 55.
33 Mayo, p. 69; Mary Volango interview, Oct. 14, 1997, p. 14.
34 Don Chipman, "Remembrances of Hawthorne Studies," *Microphone*, June–July 1985, p. 21.
35 Gillespie, *Manufacturing Knowledge*, p. 124.
36 Baritz, *Servants of Power*, p. 95.
37 Arnold S. Tannenbaum, "The Group in Organizations," in Victor H. Vroom and Edward L. Deci, *Management and Motivation* (New York: Penguin Books, 1979), p. 224.
38 Alan MacLean, "Occupational Stressors," in Cass and Zimmer, *Man and Work in Society* (New York: Van Nostrand Reinhold, 1975), pp. 178–179.
39 Alvin von Auw interview, Oct. 7, 1997, p. 14.
40 Gillespie, *Manufacturing Knowledge*, pp. 145–146.

41 F. J. Roethlisberger and William Dickson, *Management and the Worker* (Cambridge, MA: Harvard University Press, 1939), p. 203.
42 For a bibliography of their work, see Gillespie, *Manufacturing Knowledge*, pp. 274–276.
43 Richard Gillespie, *Manufacturing Knowledge: A History of the Hawthorne Experiments* (Cambridge: Cambridge University Press, 1991), p. 1.
44 Edward E. Lawler III, "Pay, Participation and Organizational Change," in Cass and Zimmer, *Man and Work in Society*, (New York: Van Nostrand Reinhold & Co., 1975), p. 137.
45 Gillespie, p. 209.
46 Fred E. Fiedler, "New Concepts for the Management of Managers," in Cass and Zimmer, *Man and Work in Society*, p. 207.
47 Victor Vroom, "Leadership Revisited," in Cass and Zimmer, *Man and Work in Society*, p. 220.
48 Jay Lorsch, "Managers, Behavioral Scientists, and the Tower of Babel," in Cass and Zimmer *Man and Work in Society*, p. 246.
49 Baritz, *Servants of Power*, pp. 77, 107.
50 Gillespie, *Manufacturing Knowledge*, p. 217.
51 Baritz, pp. 105–110.
52 William J. Dickson and F. J. Roethlisberger, *Counseling in an Organization* (Boston: Harvard University, 1966), pp. 5–7.
53 Sanford Jacoby,"Employee Attitude Testing at Sears, Roebuck and Company, 1938–1960," *Business History Review* 60 (Winter 1986): 602.
54 "Western Electric News—1932," p. 38.
55 "Western Electric Builds in Baltimore," *Western Electric News*, Dec. 1928, pp. 3–4.
56 Carroll Dulaney, "Day By Day," *The Pointer*, Oct. 1938, p. 4.
57 "Western Electric Is 'Playground That Went to Work' Back in '29," *Baltimore American*, March 4, 1951.
58 "How Western Electric Does Move," pp. 1–2, Oct. 1928, 93 01 194 05.
59 Transcript of Broadcast, 2–2:30 p.m., Wednesday, October 19 [1938], p. 6, 93 01 194 02.
60 "How Western Electric Does Move," p. 3.
61 *The Literary Digest*, Oct. 31, 1936, pp. 5–6.
62 N. R. Danielian, *AT&T: The Story of Industrial Conquest* (New York: The Vanguard Press, 1939), pp. 200–203.
63 Alvin von Auw, *Heritage and Destiny*, pp. 54–56.
64 Alvin von Auw interview, Oct. 7, 1997, p. 21.
65 *Bell System Statistical Manual*, 1900–1945, p. 701.

66 Joseph Juran interview, Sept. 5, 1996.
67 Roethlisberger and Dickson, *Management and the Worker*, p. 340.
68 Ibid., p. 341.
69 Ibid.
70 Ray Russ interview, Oct. 24, 1997.
71 Cuthbert Cuthbertson interview, Oct. 27, 1997, pp. 4–7.
72 Robert Yaverick interview, July 15, 1996.
73 S. Dan Daniels, "The Radio Division," typescript, 1944, pp. 1–6, 91-2-131-05. As an interesting sidelight: while the throat microphones were adopted by most of the Allied forces, they did not work for the British, who formed their words so high in the mouth that the throat microphone could not pick up the sounds.
74 *The Western Front* (ca. 1943), pp. 16–17.
75 Robert Buderi, *The Invention That Changed the World* (New York: Simon & Schuster, 1996), p. 28.
76 Henry E. Guerlac, *Radar in World War II* (Los Angeles: Tomash Publishers, 1987), p. 691; "Radar—A Production Triumph," *Western Electric Oscillator*, Dec. 1945, pp. 6–8, 42–43; Western Electric, *Annual Report*, 1945, p. 4.
77 "Citation to Accompany the Award of the Medal for Merit to Clarence Griffith Stoll," July 18, 1946, 92 10 188 05.
78 Alexander J. Allen, "Western Electric's Backward Step," *Opportunity: Journal of Negro Life*, July–Sept. 1944, p. 108.
79 Sandy M. Shoemaker, " 'We Shall Overcome, Someday': The Equal Rights Movement in Baltimore, 1935–1942," *Maryland Historical Magazine*, Fall 1994, p. 264.
80 Ibid., p. 268.
81 Byron Fairchild and Jonathan Grossman, *The Army and Industrial Manpower* (Washington, DC: The War Department, 1959), p. 160.
82 Ibid.
83 "500 Negroes Oppose Strike," *Baltimore Sun*, Oct. 18, 1943.
84 Fairchild and Grossman, *Army and Industrial Manpower*, pp. 160–161.
85 "WLB Warned of Possible Race Rioting," *Baltimore Sun*, Dec. 3, 1943.
86 Allen, "Western Electric's Backward Step," p. 140.
87 Ibid, p. 162.
88 "Army Takes over Five Strike-Bound Plants of Western Electric," *Baltimore Sun*, Dec. 20, 1943.
89 Allen, "Western Electric's Backward Step," p. 142.
90 Maybelle Rodgers interviews with Stephen Adams, February 16 and 19, 1998.

5. DEFENSE AND SOCIAL CONTRACTS

1   John Brooks, *Telephone: The First Hundred Years* (New York: Harper & Row, 1976), pp. 233–234.

2   "Bell Telephone Laboratories," *Western Electric Oscillator* 12, pp. 12–14, 350.

3   W. S. Magill to record, "Conference with Nippon Electric Representatives Regarding Vacuum Tube Quality and Repeater Tube Production at the Tomagawa Plant," Oct. 7 and 14, 1946, 299 09 02 04.

4   Sarasohn, et al., for the record, "The Need for a Management Training Course in the Communications Manufacturing Industry," Aug. 6, 1949, 299 09 02 04.

5   Necah Stewart Furman, *Sandia National Laboratories: The Postwar Decade* (Albuquerque: University of New Mexico Press, 1990), 333.

6   Ibid., 332.

7   Harry Truman to Wilson, May 13, 1949, AT&T Archives, 127 03 02 01.

8   Wilson to Lilienthal, July 1, 1949, 127 03 02 01.

9   "Chronology of Events Leading to Execution of Contract," quoted in Furman, *Sandia National Laboratories*, 344.

10 "Testimony of Mervin Kelly," House Committee on the Judiciary, Antitrust Subcommittee, *Part II—volume I, American Telephone & Telegraph Co., 2013*, 85th Cong., 2d sess.

11 C. E. Wilson to Herbert Brownell, July 10, 1953, reproduced in House Committee on the Judiciary, Antitrust Subcommittee, *Part II—volume I, American Telephone & Telegraph Co., 2029–30*, 85th Cong., 2d Sess.

12 Joseph Juran, "Made in USA: A Renaissance in Quality," *Harvard Business Review*, July–August 1993, pp. 43–44.

13 Ibid.

14 R. A. Pook, "A Story of Hawthorne in Years 1919–1934," *Microphone*, June–July 1985, p. 10.

15 Joseph Juran interview, Oct. 8, 1997, pp. 25–27.

16 Joseph Juran interview, Sept. 5, 1996, p. 3.

17 Leslie D. Simon, "Western Electric Research Center," ca. 1963–1964, 299 09 02 05.

18 Wayne Weeks interview, September 15, 1997, p. 39.

19 Ibid., p. 3.

20 Ibid., p. 34.

21 Alvin von Auw interview, Oct. 7, 1997.

22 Annual Report for 1958, p. 18.

23 Wayne Weeks interview, Sept. 15, 1997.

24 Brooks, *Telephone*, p. 218.

25 Gayley to Adams, Jan. 7, 1998.
26 Ibid.
27 Arnold R. Isaacs, "Hoffa Visits, Seeks Votes at Factory," *Baltimore Sun,* Oct. 12, 1963.
28 Horace, Ayres, "Teamsters Union May Contest Election Loss," *Baltimore Evening Sun,* Oct, 17, 1963.
29 "Police Guard Labor Leader Here Following Offer of Bribe, Threats," *Baltimore Evening Sun,* Oct. 15, 1963.
30 Alvin von Auw interview, Oct. 7, 1997, pp. 43–44.
31 Arnold R. Isaacs, "Western Electric Workers Vote Down Teamsters' Bid," *Baltimore Sun,* Oct. 17, 1963.
32 Brooks, *Telephone,* p. 285.
33 "Statement by Western Electric Company," Jan. 12, 1962, 189 02 02 03.
34 "Statement by Western Electric Company," Jan. 12, 1962, 189 02 02 03.
35 Richard L. Tobin, "Ma Bell's Long-Distance Runner," *Saturday Review,* Jan. 22, 1972, p. 59.
36 *Equal Opportunity in Federal Government on Federal Contracts: Executive Order 10925 Establishing the President's Committee on Equal Employment Opportunity,* March 6, 1961, p. 2.
37 "Joint Statement on 'Plan for Progress,'" July 12, 1961, 189 02 02 03.
38 "Evolution of the Plan for Progress," p. 3, 189 02 02 03.
39 "Special Meeting, Bell System Presidents: Equal Employment Opportunity," Aug. 1, 1963, 189 02 01 04.
40 Norman Rubin, interview with Stephen Adams, Apr. 3, 1998.
41 Norman Rubin and Alvin von Auw interviews, Apr. 3, 1998.
42 "Vice Presidents Meeting," July 30, 1963, 91 07 244 01A
43 Maybelle Rodgers interview, Feb. 19, 1998.
44 James Harwood to Romnes, Sept. 28, 1961, 189 02 02 03.
45 "Equal Employment Conference, Jan. 27, 1964, P. A. Gorman," p. 6, 189 02 01 05.
46 "Vice President's Meeting," July 30, 1963, p. 4, 91 07 244 01A
47 Wayne Weeks interview, Sept. 15, 1997.
48 Alvin von Auw interview, Oct. 7, 1997.
49 "Economic Breakthrough: Western Electric Plant Will Be Largest in History of the City," *Shreveport Magazine,* March 1965, p. 17.
50 Floyd Boswell interview, Dec. 22, 1997.
51 Paul A. Gorman, "Why W. E. Is Happy with Its Choice," *Shreveport Magazine,* Feb. 1967, p. 20.
52 Ibid, p. 37.

53 Ibid.

54 Theodore V. Purcell and Gerald F. Cavanagh, *Blacks in the Industrial World* (New York: The Free Press, 1972), p. 51.

55 David J. Garrow, *Bearing the Cross: Martin Luther King and the Southern Christian Leadership Conference* (New York: W. Morrow, 1986), p. 528.

56 Ibid., pp. 517–518.

57 Bob Jerich interview, Apr. 6, 1998; Garrow, p. 529.

58 Garrow, p. 549.

59 Jerich interview, Oct. 17, 1997.

60 "Hawthorne Hosts Suppliers' Opportunity Day," *The Microphone*, Oct. 1968, p. 4.

61 "George Johnsen's Gold Oilcan Award Has Greased Thousands of Rusty Doors," *Minority Supplier News*, Oct.–Nov. 1980, p. 2.

62 Val Jordan interview, Oct. 15, 1997, p. 61.

63 Ibid, p. 67.

64 Ibid., pp. 61–62, 72.

65 "Special Meeting, Bell System Presidents, Aug. 1, 1963," p. 1, 189 02 01 04; *1969: A Year of Progress: Summary Report on Equal Employment Opportunity Activities and Programs at Western Electric Company*, p. 1, 107 10 02 644 01.

66 *A Year of Progress*, p. 1; "Special Meeting," Aug. 1, 1963, p. 1.

67 Robert Cohen and Robert Rudolph, "Western Electric Loses Appeal in Sex Bias Suit," *The Star-Ledger*, Oct. 16, 1979.

68 *New York Times*, June 8, 1980, p. 53.

69 H. I. Romnes, "Excerpts from Closing Remarks, Western Electric Company Conference," May 19, 1961, 92 09 186 04B.

6. A SHOCK TO THE SYSTEM

1 Marx interview, Oct. 1, 1997, p. 11.

2 Hierarchy was a common American approach to big business in the twentieth century. Even Dale Carnegie, the master of self-help for the business world, acknowledged the ubiquitous hierarchy in his most famous training session. Attendees excitedly chant: "There are people in the ranks who will stay in the ranks. Why? Because they don't have what it takes to get things done."

3 See Sanford Jacoby, *Modern Manors* (Princeton, NJ: Princeton University Press, 1997).

4 Luncheon, Oct. 16, 1997, p. 45; Marx interview, Oct. 30, 1997, p. 3.

5 "Talk from the Tower," *WE*, Mar./Apr. 1974, p. 27.

6 Ibid., p. 29.

7 Val Jordan interview, Oct. 15, 1997, p. 67.
8 Ibid., p. 107.
9 "Talk from the Tower," p. 29.
10 Ibid., p. 27.
11 Val Jordan interview, p. 91.
12 Ibid., pp. 91–92.
13 "Factory within a Factory," *WE* 33, no.1 (Jan./Feb. 1981): 14–17.
14 Chick Gayley interview, May 5, 1998.
15 Don Procknow interview, Dec. 19, 1985.
16 John Thomas O'Neill interview, Oct. 26, 1997.
17 "Upbeat at Hawthorne. Inside Those Walls Things Are Changing," *WE*, Feb. 1970, pp. 2–5.
18 Harvey G. Mehlhouse, "1971 and Beyond," *WE*, Jan./Feb. 1971, pp. 2–5.
19 Harvey G. Mehlhouse, "1971 and Beyond," *WE*, Jan./Feb. 1971, pp. 2–5; Robert Farrell, "Atlanta—Where Things Happen," *WE*, Apr. 1972, pp. 24–29; Joe Gazdak, "The Dallas Plant," *WE*, Dec. 1973/Jan. 1974, pp. 24–29.
20 "Occupation Innovation," *WE*, Mar./Apr. 1974, p. 2.
21 Dick O'Donnell, "WE's Resident Seers," *WE*, Jan./Feb. 1971, pp. 6–9.
22 Larry Seifert interview, July 28, 1997, p 7.
23 Don Procknow interview, Mar. 24, 1997, p. 29.
24 Western Electric Annual Report for 1975, p. 1.
25 Lawrence Seifert interview, July 28, 1997.
26 "Forsgate Triumph," *WE*, Nov. 1973, pp. 12, 14–17; Larry Seifert interview, July 28, 1997.
27 John Mayo interview, May 28, 1998; David Roessner et al., *The Role of NSF's Support of Engineering in Enabling Technological Innovation* (Arlington, VA: SRI International, 1998), p. 30.
28 Larry Seifert interview, July 28, 1997.
29 "Fighting Bell: Suit to Split up AT&T Bears Out Ford Pledge of Antitrust Firmness," *Wall Street Journal*, Nov. 21, 1974; Sanford L. Jacobs, "AT&T's Western Electric and Long Lines are Prime Focus of Justice Agency Suit," *Wall Street Journal*, Nov. 21, 1974.
30 Quoted in Howard M. Anderson, "Will the Big Suit Against AT&T Be a Bonanza For Independent Manufacturers?" *Telephony*, Sept. 15, 1975, p. 78.
31 Procknow interview, Mar. 24, 1997.
32 O'Neill interview, Sept. 26, 1997, p. 65.
33 O'Neill interview, Oct. 1, 1997; Marx interview Oct. 1, 1997.
34 Procknow interview, March 24, 1997.

35 View from Broadway," *WE*, Dec. 1972/Jan. 1973, pp. 2–5.
36 Marx interview, Oct. 30, 1997, p. 40.
37 Weeks interview, Sept. 15, 1997; Marx interview, Oct. 30, 1997.
38 Marx interview, Nov. 13, 1997.
39 Dan Stanzione, May 13 advisory board meeting.
40 "ESS Goes Compact," *WE*, Jan./Feb. 1971, p. 10; Richard O'Donnell, "Summing Up—The Seventies," *WE*, March/April 1980, pp. 14–18.
41 Charles Brown Memo to Messrs. deButts, Ellinghaus Cashel, Bolger, Nurnberger, Olson, Garlinghouse, and Von Auw, Sept. 15, 1977, 294 04 02 02.
42 Arthur D. Little, Inc., *World Telecommunications, Vol. I.: Overview and Technological Trends*, pp. 67–68; H. G. Alles, "The Telecommunication Switching Networks," *IEEE Transactions on Communications*, July 1979, p. 1080; J. T. Combot and N. Epstein, "Introduction of Digital Switching to the Local Network," *IEEE Transactions on Communications*, July 1979, p. 1056.
43 O'Neill interview, Sept. 26, 1997, p. 83.
44 Ibid., p. 84.
45 Larry Seifert interview, July 28, 1997.
46 Marx interview, Nov. 13, 1997, p. 16.
47 Ibid., p. 22.
48 Procknow interview, Mar. 24, 1997, p. 26.
49 Marx interview, Nov. 13, 1997, p. 17
50 Ibid., p. 20.
51 "The View from AT&T Technologies," *AT&T Outlook*, Feb. 29, 1984, pp. 4–5.
52 Procknow interview, Mar. 24, 1997, p. 25.
53 "The View from AT&T Technologies," *AT&T Outlook*, Feb. 29, 1984, pp. 4–5.

7. AFTER THE WESTERN

1 "Click! Ma Is Ringing Off," *Time*, November 21, 1983, p. 60.
2 Marx interview, Dec. 12, 1997.
3 John O'Neill interview, Sept. 26, 1997, pp. 77–78.
4 Ibid., p. 77.
5 John O'Neill interview, Oct. 18, 1987.
6 "Quality Means Customer Delight in Manufacturing," *Focus. Celebrating Quality: How AT&T Won Two Baldrige Awards*, 1992, pp. 4–5.
7 Robert Allen interview, Dec. 8, 1997, pp. 7–8.

8 AT&T press release, Dec. 21, 1988; L. W. Tucker, "A Company Affiliation in Japan," *Western Electric News*, October 1921, pp. 9–10.
9 "Special Report, Behind AT&T's Change at the Top," *Business Week*, Nov. 6, 1978, p. 128.
10 Robert Allen interview, Dec. 8, 1997, pp. 44–45.
11 Robert Allen interview, June 16, 1998, p. 12.
12 Ibid., p. 24.

CONCLUSION

1 Stephanie N. Mehta, "Soaring Lucent Defies Wall Street's Estimates," *Wall Street Journal*, July 23, 1998, p. B4
2 N. R. Danielian, *AT&T: The Story of Industrial Conquest* (New York: The Vanguard Press, 1939), p. 367.
3 Ibid.

BIBLIOGRAPHICAL ESSAY

PRIMARY SOURCES

A principal theme running throughout most of Western Electric's history is the extent to which its possibilities were circumscribed by the desires of its parent company (Western Union, then AT&T). Therefore, for the purposes of this book, it is fitting that the abundant documents and publications of both Western Electric and its parent are housed at the AT&T Archives.

The archives include correspondence files, biographical files, speeches, manuscripts, articles, and memoirs by and about major Western Electric figures. The records from the 1880s to the 1920s are particularly abundant, ranging from the letterpress books of outgoing correspondence of Bell's presidents and general managers to the minutes of Western Electric board meetings. These documents reveal conflicting agendas: its wish to be the "department store of electrical apparatus" and the desire of its Bell parent for Western to concentrate on the telephone. Similar conflicts appear in the minutes and reports of Bell System switchboard and cable conferences from 1887 to 1892; of numerous subsequent engineering, sales, and general conferences; and in the reports of the Bell Engineering Department from 1885 to 1923.

The archives also have a number of internal company publications. *The Western Electric News* (1912–1932) is a bountiful source of biographical information, updates on overseas ventures, reports on new product development, and accounts of the company's educational, social, athletic, and entertainment programs. It offers a valuable window onto the world of Western's less prominent people. *WE* (1949–1983) has a more centralized focus, leaving more local stories to the *Hawthorne Microphone*, the *Kearnygram*, the *Pointer*, and other plant publications. *Bell Telephone Magazine* offers AT&T's perspective.

Western Electric represents a significant case study in business/government relations, both as manufacturer for the regulated Bell System and as key government contractor. Sometimes those two roles overlapped, as in the early 1950s, when the Defense Department protected one of its principal contractors by lobbying the Justice Department not to pry Western Electric loose from AT&T. The archives have a set of the documents assembled for that 1956 antitrust case, as well as those gathered for the 1935 investigation by the Federal Communications Commission and for the 1983 antitrust case. The most helpful of these collections is the set collected for the 1956 case, when lawyers from AT&T's firm (Dewey, Ballantine) took great pains to reconstruct Western's history.

Western Electric's stock was never publicly traded; indeed, after 1912, AT&T owned more than 95 percent of it. That was when the government began to scrutinize the Bell System. Therefore, instead of trying to show Wall Street how much money it was making, Western spent considerable effort showing how *little* money it made in comparison to other electrical manufacturers (GE and Westinghouse). The archives contain those comparisons, as well as quite detailed company financials among external and internal annual reports from 1880 until 1983.

Various consulting firms investigated the company's activities. In the 1960s, Western Electric commissioned McKinsey to determine how efficiently the company was handling its various operations. In the 1970s, the Federal Communications Commission hired Touche-Ross to study the efficiency of Western Electric's operations, in an attempt to determine the fairness of rates charged and profits earned by the company. The archives house copies of both the McKinsey and the Touche-Ross reports.

Western Electric's large scale, and its responses to it, helped to embody the great irony of twentieth-century quality control: whereas we associate nineteenth-century quality with the smallest-scale operations, the twentieth-century quality revolution began at one of the world's largest-scale manufacturing operations. The big breakthrough was Walter Shewhart's "control chart," which began the modern quality movement and spawned a group of experts who spread the gospel around the world. The archives have the videotape collection "A History of Quality Control and Assurance at AT&T: 1920–1970," featuring interviews with W. Edwards Deming, Joseph Juran, and others who began their careers working at Western Electric and/or with Dr. Shewhart.

In the early twentieth century, social scientists descended on Western Electric to collect data and test theories of industrial psychology and sociology. The most noted study involved the Hawthorne experiments, in which the National Research Council set out to test the impact of lighting levels on output and instead found that attention paid to workers played a greater role than working conditions per se on productivity. The archives have a complete record of the Hawthorne experiments.

Western Electric was the captive supplier for Western Union from 1872 to 1879. The Western Union Papers at the Smithsonian feature relations with Western Electric. The Smithsonian also has selected papers of Western Electric cofounder Elisha Gray.

ORAL HISTORIES

The Western Electric collection of documents is less bountiful in the 1930s and after. Fortunately, many retirees and other Western Electric veterans – from various levels of the organization, and with a wide variety of experiences – agreed to speak with us. The following interviews were taped and transcribed:

Oral History Subject	Date(s) of Interview
Robert Allen	6/16/98
Cuthbert Cuthbertson	10/27/97
Helen Grefe	12/3/97
Robert Jerich	10/17/97

Oral History Subject	Date(s) of Interview
Val Jordan	10/15/97
Joseph Juran	10/8/97
William Marx	10/1/97; 10/30/97; 11/13/97; 12/12/97
John T. O'Neill	9/26/97; 10/1/97
Don Procknow	3/13/97; 3/24/97
Ray Russ	10/24/97
Larry Seifert	7/28/97
Mary Volango	10/14/97
Alvin von Auw	10/7/97
Wayne Weeks	9/15/97

SECONDARY SOURCES

Governmental scrutiny of the company and the attention devoted to it by social scientists combine with the company's position as the Bell System's captive supplier to form an odd distinction: Western Electric was one of America's most observed but least well-known large manufacturers. This is the first full-length history of the Zeliglike Western Electric.

On the other hand, many books have been written about AT&T and the Bell System. John Brooks's *Telephone: The First Hundred Years* (New York: Harper & Row, 1976) offers an excellent overview of the Bell context in which Western was operating. Peter Temin and Louis Galambos also present that context, with an emphasis on the later twentieth century, in *The Fall of the Bell System* (New York: Cambridge University Press, 1987). Ithiel de Sola Pool, ed., *The Social Impact of the Telephone* (Cambridge, MA: MIT Press, 1977), is a collection of essays that reveal the wider ramifications of Western Electric's innovations. A critical view of the Bell System – with extensive reference to Western Electric's role – is offered by N. R. Danielian, *AT&T: The Story of Industrial Conquest* (New York: The Vanguard Press, 1939). Financial aspects are presented in J. Warren Stehman, *The Financial History of the American Telephone and Telegraph Company* (Cambridge, MA: Houghton Mifflin, 1925). A brief in-house

254

book on Western is Albert Iardella, *Western Electric and the Bell System* (New York, 1964).

Western Electric did not spring full-grown from the brow of Bell; rather, it was older than its "parent." Born in the midst of the nineteenth-century communications revolution, Western straddled the days of the preeminence of the telegraph and the early days of the telephone. The telegraph environment is described in *The Telegrapher* and Western Union's *Journal of the Telegraph*, and in Edwin Gabler, *The American Telegrapher: A Social History, 1860–1900* (New Brunswick, NJ: Rutgers University Press, 1988). The personalities of the industry are profiled in James D. Reid, *The Telegraph in America* (New York: Derby Brothers, 1879), and Matthew Josephson, *Edison: A Biography* (New York: McGraw-Hill, 1959).

The Western Electric story is a classic case of vertical integration. By treating vertical integration more as a process than as an isolated event, and by doing so from the point of view of the acquired company, our book will fill a large gap in the literature. Business historians have tended to focus on the long-term effects of vertical integration, as Alfred D. Chandler Jr. does in *The Visible Hand* (Cambridge, MA: Harvard University Press, 1977). George David Smith's *The Anatomy of a Business Strategy: Bell, Western Electric and The Origins of the American Telephone Industry* (Baltimore: The Johns Hopkins University Press, 1985) deals with Bell's acquisition of Western Electric. Smith focuses on events of the 1870s and 1880s, and writes from the point of view of Bell rather than that of Western Electric. The centerpiece of his book is the acquisition agreement and what led up to it; we have explored the subsequent process of integration, which took decades to complete.

Developments at the turn of the century in the Bell System are the focus of Robert Garnet's *The Telephone Enterprise* (Baltimore: The Johns Hopkins University Press, 1985), Ken Lipartito's *The Bell System and Regional Business* (Baltimore: The Johns Hopkins University Press, 1989), and Neil Wasserman's *From Invention to Innovation* (Baltimore: The Johns Hopkins University Press, 1985). All three help to explain why Western and Bell finally found it necessary to complete the vertical integration process during the first decade of the twentieth century. Garnet and Lipartito focus on the relationships between AT&T and the operating companies, which finally succumbed to the standardization AT&T had long sought and Western had come to embrace. Wasserman describes how Western brought research expertise inside the company in response to the challenge of long distance. The long-distance story is also told in Hugh Aitken, *The Continuous Wave* (Princeton, NJ: Princeton University Press, 1985). Lipartito describes the significance to Bell System employees of automatic switching technology, in "When Women Were Switches: Technology, Work and Gender in the Telephone Industry, 1890–1920," *American Historical Review* 99 (1984): 1074–1111.

Prior to the 1925 establishment of Bell Laboratories, Western Electric and Bell had separate research groups. The best starting point on research at Western Electric are M. D. Fagen's internally published multivolume set, *A History of Engineering and Science in the Bell System* (1975–1985), and Leonard Reich's *The Making of American Industrial Research* (New York: Cambridge University Press, 1985). For the context in which research development began at Western Electric, Paul Israel, *From Machine Shop to Industrial Laboratory* (Baltimore: The Johns Hopkins University Press, 1992) is invaluable, as is Bernard Carlson, *Innovation as a Social Process* (New York: Cambridge University Press, 1991).

During the company's early years in the Bell System, it led a double life of customizer and mass producer. Production of switchboards – the company's bellwether product – was a custom affair (each exchange seeming to have its own quirks), whereas the company's other products, such as cable and wire, could be mass-produced. The extent to which nineteenth-century customized production shifted to twentieth-century mass production is featured in Alfred D. Chandler, *Strategy and Structure* (Cambridge, MA: MIT Press, 1962); Thomas P. Hughes, *American Genesis* (New York: Viking Press, 1989), John K. Brown, *The Baldwin Locomotive Works, 1831–1915* (Baltimore: The Johns Hopkins University Press, 1985); David Hounshell, *From the American System to Mass Production* (Baltimore: The Johns Hopkins University Press, 1989); and Philip Scranton, "Diversity in Diversity: Flexible Production and American Industrialization, 1880–1930," *Business History Review* 65 (1991): 27–90.

The impact of mass production on blue-collar workers is assessed by Daniel Nelson, *Managers and Workers* (Madison: University of Wisconsin Press, 1975), and David Montgomery, *The Fall of the House of Labor* (New York: Oxford University Press, 1989). Margery Davies, *Women's Place Is at the Typewriter: Office Work and Office Workers, 1890–1930* (Philadelphia: Temple University Press, 1982), and Olivier Zunz, *Making America Corporate, 1870–1920* (Chicago: University of Chicago Press, 1990), describe the changing world for pink-collar and white-collar workers. Lizabeth Cohen details the backgrounds of Western Electric's workers in *Making a New Deal: Industrial Workers in Chicago, 1919–33* (New York: Cambridge University Press, 1990), and John Schacht discusses their union activities in *The Making of Telephone Unionism, 1920–1947* (New Brunswick, NJ: Rutgers University Press, 1985). Sanford Jacoby describes the context for Bell System labor relations in *Employing Bureaucracy: Managers, Unions and the Transformation of Work in American Industry, 1900–1945* (New York: Columbia University Press, 1985). William Julius Wilson describes the consequences of plant shutdown on the community surrounding the Hawthorne plant in *When Work Disappears* (New York: Knopf, 1996).

Until 1925, Western Electric distributed electrical apparatus, and its brethren included General Electric and Westinghouse. Harold Passer's *The Electrical Manufacturers, 1875–1900* (Cambridge, MA: Harvard University Press, 1953), Thomas Hughes's *Networks of Power* (Baltimore: The Johns Hopkins University Press, 1983), and the journal *Electrical World* all provide industry context. On General Electric and Western Electric, we used: David Loth, *Swope of GE* (New York: Simon and Schuster, 1958), George Wise, "General Electric's Century" (unpublished MS); and John Winthrop Hammond, *Men and Volts* (New York: J. B. Lippincott Company, 1941). Mira Wilkins analyzes overseas manufacture by American companies, including Western Electric, in *The Emergence of Multinational Enterprise* (Cambridge, MA: Harvard University Press, 1970), and *The Maturing of*

Multinational Enterprise (Cambridge, MA: Harvard University Press, 1974). Gerald Brock's overview, *The Telecommunications Industry: The Dynamics of Market Structure* (Cambridge, MA: Harvard University Press, 1981), was also useful.

The field of industrial psychology was still in embryonic form when Western Electric began to employ psychological testing (before World War I). The context in which social scientists came to industry is discussed by Loren Baritz, in *Servants of Power: A History of the Use of Social Science in American Industry* (New York: John Wiley & Sons, 1965) and by David Noble in *America by Design* (New York: Oxford University Press, 1977). Both devote considerable attention to Western Electric. The results of the Hawthorne experiments were summarized in F. J. Roethisberger and William Dickson, *Management and the Worker* (Cambridge, MA: Harvard University Press, 1939); Elton Mayo, *The Human Problems of an Industrial Civilization* (New York: Macmillan, 1933); and Richard Gillespie, *Manufacturing Knowledge* (New York: Cambridge University Press, 1991). Eugene L. Cass and Frederick G. Zimmer, eds., *Man and Work in Society* (New York: Van Nostrand Reinhold Company, 1975) includes papers presented by leading academicians on the fiftieth anniversary of the original Hawthorne experiments.

Government regulation and contracting shaped Western Electric's world for most of the twentieth century. An excellent overview of American business/government relations is Louis Galambos and Joseph Pratt, *The Rise of the Corporate Commonwealth: United States Business and Public Policy in the Twentieth Century* (New York: Basic Books, 1988). For the World War I era, we used Robert Cuff, *The War Industries Board: Business-Government Relations During World War I* (Baltimore: The Johns Hopkins University Press, 1973), and for World War II, Harold G. Vatter, *The U.S. Economy in World War II* (New York: Columbia University Press, 1985).

After World War II, Western Electric exported quality expertise to Japan. The American occupation force asked the company to assist the Civil Communications Section (CCS) in rebuilding Japan's communications system. The CCS arranged for Western and Bell Labs engineers to teach management fundamentals to a generation of Japanese equipment manufacturing executives, paving the way for Deming and Juran to teach quality to the same group. Then, later, the Japanese managers showed the world how valuable those lessons had been. The Western Electric–Japan story is told by Lloyd Dobyns and Clare Crawford Mason in *Quality or Else* (Boston: Houghton Mifflin Company, 1991), and by Kenneth Hopper in "Creating Japan's New Industrial Management: The Americans as Teachers," *Human Resources Management*, Summer 1982, pp. 13–34.

Unless otherwise indicated, all document references are from the AT&T Archives.

INDEX

Barton, Enos
early life and business experience, 19–22
goal to expand and diversify Western's business scope, 65–7, 85
idea for European telephone business, 48
management style of, 72–3, 76, 215–16
on organized labor, 81
partnership with Gray, 25–9
partnership with Shawk, 25–6
paternalism of, 96
as president of Western Electric (1886–1908), 6, 54–7, 62
proposed construction of Hawthorne plant (1902), 82–3, 85
as secretary/treasurer of Western Electric, 30
Becker, Leo, 168–9
Beilfuss, Wanda, 118–19, 122
Bell, Alexander Graham
demonstrates telephone (1876), 1, 62
interest in duplex telegraph, 36
interest in transmission of speech, 37
knowledge of human speech physiology, 36
lawsuit to protect patents of, 39
patent approval (1876), 37
Bellamy, Edward, 62
Bell Laboratories
established (1925), 115
invention of transistor (1947), 161, 189
Lucent's research arm, vii
optical fiber research and development, 195
outcome of 1974 antitrust suit (1982), 12, 202
Western Electric research department as part of, 121–2
Bell regional operating companies (Baby Bells), divested from AT&T, 205
Bell System
benefit and insurance plan, 90–2, 96
contribution to Cold War defense, 155
government antitrust suit against (1949), 148–50, 156–60
integration of Western Electric into, 47
Purchased Products Division, 196
Western Electric as manufacturing department of, 3
Bell Telephone Company
See also International Bell Telephone Company
action to protect Bell's patents, 39
becomes AT&T (1899), 44

display at World's Columbian Exposition, Chicago (1893) 63–4
export operation (1880), 48
integration of Western Electric into, 47
introduces long-distance service (1893), 63–4
licensed manufacturers, 42
relationship with Western Electric, 3
use agreement with Western Union (1879), 40–1
Bell Telephone Manufacturing Company, 48
Bergson, Herbert, 157
Blanz, Robert, 206
Blau, Robert T., 205
Bloom, Edgar, 130
Bond, Julian, 174
Boswell, Floyd, 178
Brown, Charles, 202
Brownell, Herbert, 157
Buckley, Oliver, 156
Burchard, Anson, 107
Butterfield, Ron, 203

Capone, Al, 161
Carnegie, Andrew, 16–17
Carty, John, 1–4
Caton, J. D., 27
Chicago Economic Development Corporation (CEDC), 180
Chicago Edison Company, 30
Chicago Inter-State Industrial Exposition (1873), 33
Chicago Purchasing Council, 180
Chicago Telephone Company, 30
Chicago World's Fair (1893), 60–2
Chipman, Don, 125
Churchill, C. H., 23
Cicero, Illinois
growth in population, 83
King's plan to march in (1966), 179
location of Western's Hawthorne plant, 55, 80, 83
civil rights
See also equal opportunity
government policy imposed on Western Electric, 11–12, 151
policy of equal opportunity, 170–2, 216
Clark, Kenneth, 175
Clark, Tom, 148
"click" test, 58

Kingsbury, Nathan, 89
Kreps, Juanita, 182
Kyes, Roger, 158
Kyriazi, Cleo, 182

La Blanc, Robert E., 211
labor relations
  at Clinton Street plant, 81
  at Hawthorne plant, 168
  strike at Kearny plant (1946), 167–8
  strike at Point Breeze plant (1943), 142–5
Lawler, Edward, 128
Leavitt, Harold, 118
Lewis, Charles, 52
Lilienthal, David, 157
Long, Russell, 177–9
Lorsch, Jay, 118, 128
loudspeakers, 112, 136
Lucent Technologies
  autonomy of, 213
  Bell Labs as part of, 213
  components of, 211
  evolution of, 217
  personnel and employment policies, 213
  slogan of, 184
  spin-off from AT&T, vii
Lynch, Stafford, 30

MacArthur, Douglas, 152–3
McClellan, George, 18
McGinn, Rich, 210
Madden, Oscar, 42
management, scientific
  separation of planning from execution, 75–6
  time-and-motion studies, 75
  at Western Electric, 76
manufacturing
  Albright's approach using functional, 78–9
  change in nature of (1970s and 80s), 187
  methods for millimeter waveguide technology, 194
  requirements of electronic production, 189
  use of scientific management in, 75–6
  Western Electric European plants, 104
  Western Electric's overseas operations, 214
  Western Electric's role in, 215
Marx, William, 184, 198, 202–3, 206, 210

Massachusetts Institute of Technology (MIT), 121
Mayo, Elton, 126, 127
Mehlhouse, Harvey, 188
Menninger, Walter, 118
microphones, 136
microwave communications network, Saudi Arabia, 209
microwave transmission, 194–5
Millikan, Robert, 4
millimeter waveguide technology, 194–5
mining detector, 106
Mississippi Valley Printing Telegraph Company, 17
Monteforte, Lou, 209
Moore, George, 191
Moore's Law, 191, 195
Morgan, J. P., 88
Morse system duplexing modification (1872), 34

Nash, George, 105–7
Nash Fish submarine detector, 106
National Association of Corporation Schools (NACS), 75
National Broadcasting Company (NBC), 110–11
National Pole Company, 97
National Research Council (NRC)
  Committee on Industrial Lighting, 121
  experiment at Western Electric Hawthorne plant (1924–33), 9
  psychology committee (1917), 119–20
National Telegraphic Union, 19
Nike guided missile program, 157, 162
Nippon Electric Company (NEC), 207

Oastler, J. R., 105
Ogilvie, Richard, 179
O'Neill, John, 188, 196–7, 201–2, 208
optical fiber transmission, 195
O'Rourke, Jean, 122–3
Orton, Thomas, 30
Orton, William, 30, 39

Panama Canal, 2
patents
  De Forest's audion vacuum tube, 4–5
  patent war related to vacumm tubes, 110

Small, Bonnie, 162–4
Smoot, William, 34, 52–3, 63
sound barrage, 106
sound systems
  amplifiers, loudspeakers, microphones, and
    electronic recording, 136–7
  for movie theaters, 138
  sound motion pictures, 137
  synchronized sound, 137
Springer, L. C., 28
Stager, Anson
  business affiliations, 30–1
  career and experience, 16–18
  as cofounder of Gray & Barton, 16, 28–9
  interest in Gray's invention, 24–5
  managerial expertise, 21
  as part owner of Gray & Barton, 29–30
  as president of midwestern telephone com-
    panies, 41-2
  as president of Western Electric, 52
standardization
  discussions related to (1880s), 59
  Western Electric's failure to achieve, 77–8
Stanley, Arthur, 31–2
Stanton, Edward M., 18
Stearns, Joseph B., 34, 36
stenographers, men and women as, 101–2
Stoll, Clarence
  as Hawthorne works manager, 121
  as president of Western Electric, 138–9, 141
  as vice president at Hawthorne, 122
  during World War I in Europe, 105
strikes
  at Kearny plant (1946), 167–8
  at McCormick Harvester (1886), 82
  at Point Breeze plant (1943), 142–5
  by Western Electric machinists (1900), 81–
    2
Summers, C. H., 35
Sunny, B. E., 59
switchboards
  automatic signals on multiple (1896), 61
  dial telephone crossbar switchboards, 139
  "express" (1893), 60
  first switchboard conference (1887), 59
  innovations providing efficiency (1870s), 58
  multiple switchboard of Firman (1879), 58
switching systems
  AT&T toll, 199

electronic, 198
modularized, 198
Swope, Gerard, 95, 104–5, 107–8

tabulating machine, 67–8
Tabulating Machine Company, 69
Tanenbaum, Morris, 191
Taylor, Frederick Winslow, 76, 164
technology
  effect on company structure and operation,
    192–3
  new products as outcome of new, 193
Telecommunications Act (1996), 211
telegraph
  invention of, 15
  printing telegraph, 68
Telegraphers' Protective League, 19
telephone
  Bell's invention of, 37–8
  demand during Great Depression, 131
  growth of telephone exchanges (1870s), 58
  increased number of (1885–1900), 69
  loud-speaking telephone (loudspeaker), 112
  telephone headset, 58
telephone operators, innovations assisting, 58
Telephone Pioneers of America, 96
telephony
  development of, 34–8
  inventions of Irwin and Voelker, 42
  Vail's vision of, 45–6
Thayer, Harry
  as AT&T vice president (1908), 6
  as head of Western's New York operations,
    55, 67
  management skills, 101–3
  as president of AT&T, 51, 103, 113–14
  as president of Western Electric, 6, 73–4,
    87–8, 107–8
  on recognition of unions, 82
  relationship with Theodore Vail, 113
Total Quality Management (TQM), 208
training programs
  for engineering recruits, 100
  retraining to meet requirements of elec-
    tronic manufacture, 189–90
Training Within Industry (TWI), 152
transistors
  Bell Labs invention of (1947), 161–2, 189
  mass production of, 162